Introduction to Microcomputers

Digital System Design Series

Arthur D. Friedman, Editor
George Washington University

Introduction
to Microcomputers

Edited by

E L Dagless

University of Bristol

and D Aspinall

University of Manchester
Institute of Science and Technology

COMPUTER SCIENCE PRESS

© Copyright D Aspinall, L A M Bennett, E L Dagless, R D Dowsing,
J S D Mason, 1982

Printed in United States

Published simultaneously in the United States of America and Great Britain by:

Computer Science Press, Inc.   Pitman Books Ltd.
11 Taft Court   39 Parker Street
Rockville, Maryland 20850   London WC2B 5PB
U.S.A.   Great Britain

1 2 3 4 Printing   Year 84 83 82 81

Library of Congress Cataloging in Publication Data

Dagless, Erik L. 1946–
    Introduction to microcomputers.
    (Digital system design series)
    Bibliography: p.
    Includes index.
    1. Minicomputers.
    I. Aspinall, David   II. Title.   III. Series.
    TK7885.A77   621.3819′5   81–5437
    ISBN 0–914894–25–0   AACR2

Contents

Preface

This text follows very closely the structure of an earlier text, *Introduction to Microprocessors* by the same authors. Some justification should be offered for writing a new volume based so heavily on, but differing markedly from, its predecessor. The original text presented the material developed on a short course aimed at introducing experienced, practising digital systems engineers to a new, alternative method using microprocessors; basically a conversion for those already knowledgeable about existing digital techniques. The new text contains a more detailed treatment, suitable for undergraduate courses in Electrical/Electronic Engineering and Computer Science. It is assumed that any lectures based on this text would be supported by courses on logic design and programming. The text sets these topics in perspective, noting their relationship to microcomputing, but makes no attempt to cover them exhaustively; the references cite suitable supporting material.

Two of the authors (E. Dagless and J. Mason) added extensively to the original material when writing a correspondence course text, and major additions were found desirable for teaching in the more conventional university environment. In rewriting for an updated edition the authors have drawn heavily on this new material. The result is an increase in detail and a more thorough treatment in many of the chapters. All the chapters conclude with an extensive selection of graded tutorial questions aimed at illustrating the main theme of the chapter and extending the readers' ideas to more advanced concepts. Every effort has been made to make the book self-contained, and detailed notes can be found in the appendices. A new form of chart is included which shows the register map of the 8085. It may be used to explain the actions of programs where a 'before' and 'after' map is produced.

Perhaps a more noticeable shift in the last few years is the greater importance of the microcomputer. The commonplace occurrence of the computer on a chip, and the increasing popularity of 'board' computers, where more power is required, places the emphasis on using the computer, rather than assembling one from circuit components. The stress placed on this issue in the earlier text has been strengthened in the new volume by adding more material on applications of computing components, and by changing the name to *Introduction to Microcomputers*. The authors have been careful to maintain a consistent terminology, using microprocessor to describe a microelectronics-based central processor and microcomputer for the combination of microprocessor together with a memory and some input/output resource.

The work is introductory because it brings together all of the many facets of applying microcomputing technology and can, therefore, only provide a superficial treatment of some topics. It is detailed in its account of computer structure (chapter 2) instruction set and addressing modes (chapters 3 and 5) pertaining, in particular, to the 8085. A comparison of the organization of memory and input/output (chapter 6) and the need for handling concurrency (chapter 7) is less specific. Here the treatment is towards giving general concepts, leaving the interested reader to study specific devices from manufacturers' literature; a far more complete source of detailed information and new ideas.

The emphasis on the application of, or the solving of a problem using, microcomputers is reflected in three chapters (chapters 4, 9, 10) and much of the appendix dealing with the design of solutions and worked examples.

The remaining three chapters summarize the other topics relevant to the successful application of microcomputing techniques. Chapter 1 relates the development of large-scale integration and the emergence of the modern microprocessor and microcomputer. Chapter 8 describes the range of software tools essential for good program production, while chapter 11 outlines the hardware equipment that is necessary to support these tools and provide a suitable environment for microcomputer product development.

The microcomputer is essentially an implementation component and its exploitation is a practical skill which requires experience and practice. Whilst it is more beneficial to use the book in conjunction with laboratory work, charts are provided to enable the student to work through the operation of a program in the absence of working equipment. Many of the tutorial questions have arisen during laboratory work and help to illustrate some of the many practical difficulties that arise. If the study of this text accompanies a laboratory activity, preferably design projects rather than set experiments, information in the text, particularly the appendix, provides ideas on the form the equipment might take.

Where necessary, a single microprocessor, the 8085, is used in the main text. (As far as the instruction set is concerned, the 8080 is used synonymously with the 8085.) There are many issues which cannot be handled without the concrete example of a specific machine and where laboratory work is concerned concentration on a single instruction set is preferable. The 6800 is used frequently for comparison; the majority of the examples being in the appendix. These two microprocessors must represent the majority used in a teaching activity today and certainly these two account for a large percentage of microcomputer-based products sold.

Since the original text was published both Editors have moved elsewhere, David Aspinall to the Department of Computation at UMIST and Erik Dagless to the Department of Electrical and Electronic Engineering at the University of Bristol. Roy Dowsing is now at the University of East Anglia, while Lincoln Bennett and John Mason remain at the University College Swansea. This has added to the already difficult task of editing and collating the material, and the organizing editors thank all the co-authors for their prompt handling of scripts in checking and proof-reading. The bulk of the organization has fallen on the shoulders of Erik Dagless to whom all co-authors are cordially grateful for his hard work in coordinating their scripts, negotiating with the publishers and maintaining the momentum of the writing.

All the authors are extremely grateful to Betty Sharples for her rapid and accurate typing and Betty McGraw for collating, copying and correspondence.

1 Components for information processing

Introduction

A generation ago, the manufacturers of digital information processing systems, such as computers, based their circuits on diodes, transistors, resistors and capacitors obtained from the component manufacturers. These components were assembled onto printed circuit boards as logic modules. The modules would then be interconnected by wires.

A family, comprising a limited number of different logic modules, would be established by the system manufacturer, each member of the family being an individual production item which could be produced in bulk. As a typical large digital computer was based on a family of twenty to a hundred logic modules, copies of each module would occur ten to several hundred times in each computer manufactured.

All system manufacturers produced their own individual family of modules, which reflected both the style of their circuit and logic designers, and also their production techniques. Though all families had many similar features, in detail they were all different.

During the last twenty years, the component manufacturers have been developing semiconductor technology which assembles the basic diodes, transistors, resistors and capacitors in a surface layer, some $10\mu m$ thick, on top of a thin wafer of silicon, and these are connected by means of a layer of metal evaporated onto the silicon, which is subsequently etched to produce the required interconnecting pattern. The wafer is packaged as a logic module, suitable for interconnection to other modules by conventional printed circuit techniques. These integrated circuit modules are less costly, more reliable, smaller, and lighter than discrete component modules.

The low cost is achieved by high-volume production. Whereas a system manufacturer could contemplate production quantities of the order of one to ten thousand copies of a discrete logic module per annum, the semiconductor manufacturer must think in terms of ten thousand to one million copies of an integrated circuit module per annum, to be competitive.

A small number of module families which satisfy the needs of most system manufacturers has been developed and is produced in large volume. These include transistor/transistor logic and emitter-coupled logic, based on the bipolar junction transistor technology and also the complementary MOS based on unipolar field-effect transistor technology.

The detailed specification of each module in a family has been arrived at as the result of an iterative process of consultation between the system and component manufacturers to produce a logic module family which satisfies wide system needs and can thus justify large production runs.

The modules comprise simple logic gates and bistable memory elements which the system designer uses as basic components. They are at a sufficiently basic level to give the designer the freedom to produce a unique system which meets its specification in a way which reflects his skill and style. They have few features which are redundant for many applications; thus the designer is able to produce a trim system in which each gate and bistable element serves a useful purpose. He has learnt to live with these families, and accepts that his rivals are also using identical basic components.

His skill as a logic designer has become more important than his skill as an electronic circuit designer. While it is necessary to analyze and evaluate the circuits offered by the manufacturers and to understand the interconnection design rules, the creative talents show in the ability to design and create elegant economic logic circuits to meet a specification which is attractive to the market.

Integrated circuit technology now makes it possible to pack over 30 000 logic gates on to a small silicon wafer. Large-scale integration (LSI) permits a system in a package smaller than a littler finger. Such systems can compete with those based on the logic module families, provided the production quantities are sufficient. The design, processing, tooling and establishment of test facilities and documentation for production and marketing of an LSI circuit are very expensive. These costs can be recovered if, for a particular circuit, it serves a large-volume market such as a pocket calculator, or watch. Attempts have been made to reduce the initial costs. By adopting a well-proven technology such as 4-phase metal oxide semiconductors (MOS), and using computer-aided design techniques, special circuits have been produced which match a specialized market. Also, semiconductor manufacturers have arranged their production facilities to provide a regular array of components in the top layer of the silicon wafer, and these may be interconnected in many different ways by unique patterns of metal layer connections. The silicon wafers are mass-produced, while the metal layers are applied in small production batches. This procedure offers the system designer an opportunity to obtain circuits which meet his unique requirements and, for the quantities he requires, are less costly than specially designed LSI circuits. Such circuits are known as uncommitted logic arrays (ULA).

LSI for digital systems

The next step that the semiconductor manufacturers are taking is to analyze many different information processing systems and partition their logic circuits into self-contained units which can be identified as universal system components. These larger components may then be offered to all system designers, and be used to augment and replace the existing families of logic modules. The most common large component in such a system is the digital computer; therefore this is the obvious starting point.

To appreciate some of the problems facing the manufacturer, let us analyze a computer structure and attempt to partition it into its component parts. The block diagram of a digital computer, which shows its four main units, appears in Fig. 1.1. Information is fed into the computer by means of peripheral input devices, and is obtained from the computer through the output devices. Both sets of devices are controlled by processes in the computer. The information held in the memory comprises both the data being processed and the instructions of the programs which define the actual operations to be carried out in the processor.

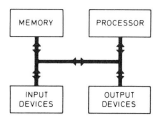

Fig. 1.1 A typical computer

There are several situations that call for the provision of input–output devices and their control, and that suggest a role for LSI components. Since their specification is affected largely by the nature of the devices rather than by memory or processor, we will not consider them in any more detail. Instead, let us consider only the memory and processor units and their interrelationship. By excluding the input/output devices, we are left with the block diagram shown in Fig. 1.2.

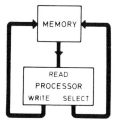

Fig. 1.2 Processor—memory relationship

Within the memory unit, information is held as binary digits, or bits, in registers comprising several bistable storage elements. The length of each register is determined by the specification of the overall computer system. Typical values are 8, 16 and 24 bits. The number of registers is also determined by the requirements of the system, depending on the amount of data to be stored and the length of the programs. Sizes range from 4K to 256K (K = 1024). Circuitry is provided to give communication between any one of the registers and the processor, and for reading the information held in the register or writing new information into it. To select a register, the processor must present an address word to the memory which is decoded by selection circuitry to open the communication channel. The length of the address word depends on the number of registers in the memory. An address length of n bits selects one of 2^n registers (12 bits selects from 4K, 18 bits selects from 256K). To achieve good computer performance, the delay between presenting an address to the memory and reading a register, the access time, should be very short, in the region of 100 ns to 1 μs.

A large memory may be constructed from sub-units of LSI random access read/write memory (RWM) modules of, say, 1K registers of 1 bit. A memory of 4K registers of 8 bits uses 32 such modules. The system specification of a RWM module is simple, since it comprises only the number and length of the registers and the access time. A joy to behold for the semiconductor manufacturer! A universal system module with an assured market! Also, other forms of memory are required universally. These include the read-only memory (ROM) for holding fixed information which does not change, a programmable version of the read-only memory (PROM) which enables the system designer to change the fixed information for different versions of the system.

The specification of the processor is a different matter. Every computer designer has his own view of the ideal processor specification, and it is unlikely that one module would embrace all in an efficient way. The factors which influence the main items in a specification, such as word length, range of processing functions, and modes of addressing information in the memory, are many and varied. They depend on the type of use for which the computer is intended, ranging over scientific calculation, business data processing, and real-time control. The software, placed between the processor and the end-user to provide high-level languages and afford automatic management of the input/output devices and flow of work through the system, also affects the detailed specification of the processor.

However, there are some general features which are common to all processors. The processor must carry out arithmetic and logical operations on the data held in the memory. Before it can do this, it must find the instruction in the memory to discover the next function; also, it must find the data operand in the memory and fetch it to the processor so that the function may be performed.

Instructions are stored as patterns of binary digits in the registers of the memory. In many cases, the consecutive instructions of the program are held in consecutive registers of the memory; thus the address of the next instruction is implicitly the address of the present instruction, plus one. A program counter register in the processor holds the address of the present instruction, its contents being incremented by one as the next instruction is fetched.

Certain instructions may explicitly specify the address of the next instruction, which may be at any address location in the memory, causing a jump to another section of the program.

The circuit block diagram of this small processor is shown in Fig. 1.3.

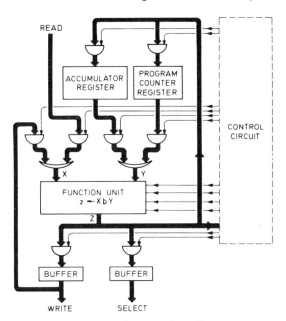

Fig. 1.3 Data paths of a typical small processor

Communication between the processor and the memory is by way of three ports labelled SELECT, READ, and WRITE. The SELECT port passes information from the processor to the memory, coded as the address of the selected register in the memory, to request either a READ or WRITE channel between the selected register and the processor. Data pass through the WRITE port to the selected register, or information passes from the selected register to the READ port of the processor. Within the processor there are two distinct regions: the data paths, and the control circuit. The data paths comprise the function unit, accumulator register, program counter register, and buffer registers, together with the gating and routing circuitry between them. The control circuit ensures the correct sequence of flow through the data paths.

The function unit carries out operations of the form $Z \leftarrow X . b . Y$. The operator b is selected by the control circuit. Typical operators are ADD, SUBTRACT, SHIFT, LOGICAL AND and NON-EQUIVALENCE. The operands, X and Y, and the result, Z, are all words composed of many bits in parallel, and the operation is performed on all bits of each operand in parallel to produce a result on all bits of Z in parallel. The operand X is selected to be either the information read from memory or that buffered on the output of the function unit at the WRITE TO MEMORY port. The operand Y is selected from either the accumulator register or the program counter register. The result may be routed to either register or to the ouput buffers, and it is also sent to the control circuit. All of these routes are many bits in parallel and, together with the registers, gates, and functional unit, represent the majority of logic modules within the processor.

There are two ways to divide the data paths into circuit modules which may be suitable for LSI. By drawing lines across the diagram, it is possible to identify five types of module. The function unit, the gating system producing operand X, the output buffer registers, the small memory unit of two registers, and the gating system for operand Y. At the boundary of each partition there must be leads to interconnect the modules together. In the case of the function unit, there must be leads to route in X and Y and route out the result Z. The number of leads required for each of X, Y and Z is equal to the number of bits processed in parallel by the function unit. In a typical system, this number may be 16—thus 48 leads are required for X, Y and Z. In addition, there must be leads to permit the input of the control signals. These are coded in a similar way to addresses, and 4 bits permit selection of 1 of 16 operators. A typical function unit permitting 16 operations on 2 operands of 16 bits could require at least 52 interconnection leads. These leads are routed from the surface of the silicon wafer to pins in the package which carry the wafer, and provide mechanical and environmental protection. Package technology has kept pace with semiconductor technology, but is only able to provide economic packages with up to 40 pins. Packages with more than 40 pins are rare and expensive.

The other modules produced by horizontal partitioning of a 16-bit processor require in the region of 30 to 50 pins, and are not an economic proposition.

The diagram may be sliced in a vertical direction into data path modules, similar to those shown in Fig. 1.3, but only 2 bits wide. Such modules would require only 20 pins. Eight such modules could enable the construction of a processor for word lengths of 16 bits. Thus, one important item in the specification of a computer, the word length, is catered for by connecting a sufficient number of the modules in parallel.

Data path modules

Let us consider how the other basic requirements of a computer are satisfied by an assemblage of such data path modules. The first requirement is an ability to control the flow of the program which is based on designating an internal register as a program counter. This register will hold the address of the present instruction. Usually, the next instruction is fetched by passing the contents of the program counter through the function unit which is controlled to carry out $Z \leftarrow Y + 1$. The output of Z is then copied to both the program counter and to the select buffer. The memory is accessed, and the next instruction appears at the READ port of the processor; it is gated to the function unit which is controlled to carry out $Z \leftarrow X$. The appropriate part of the instruction, which describes the address of the operand, is then copied from Z into the select buffer and the function digits are transferred into the control circuit, where they are decoded to control the function unit to perform $Z \leftarrow X.b.Y$ at the appropriate time. Before this time, the memory must be accessed to produce the operand at the READ port of the processor, whence it is gated to the X input of the functional unit; also the contents of the accumulator register must be gated to the Y input of the functional unit. When this operation ($Z \leftarrow S.b.A$) has been completed, Z must then be copied back to the accumulator register to complete $A \leftarrow S.b.A$. This cycle must be repeated by fetching the next instruction. This complete cycle contains the following basic sequence of activities:

(1) Fetch next instruction
(2) Decode instruction
(3) Fetch operand
(4) Execute instruction

Within each activity there is a distinct sequence of events, each of which involves the opening of gates, the control of the function unit, and the setting of bistable elements in registers or buffers. Each event requires a unique combination of control signals from the control circuit. At any particular time the pattern of signals emanating from the control circuit can be said to describe its state. Thus, the control circuit may be conceived as a machine which can change its state as it moves from event to event within the total cycle. The sequence of states is determined by the required sequence of events within each activity of the cycle. Certain sequences will always be the same. There must always be a sequence to fetch the next instruction, but the decoding of the instruction may result in different sequences. In addition to the sequence described above to execute $A \leftarrow S.b.A$, there are different sequences to execute $S \leftarrow A$ and jump of program control resulting from different instructions.

The computer which we have considered so far has very limited operand addressing capabilities and a very restricted set of operators. In other computers, the specification may require the option of processing the address field of the instruction to compute the operand address leading to many alternative states of the control circuit within the fetch operand sequence.

Arithmetic operators, such as multiply or divide, involve many passes through the simple function unit which, in turn, involve many different sequences of states within the execute instruction activity.

The data path module provides the necessary components for controlling the flow of instructions and obeying them, provided a control circuit can be designed to control the repeated use of these components, in different combinations, within the cycle of activities involved in each step of the program. Such a module would seem to satisfy the requirements of a wide range of computer functional specifications, However, it can only be used in different systems if each system has its own unique control circuit described by a unique sequence of states. The semiconductor manufacturer may have found a module which meets half of the requirements, but the complexity and variety of the control circuit still presents a problem.

LSI components for control logic

The control logic is generally described by a flowchart and corresponds conceptually to a bit serial system. The complex and varied route taken by the pre-pulse or token as it moves through the flowchart, to indicate the current region of activity in the total process, is the representation of both the specialized nature of the equipment specification and the personal design approach and ideas of the logic designer.

The control logic is characterized by its uniqueness and also by its complexity. Certain components are often used, such as counter, decoders, and delay elements, but these are generally quite small in size and are classed as MSI (not LSI).

The role which a general-purpose LSI unit could play in the area of control logic design would be to provide a unit onto which the designer could map his complex control logic. Such devices are beginning to appear. The first is the uncommitted logic array (ULA) which provides on the chip an array of standard gates which can be interconnected by a programmable mask technique to suit the particular requirements of the logic designer. The familiar circuit diagrams of the logic designer can be mapped onto the programmable mask. However, there is a limit to the complexity that can be handled by this approach. An alternative which has long-term implications is the use of memory arrays and table look-up techniques for the implementation of control logic.

Combinatorial logic

To illustrate this approach, consider the illustrated example of a typical design problem. The problem is specified by the truth table in Fig. 1.4.

Row	\multicolumn{4}{c}{Inputs}				\multicolumn{3}{c}{Outputs}		
	x_0	x_1	x_2	x_3	z_0	z_1	z_2
0	0	0	0	0	0	0	0
1	0	0	0	1	0	0	0
2	0	0	1	0	1	0	0
3	0	0	1	1	1	0	0
4	0	1	0	0	1	0	1
5	0	1	0	1	1	0	1
6	0	1	1	0	0	0	0
7	0	1	1	1	0	0	0
8	1	0	0	0	1	0	0
9	1	0	0	1	0	0	0
10	1	0	1	0	0	0	0
11	1	0	1	1	0	0	0
12	1	1	0	0	0	0	0
13	1	1	0	1	0	0	0
14	1	1	1	0	0	0	0
15	1	1	1	1	1	1	1

Fig. 1.4 Truth table

To implement these expressions in terms of NAND gates, we obtain the circuit as shown in Fig. 1.5.

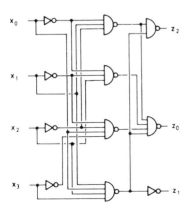

Fig. 1.5 Gate implementation

To the uninitiated, the circuit drawing bears little or no relationship to the design problem as stated in the truth table. When this circuit is implemented, either by hand-wiring of logic modules or on a printed circuit board, or ULA, the result will appear to be even more complicated and more difficult to check out.

Is it possible to implement a logic functional unit which has less complication at the later design and construction stages of the process? One obvious method is to map the truth table onto a conventional RWM or ROM. The memory would need to be of 2^n words of m bits, where

n = number of input variables
m = number of output variables

In our example,

$n = 4$
$m = 3$

Thus: 16 words of 3 bits.

In practice, the input variables would be arranged to act as the address for the memory and the word read from the line of memory by this address would act as the output, each bit of the output word corresponding to an output variable (Fig. 1.6). Thus, we see a direct correspondence between a familiar tool of the logic designer, a truth table, and an actual circuit implementation, a read-only memory. We have removed all the placement and wiring problems implicit in the implementation of the earlier logic circuit, and can see this approach as a possible way to implement combinatorial logic.

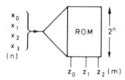

Fig. 1.6 ROM implementation

There is, however, one obvious economic disadvantage. The height of the ROM is 2^n, where n is the number of bits in the address = the number of input variables. Thus for, say, 10 input variables, the ROM must have 1024 words of length depending on the required number of output variables. An 8-input adder, producing an 8-digit sum plus carry overflow, would involve 64K words of 9 digits. Is there a method of reducing the number of words in the ROM?

Functional memory

If we return to the original truth table, we find that certain output rows contain all zeros (0, 1, 6, 7, 9, 10, 11, 12, 13, 14). Fewer rows contain at least one '1' (2, 3, 4, 5, 8, 15). If we could find a way to store these 6 rows in a ROM and access these by an associative or content-addressable memory (CAM), then we could reduce the size of the memory to 6 words instead of 16 (Fig. 1.7).

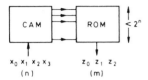

Fig. 1.7 FM (functional memory)

Thus, if we replace the conventional decoder of a ROM by an associative store and write into the associative store a bit pattern describing only those input patterns which produce an output, then we obtain a significant reduction in the number of words stored (Fig. 1.8).

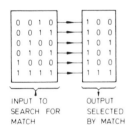

Fig. 1.8 FM implementation

If such a combination of CAM and ROM were constructed on a single silicon chip and offered as an LSI module, it would present the designer of logic functional units with a component which permits the removal of much of the drudgery inherent in the final stages of the current design process. This component may be termed a functional memory (FM).

Programmable logic arrays

This approach can be taken a stage further. If we return to the original example and examine the minimized truth table and Boolean equations, we find that by exploiting a third state, the 'don't care' state $\emptyset$, it is possible to reduce the size of the functional memory from 6 words to 4 (Fig. 1.9). This component is termed a programmable logic array (PLA).

The PLA is composed of two logic elements AND and OR gates arranged in a regular array so that their inputs may be programmed. A simple configuration is shown in Fig. 1.10.

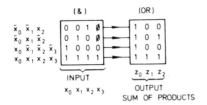

Fig. 1.9 PLA (programmable logic array)

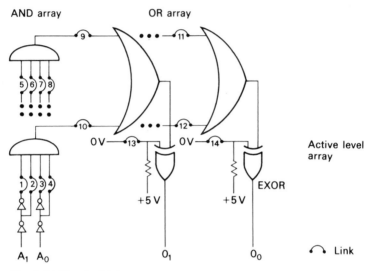

Fig. 1.10 Simple PLA

An additional programming feature is the inversion logic at the output, which makes the output either active-high, e.g. link 13 left alone, or active-low, e.g. link 13 removed.

For each input term a gate can be programmed to one of four states. Taking links 1 and 2 as an example,

1	2	Gate function
–	–	Disabled
–	×	Responds to $A1 = 1$
×	–	Responds to $A1 = 0$
×	×	Always responds (don't care)

(× link removed;   – link present)

The array circuits come in many forms now, the most powerful being the programmable logic sequencer. This is a PLA with a register contained on the chip and connected to the inputs and outputs internally to provide feedback (see next section).

A PLA with 16 inputs and 8 outputs is equivalent to a memory of 64K bytes. Most PLAs of this size have about 90 product terms. A field programmable array, FPLA or FPLS, has fusible-link type connections which can be removed by an electronic programmer. This makes for a more cost effective component for low-volume products. A FPLA will usually have about 50 product terms. An FPLS with a 6-bit register internally connected to both outputs and inputs has the logical power of about a 4M byte memory.

Sequential logic

Control circuits are more frequently needed to control the sequence of actions, say counting a number sequence 0, 1, 2, 3, 5, 7, 11, 13. This is usually achieved by incorporating a register with a combinatorial circuit. The circuit generates the register inputs which are copied to the output when the clock signal is active, usually on the rising edge.

The register output generates the output sequence and is also fed back to the input of the combinatorial circuit. The circuit and truth table are shown in Fig. 1.11.

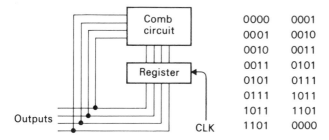

0000	0001
0001	0010
0010	0011
0011	0101
0101	0111
0111	1011
1011	1101
1101	0000

Fig. 1.11(a) Simple sequential machine   *Fig. 1.11(b)* Truth table for machine

Development of microprogramming

The combinatorial circuit could be implemented by a simple ROM. In the example shown in Fig. 1.11(a), there are four flip-flops which together may represent up to 2^4, i.e. 16, possible states. The number of states permitted in the design is restricted to eight (0, 1, 2, 3, 5, 7, 11, 13). Thus the ROM must have 2^4 words each of 4 bits, i.e. 16 words of 4 bits each. Only half of these words will be populated according to the table contained in Fig. 1.11(b). The size of the ROM would be $16 \times 4 = 64$ bits. An alternative solution which reduces the memory size is shown in Fig. 1.12.

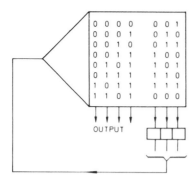

Fig. 1.12 ROM sequencer

The address of the next number is held alongside the present number in the counting sequence. The size of this ROM is $7 \times 8 = 56$ bits. The obvious final step is to dispense with the 3-bit binary counter field within the ROM and replace the D-type flip-flop by a 3-bit counter. At the expense of extra logic external to the memory, this reduces the ROM size to 32 bits.

We have seen how we can generate a repetitive control sequence by a completely table-driven approach, and also by a combination of table plus external logic. The next stage of the problem is to consider ways of controlling the number of times the complete counting sequence or control loop is executed, and also ways of initiating the next counting sequence or stage of control that is required. Both these decisions may be conditional on the value of data in the data path generated as a result of the data path operations initiated by the current sequence, or by some external event. To solve these problems we need a system as shown in Fig. 1.13.

With this system, it is possible to map control patterns of up to m bits into the memory and permit the next pattern to be either the content of the next word in memory (ADDRESS + 1) *or* the content of the word specified by the next start address, either unconditionally or conditional on one of the external conditions K.

The design process consists of determining the control patterns, placing them in the memory, and organizing the linkage between patterns by writing a pattern into the JUMP ADDRESS, JUMP UNCONDITIONAL and JUMP CONDITION fields of the memory.

The choice of m, n and l is determined by the problem. This system, which has been described briefly, is of course the *microprocessor* suggested by Wilkes in 1950, for which one could write microprograms to provide the control sequences necessary for the control of the data paths of a computer.

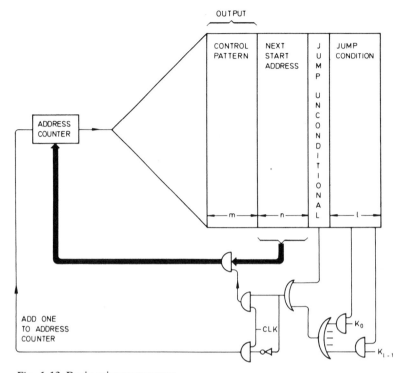

Fig. 1.13 Basic microprocessor

A generalized microprogram control system is shown in Fig. 1.14. Each line in the memory contains 4 fields: the control pattern to define the control signals to produce the required operation of the data paths; the

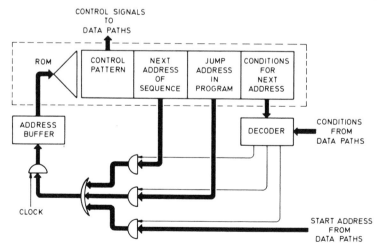

Fig. 1.14 Simplified microprogram control unit

address of the next microprogram instruction in the sequence; the address of the instruction to be jumped to, out of sequence; the pattern of conditions which must be combined with condition data from the data paths to determine the type of next address. External to the memory are the connections from and to the data paths, which provide the conditions and start address if required. The decoder selects the address of the next instruction which is clocked into the address buffer to begin the next stage in the control sequence.

This external circuitry may be placed on an LSI chip to provide a general-purpose microprogram control module. This is then used in conjunction with a memory module which can be either ROM or PROM or RWM, to provide the control circuit for the processor.

Microcomputer morphology

The data paths and control circuit may also be integrated into one component which is popularly termed a microprocessor. In this case the prefix 'micro' refers to the small physical size of the component and does not convey the same meaning as in its earlier use by Wilkes. The present use of the word 'microprocessor' refers to a small processor which can support a computer instruction set and when connected to memory and peripheral devices comprises a small computer. Furthermore the processor, memory and facilities for interfacing peripheral devices can all be combined into one component, termed a microcomputer.

The basic structure of a small computer based on the microprocessor, or of the complete microcomputer, is shown in Fig. 1.15. The physical components and their interconnection are shown in Fig. 1.15(*a*), while their abstract nature is shown in Fig. 1.15(*b*).

The timing of the actions within the data path and control circuit are ordained by an external clock. The READ and WRITE ports between the data path and the memory are usually passed through a time-division multiplexer, or switch, which provides a bi-directional port to a bi-directional bus system for READ and WRITE data. A separate SELECT bus passes the address to the memories and input/output devices.

The read-only memory and read/write memory units each consist of a collection of separate memory modules, which must be interfaced to the bi-directional bus and the address bus. The input/output must be arranged so that each individual device may be selected for connection to the READ and WRITE ports of the data paths through the buses and switch. Control signals must also pass between the control circuit and all the other units. The detailed interconnection of the units depends on the electrical and logical characteristics of the components used, as set out in the manufacturer's data sheets.

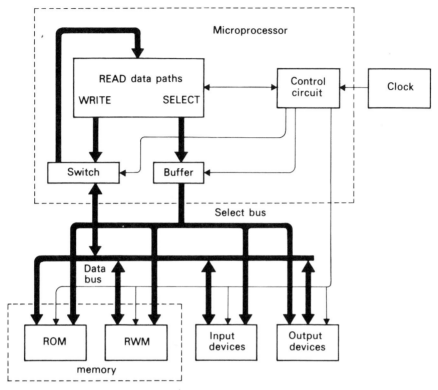

Fig. 1.15(a) Microcomputer: a physical schematic

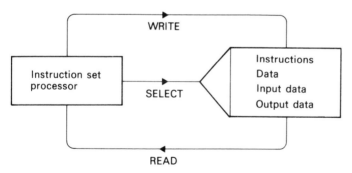

Fig. 1.15(b) Microcomputer: an abstract schematic

These characteristics are discussed in later chapters to give an understanding of the structure of the total microcomputer system necessary to support the programs which will execute the information processing task of the finished product or system.

The program itself may be considered as a representation of the solution to a logical design problem, as an alternative to the former wiring diagram. It consists of a list of instructions each based on a member of the instruction set of the microprocessor. This list will be stored, usually on ROM, within the addressable memory space of the microprocessor and will be selected, in sequence, by the microprocessor to execute the processing task. Each instruction, as it is obeyed by the microprocessor, will access data within the memory space. These data may be held in ROM or more usually in read/write memory (RWM). The input and output devices will also be arranged within an addressable memory space and may be accessed as data by certain instructions.

The instruction set and permissible microcomputer structures are explained within the data sheet of the microprocessor. The characteristic properties and limitations of these will be considered in later chapters, together with an introduction to programming techniques.

Summary of basic components

A set of basic universal system components has been identified and described in the context of the set required to make up the main frame of a typical computer. The computer was chosen as a convenient example and it must be stressed at this point that the set of components may also be used

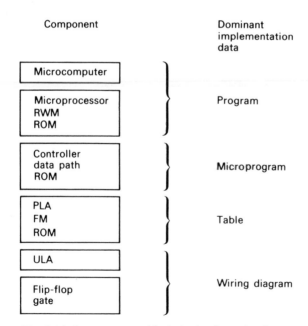

Fig. 1.16 Components with their dominant implementation data

in the implementation of the hardware of a wide range of information processing products or systems. Furthermore the design techniques necessary for the correct application of these components are a direct development of the familiar logic circuit design techniques which are used for the application of the basic gate and flip-flop components. The range of components extends through the memory and microprogrammable bit slice components to the complete microcomputer as shown in Fig. 1.16. As one moves up the range, the wiring diagram, which describes the physical interconnection of the components, is supplemented to an increasing extent by more abstract design data such as tables and programs. At the level of the microcomputer the dominant design activity is programming. Traditional logic design techniques must be developed to facilitate the interworking of both the physical wiring and the abstract program. The representation of design data must now be based not only on the familiar symbols for the logic elements but also the statements which represent the program steps.

Problems

P1.1 What are the Boolean expressions for the function of Fig. 1.4?

P1.2 The circuit of Fig. P1.1 is composed of AND, OR, and INV logic elements. Write out the Boolean expressions for the function.

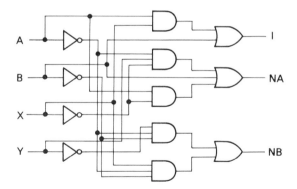

Fig. P1.1 Logic circuit

P1.3 The De-Morgan relationships are:

$$A + B = \overline{\overline{A}.\overline{B}} \text{ and } A.B = \overline{\overline{A} + \overline{B}}$$

Draw the logic diagram for these equalities.

Redraw the circuit of Fig. P1.1 using (*a*) only NAND elements, and (*b*) only NOR elements (NAND is $\overline{A.B}$, i.e. Not AND; and NOR is $\overline{A + B}$, i.e. Not OR)

P1.4 The EXCLUSIVE-OR function (EXOR or $\oplus$) is expressed logically as $A\bar{B} + \bar{A}B$. Draw the truth tables for:

$A \oplus 1, A \oplus 0, A \oplus A, A \oplus B$.

Can you explain the value of these operations and why the complement of EXOR is the equivalence function?

P1.5 The function unit of a computer operates on more than one binary digit in parallel. For example, if A represents an 8-bit quantity, where A_0 is the least significant (right-most) bit, and A_7 is the most significant (left-most) bit, then the function unit will perform the general operation $A_n \leftarrow A_n \cdot b \cdot S_n$, where b is a binary operation and A and S are 8-bit registers. What are the results of the operations AND, OR, EXOR, ADD, on the following patterns?

$A = 0\,1\,0\,0\,1\,1\,0\,0 \quad S = 1\,0\,0\,0\,1\,1\,1\,1$
$A = 1\,0\,0\,0\,1\,1\,1\,0 \quad S = 1\,1\,1\,1\,0\,0\,0\,0$

P1.6 In a computer, the operation required can often only be produced by performing a sequence of operations. Calculate the outcome of the following, and explain a possible use of such a sequence:

$A = 0\,0\,1\,1\,1\,1\,0\,0$ then AND with
$S = 0\,0\,0\,0\,1\,1\,1\,1$ then OR with
$S = 1\,0\,0\,0\,0\,0\,0\,1$ then EXOR with
$S = 1\,1\,1\,1\,0\,0\,0\,0$

P1.7 The function unit of a computer can usually perform some or all of the following shift operations:

	Left	Right
Arithmetic	$A_0 \leftarrow 0$	$A_7 \leftarrow A_7$ (sign extend)
Logical	$A_0 \leftarrow 0$	$A_7 \leftarrow 0$
Cyclic 8-bit	$A_0 \leftarrow A_7$	$A_7 \leftarrow A_0$
Cyclic 9-bit	$A_0 \leftarrow C, C \leftarrow A_7$	$A_7 \leftarrow C, C \leftarrow A_0$

where C is a ninth bit or carry bit.

The table describes only the end operations; the rest are obvious. Describe how a shift register works, and calculate the result of shifting the following two patterns three times, using all eight of the above modes:

(i) $A = 1\,0\,0\,1\,1\,1\,0\,1$; (ii) $A = 0\,0\,1\,1\,0\,1\,1\,1$

Assume $C = 1$ initially.

P1.8 Describe the operation of a binary counter, and show the sequence for a 4-bit counter.

What is the counting sequence for a binary coded decimal (BCD) counter?

Describe how counters are cascaded to provide an extended range, illustrating with examples for binary and BCD.

What are the benefits and drawbacks of binary and decade counters?

P1.9 A read-only memory is often implemented using the circuit of P1.2. It contains 16 rows of diodes, one for each of the product terms decoded.

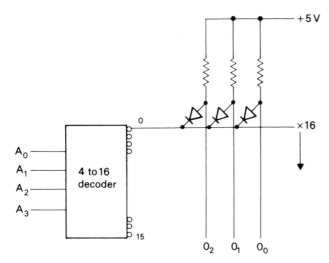

Fig. P1.2 Simple read-only memory

Using a grid of 16 × 3 to signify each diode, show the ROM pattern for the two truth tables of P1.1 and P1.2, using a cross to indicate a diode present. Remember to identify clearly connections to the ROM input.

P1.10 What size of ROM is required for P1.9, and how big is the ROM for a circuit with 10 inputs and 13 outputs?

P1.11 Fig. 1.10 shows the logical structure of a programmable logic array (PLA). If all the links numbered are normally connected as shown, what are the output functions 0_0 and 0_1 in terms of A_0 and A_1 if the following links are removed?

    (a) 1, 3, 4, 6, 8, 9
    (b) 2, 3, 5, 7, 8, 9, 10, 14
    (c) 1, 3, 5, 6, 9, 11, 13

P1.12 The matrix of Fig. P1.3 is a symbolic arrangement of the field PLA (FPLA) structure of Fig. 1.10, which shows the links for P1.11(c). Draw similar matrices for the truth tables of P1.1 and P1.2. (Hint: first reduce the truth tables to their minimum form, using Boolean algebra or any other method.)

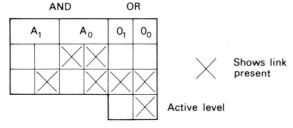

Fig. P1.3 FPLA symbolic matrix

2 The computer structure

A microprocessor is the central processing unit of a computer fabricated onto a single integrated circuit (IC) or, at most, two or three ICs. A computer is a processing system capable of obeying a program, which is a set of instructions that perform the required task. This chapter describes the structure of the computer and, in particular, one based on a micro-processor. The functions of the principal components are described in detail.

A computer-based solution to an engineering problem is shown in block diagram form in Fig. 2.1. Here, the system is the complete design solution

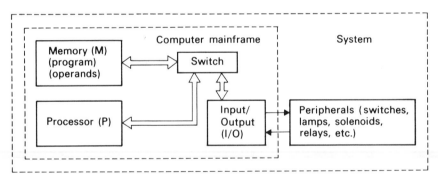

Fig. 2.1 Basic microprocessor system

which contains the peripherals and a computer mainframe. The peripherals are *all* the components or sub-systems which are not contained within the computer. Examples include, at one end of the spectrum, switches, lamps, relays and amplifiers; in the middle of the range, convertor circuits, and small motors; while at the top there are complete sub-systems like video display units (VDUs), floppy disk drives, high-power motor control sets, and plant equipment. In the peripheral domain, the traditional engineering disciplines are still applied, although more and more of the system tasks are moving into the computer as the technology becomes better under-stood. The problem for the systems engineer is to identify the optimum boundary between the computer and the peripheral space, to produce the most cost-effective solution.

A computer mainframe can be obtained in many forms. A large mainframe for large data processing applications; a minicomputer for plant control; a microcomputer system for small to medium scale applications; and a set of integrated circuits which first must be assembled into a mainframe configuration. It is the latter approach that the microprocessor has spawned and which has created the need for the specialist skills of the microprocessor engineer.

Computer mainframe

The mainframe consists of three components, linked by a switch. The switch provides the routes which enable these components to communicate. The switch will be explained in more detail in Chapter 6.

Processor: The processor (P) forms the heart of the computer system. It contains an *arithmetic and logic unit* (ALU), *registers* (R) containing operands and addresses, and a *control unit* which obeys the *instructions* to perform the specified task. The microprocessor is a processor or central processing unit (CPU) on a single integrated circuit. Figure 2.2 shows a detailed diagram of a hypothetical processor and memory; the lower-case letters (a–r) used in the text refer to the routes on this diagram.

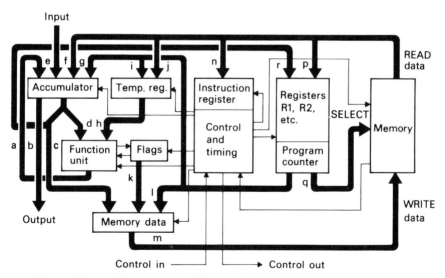

Fig. 2.2 Small central processor and its memory

Memory: The memory (M) is a vector or block of registers (binary words), together with an address decoder. An address (q) is input to the decoder which selects one of the register locations. If the registers can only be read (p n j f), i.e. data output from the memory, then it is a read-only memory (ROM). If the registers can be written (m), i.e. data input to the memory as well as read, then the memory is a read/write memory (RWM). The memory contains the *program*, which is normally only read, and *operands* (data) which are read or written by the processor.

Input/output: The input/output (I/O) is a vector of registers which are connected to peripheral devices. As with the memory each register has a unique address which is selected by an address decoder. A register that is read is called an input port, since it allows data to enter the processor. A register that is written to by the processor is called an output port, since it lets data out of the processor. Each port will have *n* bits of data, where *n* is the word length of the processor. For an 8-bit machine, an input port can allow the computer to read up to 8 switches at once, or two 4-bit thumbwheel digits, or one 8-bit ADC, or up to 8 photosensors, etc. One output port will provide signals for up to 8 indicator lamps, or 8 solenoids or relays, or 2 decimal digit displays, or one 8-bit DAC, etc. Further examples and a fuller description are given in Chapter 6. For simplicity the hypothetical processor of Fig. 2.2 only illustrates one input port route (c) and one output port route (b).

Program: The program is a set of instructions which has been created by the programmer and loaded into the memory. The instructions are stored in sequential order and obeyed one at a time by the processor. The program performs operations on the operands stored in the memory, and controls the data transferred between the processor and peripherals via the input/output ports. It is the program that defines the task that a computer performs. The program is addressed by a special register called the *program counter* (PC).

Operands: An operand is the information or datum stored in the computer which is operated on by the processor when executing an instruction. Operands may reside in registers within the processor, or in the memory, in which case an operand address selects the operand required. The operand address can be specified in many ways, collectively called addressing modes. The address may be provided directly in the instruction, or many arithmetic operations may be performed before the final address is generated. This topic is treated more fully in Chapter 5.

Instruction: An instruction is a command executed by the processor, and a program is a sequence of instructions. There are two basic types of instruction (although there are often a few minor exceptions):

(*a*) Operation instructions perform operations on the operands. The instruction must define both the operator and the operands involved, either explicitly or implicitly.

Explicit operands are defined by the programmer and appear as operands or operand addresses in the instruction field (see Chapter 3 for examples). Implicit operands are fixed by the processor designer; there is no freedom of choice for the programmer.

(*b*) Control instructions modify the normal sequence of operations in the program, i.e. they control the flow through the program. Normally the program is executed in sequence, obtained by adding 1 to the program counter; the next instruction is always placed immediately after the one being executed. Control orders can conditionally or unconditionally change this sequence so that loops, i.e. jumping back to a previously executed section of code, or branches, i.e. jumping over sections of code, can be constructed by the programmer. Control orders must define the type of control action to be performed, the address in the program where the next instruction resides, and the condition to be tested.

Registers: The term register normally refers to a location containing either an operand or an address which resides inside the processor, e.g. R1, R2 in Fig. 2.2 which is distinct from the memory. The processor registers are few in number, to keep the physical size small, and can be accessed more quickly than the memory, therefore making the instruction execution quicker. Some registers on the processor may perform a unique function and are usually given a special name; for example, the program counter, the accumulator, and the stack pointer.

Program counter: The program counter is a special register in the processor which contains the address of the next instruction to be executed. When an instruction is fetched from the memory, the program counter value is increased by one, i.e. it counts, and so points to the next location in the memory. Control orders modify the value of the program counter to force the processor to alter the normal sequential accessing of the program.

Accumulator: The accumulator is a dedicated register which receives the results of the operations performed by the ALU. Most microprocessors have accumulator-based instruction sets, which means that the destination of most operations is this special register; i.e. $A \leftarrow A.b.S$, $A \leftarrow S.u$ or $A \leftarrow X.b.Y$ are typical assignment operations for such processors.

Stack pointer: The stack is a special data structure used to store subroutine return addresses in the main read/write memory. The current top of the stack is defined by the contents of the *stack pointer*. The use and function of the stack and the stack pointer are described more fully in Chapters 3 and 5.

Control unit: The control unit is the core of the processor, and it controls the activity of the complete computer system. The sequence of activity is governed by the instruction, which passes to the control unit via the instruction register after being fetched from the memory (n). The control circuitry will select the correct register in the processor or cause the correct address to be used to access memory to fetch operands. It controls the arithmetic unit to perform the operation on the operands and generates all the waveforms necessary for the switch to set the correct routes, at the right time. The control unit is driven by a clock which may be supplied externally, as in the 8080 and 6800, or it may be an internal circuit with external timing components, as in 8085. The clock provides the main beat of the processor and its immediate circuits, like memory and static input-output. The clock supplies the datum for the detailed timing information for the circuit designer.

Arithmetic and logic unit: The arithmetic and logic unit (ALU) performs the operation, selected by the instruction, on the operands fetched by the control unit. A typical selection of operations include ADD, SUBTRACT, AND, OR, COMPARE, SHIFT, etc. The ALU also contains bi-stables or flip-flops which store the state of the result of the operation. These usually include a logical overflow or carry, sign, zero, and sometimes arithmetic overflow and others which vary from processor to processor. These status bits are used by conditional control instructions as logical conditions and are often called *condition flags*, or condition flip-flops.

Word length: The word length of a processor is the number of binary digits (bits) in the arithmetic unit. This governs the minimum processing width and defines the primary storage requirement within the internal registers and the memory. The word length governs the basic numerical range, the number of binary variables available and the number of states available in a word, as shown in Fig. 2.3(a).

Word length	n	8
Integer range	0 to + $(2^n - 1)$	0 to 255
Signed integer*	2^{n-1} to + $(2^{n-1} - 1)$	− 128 to +127
No. of binary variables	n	8
No. of states	2^n	256

Fig. 2.3(a) Features of word length   * 2's complement

No. of bits	Numerical data Range 2's complement		No. words for 1 million	Memory address Memory size	No. words for 64K memory
4	−8 to	+7	6	16	4
4 BCD	0	+9	7	—	—
8	−128	+127	3	256	2
16	− 32 768	+32 767	2	65 536	1
32	-10^{10}	$+10^{10}$	1	2×10^{10}	$\frac{1}{2}$

Fig. 2.3(b) Numerical and address range capability

Since most processors operate with the instructions and basic operands of the same length, the word length normally determines the instruction length. Early computers worked with instructions, addresses and operands of the same length, but 8-bit microcomputers have exploited multiword formats. The basic operand is 8 bits long, the addresses are 16 bits or more, while the instructions can be represented by up to 5 bytes of information. This approach frees the computer designer from many of the constraints that early designers laboured under. It does, however, make the meaning of word length less clear, but the definition above still seems to apply.

Thus a microcomputer like the 8085 will perform arithmetic and logical operations, on operands in the memory, 8 bits at a time, but has 16 bit address variables which can be manipulated by a 16-bit adder/incrementer. The instructions can occupy from 1 to 3 consecutive memory words.

High precision: Many applications require greater precision than that shown in Fig. 2.3(*a*) for 8-bit machines. Operands can be represented by more than one memory word although they are processed a word at a time. A long word length gives better precision but can lead to redundancy when only a few bits of a word are used (see Fig. 2.3(*b*)). For multiword working the processor must include special instructions to manipulate the operands.

Data paths of a fixed instruction set processor

The paths of a hypothetical processor based on the 8080 are shown in Fig. 2.2. The main memory and a simple input and output facility are shown. The processor is of the fixed instruction-set type, which represents the majority of the microprocessors available today. This arises from the implementation of the control circuit which defines the response of the processor to the instruction commands received from the memory, route (n). The control circuit is fixed by random logic connections, or connections in a PLA or ROM and the instruction set cannot be changed by the user.

The routes shown describe the basic paths available for communication between the various units. In practice, these paths would be provided by a single route which is time-multiplexed; this makes for efficient chip designs and economical layout but obscures the basic detail required to understand the routes of the machine.

An accumulator-based machine is shown. The function unit derives its inputs from the accumulator, route (d), and another source represented by the temporary register, route (h). The result is delivered to the accumulator by route (a). The result can then be moved to the internal registers, route (r), to memory via routes (c) and (m), or to the output by route (b). The accumulator can be loaded from input, route (e), memory, route (f), or the registers, route (g), and the temporary register can be loaded from memory, route (j), or from the internal registers by route (i).

The register bank contains the internal registers used for operands or for operand addresses. The program counter is emphasized because of its important role in the basic machine activity. During the instruction fetch cycle (see below) the program counter addresses the memory by route (q) and the instruction passes to the instruction register via route (n). All other memory addresses are derived from the register bank and directed via route (q) to the memory.

Operands are moved from the memory to the registers via route (p) and from the registers to memory via routes (l) and (m). These routes show all the major paths required for understanding the activity of the 8080/85 microprocessors while obeying their respective instructions.

Processor activity

Under normal program execution, the processor performs an extremely simple sequence of activity. At the top level, the sequence may be described as

(i) obey instruction; point to next instruction
(ii) jump to (i).

The sequence (i)–(ii) is called the instruction cycle. The time to execute an instruction cycle depends on the type of instruction being performed. The instruction cycle is divided into beats, called machine cycles, which usually include a memory access. Each machine cycle takes a number of clock cycles as required for the type of sequence selected. The complete instruction cycle consists of 3 major machine cycles, A–C, as follows (references in brackets refer to Fig. 2.2):

A1. *Fetch instruction*
Send contents of PC to the memory (q). Read back instruction into the instruction register (n). Add 1 to the program counter to point to the next instruction.
a2. *Decode instruction*
The control unit identifies the operator and operands, and generates the signals required for this instruction cycle.
B. *Fetch operands*
The control unit identifies any operands required for the current operation. If a memory operand is required, the operand address is sent to the memory (q) and the operand is read into the processor (f, j or p).
C. *Execute instruction*
The control unit instructs the ALU to perform the operation on the operands fetched (d, h, a). The results are returned to the destination operand in a register (r), or in a memory (c, m) or the accumulator.

The actions A1 and a2 constitute the first machine cycle and are present in all instructions. Cycles B and C may or may not occur, depending on the actions of a2. Also, the actions of B and C may take two or more machine cycles. For example, to fetch a 16-bit operand from an 8-bit memory requires two consecutive memory accesses, i.e. two machine cycles.

The actions of B and C may not require extra machine cycles if the operands are in the internal registers of the machine. These instructions may be described as A1.a2.b.c. instruction cycles, where the lower-case letters indicate internal cycles, while ones involving two cycles in B and C would be A1.a2.B1.B2.C1.C2 instruction cycles. Examples of these will be illustrated in the tutorial problems at the end of the chapter.

Types of data

Two forms of data have been specifically referred to so far: instructions and operands. All are stored in binary form in the memory of the processor and can only be distinguished by the way the processor uses the information. Data are interpreted as instructions if accessed during the instruction fetch machine cycle. The data are operands if accessed during all other machine cycles of the instruction cycle.

Instructions and their representations usually differ from machine to machine. For example, the instruction

$$A \leftarrow A + B \qquad \text{(Add B to A)}$$

can be performed in the 8080/85, and the 6800 (and many other processors), but the binary pattern for these instructions is 10000000, and 00011011, respectively. Thus to interpret the data stored in the memory of a processor, one must not only distinguish between operands and instructions, but also identify the processor.

The operand information can be interpreted in many ways. The most common is as binary integers representing numbers or addresses. For an n-bit word, integers in the range 0 to $2^n - 1$ can be represented. For example, the number 130 is 10000010 (128 + 2) in 8-bit binary, while 01011010 is equivalent to 64 + 16 + 8 + 2 = 90.

For arithmetic operations, signed integers are required, and they are usually represented in 2's complement form. For an n-bit word, the number range is -2^{n-1} to $+(2^{n-1} -1)$, i.e. for 8 bits, -128 to $+127$. The number -25 is 11100111 in binary, 10111100 is the number -68, and 00110110 is 54. More examples and the algorithm for conversion are given in the tutorial problems.

It should be obvious that mixing representations can cause difficulties, i.e. a number cannot be used as an n-bit integer at one point in a program and as an n-bit signed integer somewhere else.

Often it is necessary to represent characters in the computer memory, e.g. 'A', 'B', ';', '!'. A convention called the ASCII character code is the standard adopted by many computer users. It uses a 7-bit code to represent the alphabet, upper and lower case, the numbers 0–9, and the standard symbols, e.g. * £ : ? +, etc. (see Table 2.1). Some of these codes, namely the numbers 0–31, are control or non-printing characters; for example, Line Feed makes the paper on a printer feed one line upwards. The ASCII character set is used for sub-systems which communicate with humans in textual form, e.g. VDUs, printers, keyboards, etc.

In all cases the information stored in the memory is in binary form. Of course, one could use binary in written documents, but a more convenient way to represent the stored information—be it instructions, addresses, signed or unsigned integers, or characters—is octal, base-8 representation, or hexadecimal, base-16, which are more compact representations. Both are shown together with the decimal equivalents for the numbers 0–127 on the ASCII table (Table 2.1). Octal and hexadecimal conversion is shown in Appendix 1.

Operands of 8080/85

The operands can be located in the registers of the processor, the main memory or in the input/output memory (image memory). The register structure of the 8080/85 is shown in Fig. 2.4.

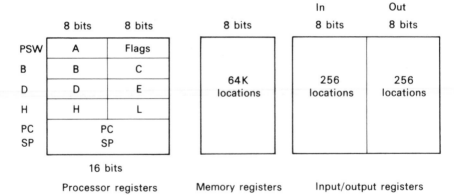

Fig. 2.4 8080/85 operand register structure

The program counter (PC) is 16 bits, permitting a directly addressed memory of 64K bytes for storing programs. There is a stack pointer (SP) of 16 bits, allowing the return address store to reside anywhere in the 64K byte memory. The 8080/85 has seven 8-bit general registers and a condition flag register. Pairs of 8-bit registers may be combined and used as a single 16-bit register as depicted in Fig. 2.4.

The 8080/85 has the capability of addressing 65 536 8-bit operands in memory directly. Thus the memory is required to accommodate instructions, operands and return addresses all within the 64K address space. In some processors the memory will also contain the peripheral registers, or input/output ports. The programmer must balance out these demands on the memory resource, often having to compromise between program and data if a smaller memory is to be used.

Frequently operands or addresses longer than 8-bits are stored in the memory, in which case additional memory locations are used; 2 for 16 bits, 3 for 24 bits, etc.

Operand addressing

The methods of accessing or defining an operand in an instruction are known collectively as addressing modes. They are treated fully in Chapter 5 so only a brief résumé of the relevant ones is given here.

(i) *Immediate*—the operand is located immediately after the instruction in the next location for an 8-bit operand, or the next two locations for a 16-bit operand. After fetching the instruction the program counter is already pointing to the next location and can be used to address the operand when reading memory. Constants are stored as immediate operands. The 8080/85 supports both 8-bit and 16-bit immediate addressing; using one or two locations in memory, respectively, for the operand.

(ii) *Direct register*—the operand is located in one of the processor registers or register pairs; both 8-bit and 16-bit operands are supported in the 8080/85.

Because of the limited number of registers the register address is short, 3 bits for the 8080/85 (see Fig. 2.5(*a*) and (*b*)) and can be readily accommodated in the 8-bit instruction word.

8080/85 contains seven 8-bit (four 16-bit) registers and 2 16-bit registers. The processor identifies the registers by the octal code shown in Figs. 2.5(*a*) and 2.5(*b*) for 8-bit and 16-bit operands, respectively. This code will appear in the instruction field (see Chapter 3) as designated by the programmer. The registers are identified also by symbols for ease of programming and clarity of understanding. A,B,C,D,E,H,L are all 8-bit operands, while B, D, H, PSW, SP and PC are 16-bit operands. (Note that PC may be used as an operand destination as shown later.)

A register can be used as the source, S, or destination, D, in the operand field of an instruction. When used as a source the contents of the register are copied and remain unchanged. When used as the destination the current contents are destroyed and the new value (the source value) is loaded into the register.

All the registers have a general purpose role, in which case they may be

Table 2.1 ASCII character codes

D	O	H	Char.	D	O	H	Char.
0	000	00	NULL	32	040	20	Space
1	001	01	SOH	33	041	21	!
2	002	02	STX	34	042	22	"
3	003	03	ETX	35	043	23	#
4	004	04	EOT	36	044	24	$
5	005	05	ENQ	37	045	25	%
6	006	06	ACK	38	046	26	&
7	007	07	BELL	39	047	27	'
8	010	08	BS	40	050	28	(
9	011	09	HT	41	051	29	)
10	012	0A	Line Feed	42	052	2A	*
11	013	0B	VT	43	053	2B	+
12	014	0C	Form Feed	44	054	2C	,
13	015	0D	Carr Ret	45	055	2D	-
14	016	0E	SO	46	056	2E	.
15	017	0F	SI	47	057	2F	/
16	020	10	DLE	48	060	30	0
17	021	11	X ON (DC1)	49	061	31	1
18	022	12	TAPE (DC2)	50	062	32	2
19	023	13	X OFF (DC3)	51	063	33	3
20	024	14	(DC4)	52	064	34	4
21	025	15	NAK	53	065	35	5
22	026	16	SYN	54	066	36	6
23	027	17	ETB	55	067	37	7
24	030	18	CAN	56	070	38	8
25	031	19	EM	57	071	39	9
26	032	1A	SUB	58	072	3A	:
27	033	1B	ESCape	59	073	3B	;
28	034	1C	FS	60	074	3C	<
29	035	1D	GS	61	075	3D	=
30	036	1E	RS	62	076	3E	>
31	037	1F	US	63	077	3F	?

D—decimal, O—octal, H—hexadecimal, Char.—character

D	O	H	Char.	D	O	H	Char.
64	100	40	@	96	140	60	`
65	101	41	A	97	141	61	a
66	102	42	B	98	142	62	b
67	103	43	C	99	143	63	c
68	104	44	D	100	144	64	d
69	105	45	E	101	145	65	e
70	106	46	F	102	146	66	f
71	107	47	G	103	147	67	g
72	110	48	H	104	150	68	h
73	111	49	I	105	151	69	i
74	112	4A	J	106	152	6A	j
75	113	4B	K	107	153	6B	k
76	114	4C	L	108	154	6C	l
77	115	4D	M	109	155	6D	m
78	116	4E	N	110	156	6E	n
79	117	4F	O	111	157	6F	o
80	120	50	P	112	160	70	p
81	121	51	Q	113	161	71	q
82	122	52	R	114	162	72	r
83	123	53	S	115	163	73	s
84	124	54	T	116	164	74	t
85	125	55	U	117	165	75	u
86	126	56	V	118	166	76	v
87	127	57	W	119	167	77	w
88	130	58	X	120	170	78	x
89	131	59	Y	121	171	79	y
90	132	5A	Z	122	172	7A	z
91	133	5B	[	123	173	7B	{
92	134	5C	\	124	174	7C	\
93	135	5D	]	125	175	7D	}
94	136	5E	Λ	126	176	7E	~
95	137	5F	—	127	177	7F	DELete

Code octal D or S	Symbol 8-bit operand R1, R2	Function
0	B ⎤	General
1	C ⎟	purpose
2	D ⎟	(GP)
3	E ⎦	
4	H ⎤	GP or memory
5	L ⎦	Operand address
6	M	Operand in memory at (H.L)
7	A	Accumulator

Fig. 2.5(a) 8-bit operand register identifiers

Code octal	Symbol 16-bit operand	Register pair	Function
V	RP1		
0	B	B.C	General registers
2	D	D.E	as source or
4	H	H.L	destination
6	SP	SP	
x	RP2		
0	B	B.C	Memory indirect
2	D	D.E	address registers
Y	RP3		
0	B	B.C	Source and
2	D	D.E	destination for
4	H	H.L	stack move
6	PSW	Acc + Flags	operations

Fig. 2.5(b) 16-bit operand register identifiers

used by the programmer to store variables or temporary results. In some instructions the registers also perform special functions which are elaborated later where relevant.

The symbols R1, R2, RP1, RP2 and RP3 in Fig. 2.5 are used in the instruction set to refer collectively to the registers listed under the respective columns. The letters D, S, V, X and Y appear in the instruction words and represent the value of the octal code shown in the tables of Fig. 2.5.

The provision of both 8- and 16-bit operands makes programming easier, although in the case of the 8080/85 the 16-bit operands are principally address operands, i.e. 16-bit positive integers.

(iii) *Direct memory*—in this addressing mode, the instruction contains the address of the location in memory which contains the operand. This makes the instruction very long because of the large number of bits required for the address. Often both 8-bit and 16-bit addresses are used. For the former the other 8 bits, usually the top 8, are either zero or provided by a register in the processor. The 8080/85 supports 3 direct addressing modes; one for 8-bit operands stored in a single memory location, the second for 16-bit operands stored in two consecutive memory locations, the third for input/output registers of 8 bits.

(iv) *Memory indirect*—in the memory indirect mode the operand is in memory. The address of the location is contained in a register pair B.C, D.E or H.L; the first register (B,D,H) contains the higher-order 8-bits, while C,E,L contain the low-order 8-bits. When the processor detects this mode in the instruction field it sends the contents of the register pair onto the address bus (route (q) in Fig. 2.2). It then either copies (read) the memory operand (source) into the destination register, or copies (write) the source register into the memory location (destination).

Because the instruction only needs a few bits to identify the register containing the address, the indirect mode is economical in its use of instruction codes.

(v) *Implied register pair*—one addressing mode uses the register pair H.L when the M register, octal code 6, is specified as the operand. Since the programmer has no choice in the selection of the address register it is called an implied addressing mode.

Summary of addressing modes in the 8080/85

The 8080/85 supports the following addressing modes:

Immediate: for both 8-bit and 16-bit operands.
Direct: for 8-bit processor register operands, for 8-bit and 16-bit memory operands, and for 8-bit input/output operands.
Indirect: for 8-bit memory operands.

In many instructions the source or destination operand is fixed, in which case it is implied. In the 8080/85 these are identified in the operation code mnemonic as shown later.

Operation unit

The operators of a computer are provided by a logic circuit called the function unit, or more specifically the arithmetic-logic unit, ALU. The general ALU, shown in Fig. 2.6, has two input operands X and Y, a result operand Z, a function unit which performs the operation and a status register which stores the state of the result.

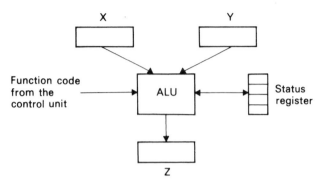

Fig. 2.6 A general operation unit

Binary operations are those which require both X and Y to be present, e.g. ADD. These operations will require 3 operands to be specified in the instruction, i.e. X, Y and Z. Unary operations only require X or Y, but not both, to be specified. Unary operation orders only require two operands to be specified.

The status register stores information for use by the ALU next time it is activated. The status bits are frequently called condition flags because they are tested by the conditional jump instructions. They are either set to logic '1' or reset to logic '0' according to the result of the current operations. The 8080/85 condition flags (i.e. flags which affect the jump instructions) are:

Carry: is set if the result produced an overflow into the 9th bit, otherwise it is reset.

Zero: is set if the result is zero, otherwise it is reset.

Sign: is set if bit 7 of the result is set and reset otherwise.

Note: bit 7 is the negative sign bit in 8-bit 2's complement notation.

Parity: is set if there is an even number of ones in the result, otherwise it is reset.

A further status bit, auxilliary carry or half carry is stored if overflow occurs from the fourth to the fifth bit. This is used only by the decimal adjust instruction so is not strictly a condition flag, since no decision can be based on its state.

Operators

Operators may be classified into those which change and those which do not change the information in the computer. The latter perform the basic move, really copy, operations of the machine and only require a variety of routing functions in the computer system. The former require an operation unit as discussed above.

Move: A move operation (really a copy operation) copies the contents of the source operand, X, into the destination operand Z. There are many move orders in the 8080/85. The move is unusual in that it is a unary operation (only one source operand) that must have two operands specified; the source and destination must be different to perform a useful function. All other unary operators can operate usefully with the same source and destination operand. The 8080/85 supports both 8-bit and 16-bit move operations which will be elaborated more fully in the instruction set.

Many forms of move operation are given special names which contain implicit information about either the source or destination. A load operation usually copies the contents of a memory location to a specified processor register while store performs the reverse operation. A push operation copies the contents of a register onto the stack. Pop copies the contents of the top of the stack into a specified register.

The exchange operation is an extremely useful copy operation. The source (destination) operand is copied into the destination (source) register and the destination (source) operand is copied into the source (destination) register. Thus no information is lost and the operation is completely symmetrical.

Eight-bit operators

The majority of the 8080/85 operations are performed on 8-bit operands in the processor registers or memory.

The operators executed by the ALU are described below. They are summarized in two columns in Fig. 2.7, which contain three descriptions of

Binary operators	Operation mnemonic		Octal
	OPb	OPIb	
Add (+)	ADD	ADI	0
Add with carry (+)	ADC	ACI	1
Subtract (−)	SUB	SUI	2
Subtract with borrow (−)	SBB	SBI	3
Logical AND (∧)	ANA	ANI	4
Logical EXOR (⊕)	XRA	XRI	5
Logical OR (∨)	ORA	ORI	6
Compare	CMP	CPI	7

Fig. 2.7 Basic binary operators of 8080

the operations. A brief written description is followed by the standard mathematical symbol where relevant. The second column shows the symbolic operation code (op-code) used when writing programs. In the 8080/85 symbolic code a different operation code is used for the immediate addressing mode. The symbolic op-codes, which end in I, e.g. SBI, for the immediate modes are shown together with the basic form of the operation code. The third column shows, in octal, the machine codes that appear in the operation field of the instruction.

Binary operators

There are eight binary operators listed in Fig. 2.7.

Add: The two source operands are added to produce an 8-bit result. If overflow occurs the carry is set; zero, sign and parity are set or reset according to the result. Because the 2's complement convention is used, the result can be an 8-bit integer, or a 7-bit signed integer. In the latter case the result may be negative, i.e. bit 7 is set, which may or may not be correct depending on the original values of the operands. The rules relating to arithmetic overflow are listed in Fig. 2.8. Therefore there are two conditions when addition can result in arithmetic overflow.

Original operands		Operator	Result overflow
X	Y	f	if Z is:
+ve	+ve	ADD	negative
−ve	−ve	ADD	positive
+ve	−ve	SUBTRACT	negative
−ve	+ve	SUBTRACT	positive

The operation is $Z \leftarrow X \cdot f \cdot Y$

Fig. 2.8 Arithmetic overflow with 2's complement numbers

Subtract: The second source operand, Y, is subtracted from the first, X, to produce an 8-bit result. Again, the flags are set or reset according to the result and the rules for arithmetic overflow of 2's complement numbers apply as shown above.

Add with carry: This operation also adds in the value of the carry bit to the two operands. It permits the programmer to add numbers of more than 8 bits in length. Consider two numbers, X and Y, in consecutive locations in memory, each 16 bits long, being added to produce a result, Z, another 16-bit operand which is stored in memory (see Fig. 2.9).

Since the ALU is only 8 bits wide, the addition of 16-bit operands proceeds in two steps. First the low operands, XL and YL, are added producing the result ZL, which is stored in the memory. The carry bit will be set or reset by the addition. It can then be included in the addition operation when the high operands, XH and YH, are added with carry, as depicted in Fig. 2.9. The result, ZH, is then stored in memory. This operation permits high precision arithmetic in an 8-bit machine.

Subtract with borrow: This is the corresponding subtraction for multi-word arithmetic. Both affect the flags carry, zero, sign and parity.

Memory

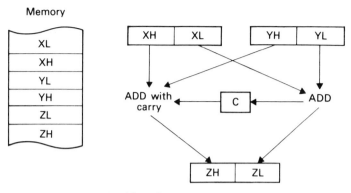

Fig. 2.9 Multi-word arithmetic

Logical AND, OR, EXOR: These operators perform logical operations on the two source operands. A bit-by-bit operation is performed; bit n of operand X and bit n of operand Y are operated on and the result placed in bit n of operand Z. There is no sideways propagation, therefore carry is always reset. The sign bit is set if bit 7 is a logic '1' but obviously the result is not strictly negative. Zero and parity are affected as normal. The logical functions are described in detail in Chapter 1.

Compare: The second operand, Y, is subtracted from the first operand, X, but the result operand, Z, is not affected. The flags are set or reset as for a normal subtraction. Compare permits a non-destructive test of the value of an operand.

Unary operators

There are nine basic unary operators as shown in the table in Fig. 2.10.

Rotate: In the 8080/85 there are two types of rotate, or shift, operator and two directions of movement, giving four different orders. The orders

Unary operators	Operation mnemonic OPU	Octal u code
Rotate left round carry	RLC	0
Rotate right round carry	RRC	1
Rotate left through carry	RAL	2
Rotate right through carry	RAR	3
Decimal adjust	DAA	4
Complement	CMA	5
	OP u*	u* code
Increment	INR	4
Decrement	DCR	5

Fig. 2.10 Basic unary operators of 8080

that move round the carry, RLC and RRC, perform an 8-bit cyclic shift; i.e. bit 7 enters bit 0 or vice versa for left and right shift, respectively. The carry flag takes the value of the end bit; i.e. but 7 or bit 0 for left and right, respectively. A 9-bit cyclic shift, which includes the carry bit, is performed by the rotate-through-carry operators, RAL and RAR. These operators are illustrated in more detail in P1.7 of Chapter 1.

Decimal adjust: This order performs a binary coded decimal adjust on positive binary integers. It adds 6 if the BCD digit is greater than 9. The adjust normally follows an addition operation using binary coded decimal digits.

Complement: A 1's complement operation is performed by the complement operator; it inverts each bit of the source operand. This function is identical to performing an exclusive-OR operation with all ones, i.e. 377 octal or FF hexadecimal.

Sixteen-bit operations

In addition to the main ALU unit which operates on 8-bit operands there is another function unit in the 8080/85, with limited capability, which operates on 16-bit operands. The operations are:

> Add 16-bit integers (DAD)
> Increment 16-bit integers (INX)
> Decrement 16-bit integers (DCX)

This function unit does not have separate flags but the result of the add operation does affect the carry bit of the main ALU.

One-bit operations

There are two operations, namely set and clear, which operate on the one-bit status flags.

Summary of operations

The 8080/85 performs operations on 1-bit, 8-bit and 16-bit operands, although the latter are rather restricted. The operators described occur in many other processors and the general treatment given provides an introduction to other types. The instruction set, i.e. combinations of operations and operands, is presented in the next chapter.

Problems

P2.1 Draw a block diagram of a computer and show the processor, memory, and input/output systems. Describe the function of each block.

P2.2 Describe the terms: Program counter, arithmetic logic unit, registers, control unit, operand register.

P2.3 What information is stored in the memory of a processor, and how is it accessed? What are the benefits of having the program and data in the same memory?

P2.4 The data routes of Fig. 2.2 have been labelled a–r. Using these labels, describe the action of the instruction fetch machine cycle and identify the data on each route used. If the instruction fetched specified 'add register R1 to the accumulator' describe this activity as well.

P2.5 What is the purpose of input/output on a computer? What are the differences and similarities between memory and input/output? Describe the execution of an input instruction on the machine of Fig. 2.2

P2.6 Describe in detail the execution of an instruction which adds a register R1 to a memory location addressed by R2, leaving the result in the same memory location. Use any temporary registers necessary.

Number representation

P2.7 Convert the following positive numbers to decimal:

00101011, 11000010, 10101010, 01110001
00001101, 11110111, 01011000, 10000000

P2.8 Convert the above numbers to octal (base 8) and hexadecimal (base 16). Use the letters A B C D E F to represent 10–15.

P2.9 Most microprocessors use the 2's complement representation for signed integers, in which case the most significant bit is the sign. To generate a 2's complement negative number $(-N)$, express N as a positive binary number, invert all the bits, and add '1'. What are the 2's complement negative numbers in 8-bit binary form for the following positive integers:

1, 11, 47, 69, 4, 127, 128?

What are they in 10-bit binary form?

P2.10 To convert from a 2's complement negative number into a signed integer, the reverse of the above process can be used. Convert the following to signed decimal integers:

11111100, 10111111, 11010101, 10000000, 10011111.

P2.11 An alternative method of conversion is to subtract the binary representation of the number from zero. This works for conversion in both directions. Convert the numbers in P2.9 and P2.10 to prove this.

P2.12 What are the 2's complement values of the binary codes of P2.7?

P2.13 There is a CCITT standard for representing the character set of a keyboard, called the ASCII codes. What are the characters represented by the eight codes in P2.7? (Note: ignore the left-hand bit—use only the right-most seven bits.)

P2.14 The binary numbers of P2.7 can also represent the instructions of a processor. What are the assembler instructions for the 8 combinations for an

8080 microprocessor? (See Appendix 3 for details of the instruction set.)

P2.15 Repeat P2.14 for the 6800 microprocessor. (See Appendix 4 for the instruction set.)

8080/85 operands

P2.16 Describe and discuss the 8-bit operands available in the 8080/85. Describe how 16-bit operands are accommodated within this structure. What is the main purpose of 16-bit operands in the 8080/85?

P2.17 One memory addressing mode treats the memory location (M) like a register. Name the addressing mode and describe how a memory operand may be accessed using it. Use the diagram of Fig. 2.2 to illustrate your answer.

P2.18 Describe how immediate and direct addressing modes work in the 8080. Compare their use in a program. If direct addressing is used to access an operand in ROM, how does it differ from the immediate mode? (Explain your answers using the notation of Fig. 2.2.)

Operation unit

P2.19 Describe with the aid of a block diagram the general arrangement of the operation unit. What is the more common name for the unit? Outline the requirements for binary (diadic) or unary (monadic) operations.

P2.20 What purposes do the status flags fulfill in the operation unit? Describe them and their function. Use examples to explain how each is set and cleared.

P2.21 An operation unit is shown in Fig. 2.6. The 8080/85 operation unit differs slightly in that the results (Z) appear in the A register and one of the operands (Y) is supplied by the A register. Draw the new arrangement, replacing Z and Y by the A register. If the A register contains 85 and the X register 20 (both decimal) what are the contents of A after performing the following operations?

ADD, ORA, XRA, ANA, CMP, CMA, RRC, RAL.

(The unary operations use only the A register.)

P2.22 If the flags are initially zero, what are the flag values after performing the operations in P2.21?

P2.23 Discuss why 16-bit operations might be useful in an 8-bit microcomputer.

3 The instruction set

The instruction set of the 8080/85 is described in a structured way in this chapter. In an earlier text by the authors both the 8008 and the 6800 were described to present a comparative assessment. The object of this chapter is to introduce the elements of instruction sets by example. To clutter this by using two processors, as before, is considered to be detrimental to the main purpose of the chapter. The 6800 is described in the same style in Appendix 4.

The microcomputer obeys commands or instructions, stored in its memory, under the control of the central processing unit (CPU). The list of commands a computer can obey is known as its instruction set, and this set is defined by the logic circuits in the control unit of the central processor and the arithmetic logic unit. The instruction set governs the processing power of the computer and is the most important single feature.

The instruction set defines the combination of operations (of the ALU) and operands (in memory or registers) that can be activated by the control unit in one instruction cycle. In the previous chapter the hardware components, operands and operations were described and no explicit restriction on operands and operations was stressed; these can only be determined by examining the instructions (or possibly the control circuit). Restrictions on combinations of operand–operator pairs are imposed by the designer of the control circuit because of limited chip area for the logic or because no space exists in the instruction word. The more flexible the combinations of operands and operators, the richer is the instruction set of the processor and the easier it is to program.

An instruction set contains two main types of instruction: the operation orders, and the control orders. The operation orders are treated first, followed by a description of the control orders.

The instructions about to be described are in a structured tabular form which makes for easier interpretation and understanding. To do this successfully with the 8080, base-8 (octal) representation of the machine code is used. The tables provide a brief description of the instructions, a mathematical notation, a symbolic description and the machine code. These tables are supplemented by more detailed written descriptions.

The material on 16-bit instructions can be omitted on the first reading–

being the more advanced instructions–and the following chapters studied before returning to these sections.

Operation instructions

Operation instructions are the orders which perform operations on operands (data), stored in registers in the CPU, the memory or in the input/output space. They all execute the general assignment statement

$$(Z) \leftarrow (X).f.(Y)$$

where f is an operator, X and Y are the source operands (one of which may be omitted), and $\leftarrow$ is the assignment operation which makes the destination operand, Z, take on the value of the right-hand side of the assignment statement. The brackets denote 'the contents of'; for example

$(A) \leftarrow (A) + (E)$; adds the contents of register E to the contents of register A, leaving the result in register A;

$(A) \leftarrow (A) \wedge 23\ O$; performs a logical AND of the contents of register A with 23_8 (23 octal, the letter 'O' indicating octal), leaving the result in register A.

An operation instruction must define all of the pertaining operands Z, X, Y and the operator, f, to specify the order completely.

Instructions which allow all three operands to be specified are classed as 3-address orders. Those allowing only two, one or zero operands to be specified are 2- 1- or zero-address orders, respectively. Operands not explicitly specified by the programmer are implied or implicit operands.

The arithmetic orders of the 8085 are 1-address; Z and X are replaced by the A register or accumulator resulting in the standard 1-address binary or diadic operation order:

(i) $(A) \leftarrow (A).b.R2$; where R2 replaces Y as the source operand.

The unary or monadic operators form instructions with 1- or zero-address of the form:

(ii) $(R1) \leftarrow (R1).u$
(iii) $(A) \leftarrow (A).u$

Only R1, R2, b and u can be defined by the programmer. The rest are fixed by the logic circuits in the processor.

The arithmetic and logical orders may be further sub-divided into 1-bit, 8-bit and 16-bit operations and are described first.

The 8080/85 is rich in move instructions and these are described separately. The key to the figures used in this section is given in Table 3.1, and will be referred to frequently.

Table 3.1 Key to Figs 3.1 and 3.2

R1	Destination operand mnemonic (see Fig. 2.5(a))
R2	Source operand mnemonic (see Fig. 2.5(a))
S	Source operand code (see Fig. 2.5(a))
D	Destination operand code (see Fig. 2.5(a))
RP1, RP2, RP3	Register pair mnemonics (see Fig 2.5(b))
V, X, Y	Register pair codes (see Fig. 2.5(b))
n	Literal mnemonic
n8	Literal code in octal
b	Binary or diadic operation code (see Fig. 2.7)
u, u*	Unary or monadic operation code (see Fig. 2.10)
OPb, OPIb	Binary operation mnemonic (see Fig. 2.7)
OPu, OPu*	Unary operation mnemonic (see Fig. 2.10)
ADDR	Memory address
ADDRH8, ADDRL8	High and low bytes of address in octal
SP	Stack pointer
SPH, SPL	High and low bytes of stack pointer
IWP	Immediate word pair
IWPH8, IWPL8	High and low bytes of IWP in octal
RP1H, RP1L, etc.	High and low bytes of register pairs

One-bit operation instructions (Fig. 3.1(a))

Two instructions, set carry to logic 1 (STC) and complement carry (CMC) are available. These instructions are most useful for setting a condition, in a subroutine, which is tested by the main program after returning from the routine. They are also useful for setting or clearing carry before arithmetic or rotate operations.

Instruction	Type and function	Mnemonic	Machine code (octal)
Zero-address 3.1 A	Set carry $C \leftarrow 1$	STC	0 6 7
3.1 B	Complement carry $C \leftarrow \overline{C}$	CMC	0 7 7

Fig. 3.1(a) 1-bit operation orders for 8080/85 (see Table 3.1 for key)

Eight-bit operation instructions (Fig. 3.1(b))

There are four basic groups of instructions in this class (3.1C–3.1F). The register, memory indirect (3.1C) and immediate (3.1D) arithmetic and

Instruction	Type and function	Instruction mnemonic	Machine code (octal)
1-address: 3.1C	Register and memory arithmetic $(A) \leftarrow (A).b.(R2)$	OPb R2	2 | b | S
3.1D	Immediate arithmetic $(A) \leftarrow (A).b.n$	OPlb n	3 | b | 6 n_8
3.1E	Increment and decrement $(R1) \leftarrow (R1).u^*$	OPu* D	0 | d | u*
Zero-address: 3.1F	Register A implied Accumulator operations $(A) \leftarrow (A).u$	OPu	0 | u | 7

Fig. 3.1(b) 8-bit operation orders for 8080/85 (see Table 3.1 for key)

Instruction	Type and function	Instruction mnemonic	Machine code (octal)
1-address: 3.1G	Register-pair increment $(RP1) \leftarrow (RP1) + 1$	INX RP1	0 | V | 3
3.1H	Register-pair decrement $RP1 \leftarrow (RP1) - 1$	DCX RP1	0 | V+1 | 3
3.1J	Register-pair addition $(H.L) \leftarrow (H.L) + (RP1)$	DAD RP1	0 | V+1 | 1

Fig. 3.1(c) 16-bit arithmetic orders (see Table 3.1 for key)

logical orders all execute the full set of binary operations OPb and OPIb shown in Fig. 2.7. Any of the registers of Fig. 2.5(a) can be used for the register and memory indirect orders. These orders require no further explanation since the component parts have been fully described in Chapter 2.

The increment/decrement orders (3.1E) operate on any of the registers

A, B, C, D, E, H, L and the memory M(H.L). In the latter case the location pointed to by H.L will be incremented or decremented.

The zero-address orders (3.1F) only operate on the A register, restricting the use of the rotate, decimal adjust and complement operations to a single destination register.

These groups require little further explanation since they are so regularly organized. The reader should refer to Chapter 2 to study the full complement of instructions available.

Examples of instructions with 8-bit operands:

Description	Mnemonic	Machine code (octal)
(i) Add 21 to register A	ADI 21	306
(A) ← (A) + 21 or	ADI 25Q	025
or (A) ← (A) + 25Q		
(ii) Compare register E with A	CMP E	273
(A)—(E)		
(iii) Complement register A	CMA	057
(iv) AND the contents of memory		
location 001.015* with register A		
(A) ← (A) ∧ M(001.015)	MVI L,15Q	056
		015
	MVI H,1Q	046
		001
	ANA M	246

Note: Q or O are used to indicate octal numbers.

The last case (iv) needs three instructions, the first two to set up the memory pointer H.L, and the third to perform the operation.

Sixteen-bit operation instructions (Fig. 3.1(c))

These arithmetic operations provide address manipulation and perform positive 16-bit integer operations. INX and DCX (3.1G and 3.1H) are increment and decrement operations, respectively, on register pairs B, D, H, and SP.

Example (v): INX B will add 1 to register pair B and C. If register C is decimal 255 before this operation, then it will be zero after the operation, and B will have 1 added to it. This is equivalent to three instructions, 5 bytes of memory, using 8-bit operations.

The DAD instruction (3.1J) is a register pair addition which uses the

---

* The address is shown as two 8-bit numbers joined by the full-stop concatenation symbol.

H.L pair as the accumulator. Register pairs B, D, H, and SP can be added to H.L and the result is left in registers H and L.

Example (vi): DAD D adds the register pair D.E to register pair H.L (overflow is ignored). If DE contains decimal 100 and HL contains decimal 157 before the instruction is executed, then the pair DE remains unchanged, while register H contains decimal 1 and register L contains decimal 1 after execution, i.e. H.L contains 257 (256 + 1).

Copy instructions: 8-bit operands (Fig. 3.2(a))

The 8-bit copy orders, frequently called move orders are available with immediate, register-direct, memory-direct and register-indirect modes.

Instruction	Type and function	Mnemonic	Machine code (octal)
2-address: 3.2A	Register direct and memory indirect transfer (R1) ← (R2) (M ≡ M(H.L))	MOV R1,R2	1 D S
3.2B	Immediate transfer (R1) ← n	MVI R1,n	0 D 6 / n_8
1-address: 3.2C	Memory direct transfer (load A register) (A) ← M(ADDR)	LDA ADDR	0 7 2 / ADDRL8 / ADDRH8
3.2D	Memory direct transfer (store A register) M(ADDR) ← (A)	STA ADDR	0 6 2 / ADDRL8 / ADDRH8
3.2E	Indirect transfer (load A register) (A) ← M((RP2))	LDAX RP2	0 X+1 2
3.2F	Indirect transfer (store A register) M((RP2)) ← (A)	STAX RP2	0 X 2

Fig. 3.2(a) 8-bit move instructions for 8080/85 (see Table 3.1 for key)

Instruction	Type and function	Mnemonic	Machine code (octal)
2-address: 3.2G	Immediate transfer (RP1 L) ← IWP L (RP1 H) ← IWP H	LXI RP1, 1WP	0 | V | 1 IWPL8 IWPH8
1-address: 3.2H	Direct transfer (load register pair H.L) (L) ← M(ADDR) (H) ← M(ADDR + 1)	LHLD ADDR	0 | 5 | 2 ADDRL8 ADDRH8
3.2I	Direct transfer (store register pair H.L) M(ADDR) ← (L) M(ADDR +1) ← (H)	SHLD ADDR	0 | 4 | 2 ADDRL8 ADDRH8
3.2J	Stack implied transfer (push to stack) M((SP)−1) ← (RP3 H) M((SP)−2) ← (RP3 L); (SP) ← (SP)−2	PUSH RP3	3 | Y | 5
3.2K	Stack implied transfer (Pop from stack) (RP3 L) ← M((SP)) (RP3 H) ← M((SP)+1);(SP) ← (SP)+ 2	POP RP3	3 | Y | 1
Zero-address: 3.2L	Register transfer (load SP from register H.L) (SPL) ← (L) (SPH) ← (H)	SPHL	3 | 7 | 1
3.2M	Register exchange (exchange D.E with H.L) (D) ↔ (H) (E) ↔ (L)	XCHG	3 | 5 | 3
3.2N	Register-Stack exchange (H) ↔ M((SP)+1) (L) ↔ M((SP))	XTHL	3 | 4 | 3

Fig. 3.2(b) 16-bit move instructions of 8080/85 (see Table 3.1 for key)

Two of them are 2-address types giving the programmer the freedom to choose both source and destination. The rest all have register A as an implied source or destination.

Register and immediate byte. Register-direct and memory-indirect using H.L (3.2A) and immediate modes (3.2B) allow all registers and register combinations (except MOV M, M, which is useless anyway but if coded according to the rules generates a halt instruction).

As with the 8-bit operation instructions, these two orders are well structured and therefore require little further explanation.

Examples (vii):

Copy the contents of C to H.	MOV	H, C	141
Copy the contents of H to C.	MOV	C, H	114
Copy the contents of A to L.	MOV	L, A	157

(Use Figs 3.2(*a*) and 2.5(*a*) to prove these correct.)

Direct memory byte. The load and store accumulator instructions use a direct memory address ADDR provided in the second and third byte of the instruction. The processor uses the address ADDR to access memory and copies of byte of data from the location to the accumulator (LDA) see 3.2C), or moves a byte of data from the accumulator to the location in memory (STA: see 3.2D).

Indirect memory byte. The load and store indirect instructions use the contents of a register pair, RP2, (either B and C or D and E) as the address for memory. The processor uses the contents of the register specified by RP2 to address the memory, then either moves the contents of this location to the accumulator (LDAX: see 3.2E), or moves the contents of the accumulator to the location addressed (STAX: see 3.2F). This addressing mode is identical in operation to using the memory register mode, M, using H.L indirectly.

Example (viii):

Copy contents of memory location 020.157 into the accumulator.

Two examples are given using LDA and LDAX B.

(*a*) Copy direct to A	LDA	020.157Q	072
			157
			020
(*b*) Load B and C with address	MVI	B, 020Q	006
			020
	MVI	C, 157Q	016
			157
Copy indirect to A	LDAX	B	012

A copy operation from A to memory could be performed using STA and STAX appropriately. Note that example (viii) (*b*) is similar in form to Example (iv).

Copy instructions: 16-bit operands (Fig. 3.2(b))

Immediate word. The most basic 16-bit (word) operation is the load immediate register pair RP1 (3.2G). The 16-bit operand, IWP, is stored in the second and third bytes of the instruction and 4 register destinations are available: B, D, H, SP (see Fig. 2.5(*b*)). This instruction permits initial loading of 16-bit registers, e.g. the stack pointer.

Example (ix):

LXI   SP, 000.100Q will load the stack pointer with 000.100 octal or 128 decimal. LXI B, 520 will load B with decimal 2 and C with decimal 8. (LXI   H, 001.015Q is identical to the first two instructions of Example (iv), and LXI B, 020.157Q is identical to the first two instructions of Example (viii) (*b*)).

Direct memory word. The register pair H.L can be loaded directly from memory or stored directly into memory, using the two instructions LHLD and SHLD (3.2H and 3.2I). The direct address ADDR is stored in the second and third bytes of the instruction group. The processor uses the address ADDR to directly access memory to move a 16-bit variable into H.L. (LHLD), or to move a 16-bit variable from H.L into the two consecutive memory locations (SHLD). The address ADDR points to the least significant byte (i.e. lower address) and the most significant byte is in location ADDR + 1.

Example (x):

LHLD   2.010 B will load the contents of memory locations decimal 520, and decimal 521 into registers L and H, respectively.

Implied word. There are two special instructions which move 16-bit operands between fixed register pairs. The first, SPHL (3.2L), copies the contents of register pair H.L into the stack pointer register. Registers H and L remain unchanged. The second, XCHG (3.2M), performs an exchange between register pairs H.L and D.E. Thus, D takes the value of H, and H takes the value of D, while E takes the value of L, and L the value of E.

The stack was described briefly in Chapter 2; its use in the 8080/85 is detailed in the next section, and a general treatment is given in Chapter 5. The use of the stack for operand storage logically fits in at this point, but rather than duplicate a description of the stack the reader is advised to complete this chapter before a full understanding of this section may be obtained. The stack provides a storage area for return addresses, and when it is located in the memory of a processor, its depth effectively becomes infinite, and therefore it can be used to store operands as well as return addresses. PUSH (3.2J) writes a 16-bit operand to the stack, while POP (3.2K) removes a 16-bit operand from the stack. PUSH automatically decrements the stack pointer by 2, and POP increments the stack pointer by 2. The register pairs, RP3, that can be used as source operands for PUSH, and destination operands for POP, are B, D, H and PSW (the accumulator and flags). The most useful function of these two instructions is the ability to store (PUSH) the processor state vector when entering a subroutine and retrieve it (POP) when leaving.

The register-stack exchange instruction, XTHL, (3.2N) swaps the 16-bit word at the top of stack with the contents of H and L. The stack pointer remains unchanged by this operation.

Program control

A variety of control mechanisms are needed to allow the programmer the freedom to modify the flow of control through a program. The general control instruction contains

  (i) destination address
 (ii) control mechanism
(iii) condition to be tested.

All three items are present either explicitly or implicitly in the instruction.

Destination address

In general the destination address can be defined using one of the many addressing modes described earlier or in Chapter 5.

Direct: The majority of the 8080/85 instructions include a 16-bit address as part of the instruction. This may be called immediate addressing if the program counter is viewed as the destination register; i.e. load the PC with the immediate word pair. Alternatively, it can be considered as direct addressing if one views the next instruction as the 'operand'; i.e. fetch the next instruction ('operand'), from the location specified by the instruction. In both cases the effect is the same, execution continues from the location specified by the destination address.

Indirect: A second method in the 8080/85 is for the address to be located in the register pair H.L. It is loaded into the program counter to effect an indirect jump. The contents of H.L can be computed prior to making the jump. Chapter 10 shows an example of using this instruction.

Control mechanisms

Jump: The basic control mechanism is the jump or goto. The destination address is loaded into the program counter and thereby causes execution to continue from the new location. If the jump is conditional on some status bit, it may only perform the loading operation if the condition is true.

Jump to subroutine: There are many situations where a particular sequence of instructions is required many times at different points in a program. To insert the code each time is wasteful of space, tedious to carry out and difficult to manage if modifications are made; it is easy to forget to correct every occurrence of the code. To overcome this problem a special jump mechanism is provided in the instruction set. To illustrate the problem a simple example will be described.

In Fig. 3.3 a main program is shown which enters a subroutine (the name used for the common section of program) from two places, location A and location B.

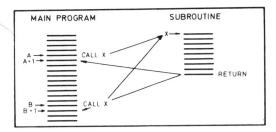

Fig. 3.3 The 'jump-to-sub-routine' operation

At the address A in the memory is a jump instruction which makes the processor continue execution at address X. However, before jumping the program counter will be pointing to the next instruction at, say, A + 1, and the processor must store this address in order to remember the location to return to after completing the subroutine. On completion of the routine a special instruction, called return, will make the processor retrieve the address stored away and load it into the program counter causing it to continue execution from location A + 1.

When the sequence is repeated at location B, the address B + 1 will be stored away and used as the return address at the end of the subroutine. A call instruction can occur as many times as it is needed in the main program, and each time the return address will be stored ready for re-entering the main program at the end of the subroutine.

When in a subroutine, a call can be executed. This creates a second return address which has to be stored away. The process is illustrated in Fig. 3.4. At level 0 of the program the store is vacant. When entering level 1 the return address A is stored for returning to level 0. Entering level 2 stores address B and entering level 3 stores address C. Returning to a new level automatically causes the return address of the next highest level to be made available, as the most recently used return address is wiped out. The mechanism described is a last-in first-out store, often called a stack.

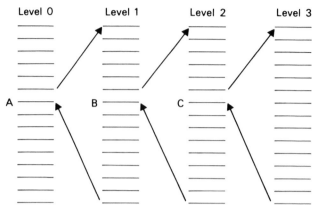

Fig. 3.4 Nesting of sub-routine return addresses

The stack: The return address store or stack must be able to accommo-date many levels of return addresses. The space on the processor is likely to be inadequate and so the main memory is often used. A stack pointer register contains the address of the location in memory which contains the latest stack entry. (Further details can be found in Chapter 5.) The stack pointer is automatically modified as return addresses are stored and retrieved. The stack pointer can be initialized using the 16-bit move-immediate instruction, LXI SP, INIT.

In practice, the stored value will depend on the length of the jump-to-subroutine instruction. In the example of Fig. 3.3 it is assumed that the next instruction is 1 word away from the current order being executed. For the 8080/85 the next instruction is 3 words (bytes) ahead for a CALL instruction and the return address stored will be PC + 3. For the restart instruction the stored value is PC + 1.

Condition

A condition may or may not be specified with the control order. If not specified then the jump is unconditional; i.e. it will always continue execution from the destination address.

The conditional jump is more useful since it provides the processor with the ability to make a simple decision based on some condition status flag. Conditional jumps, sometimes called branch instructions, perform the operations:

If condition true **then** $(PC) \leftarrow DA$
else $(PC) \leftarrow (PC) + n$

Thus if the condition specified by the instruction is true the program counter is loaded with the destination address and execution continues from that location. If the condition is false then execution proceeds in the normal way. The description shows the PC having *n* added to it, which may be, in fact, 2 or 3 if an 8- or 16-bit address is located immediately after the instruction word.

The 8080/85 provides a wide selection of conditions, as shown in Fig. 3.5.

Condition	Mnemonic c	Code C
Carry cleared	NC	2
Carry set	C	3
Zero cleared	NZ	0
Zero set	Z	1
Positive	P	6
Minus	M	7
Parity even	PE	5
Parity odd	PO	4

Fig. 3.5 Condition codes for 8080/85

The mnemonic shown is used in the symbolic form of the instruction together with the control information and destination address. The codes shown appear in the instruction and represent the information interpreted by the processor. Positive refers to sign-bit cleared and minus is sign-bit set.

Summary of control instructions

The constituent parts may be summarized as follows:

(*a*) *destination address*
    (i) direct using 16-bit in instruction
    (ii) indirect using contents of H.L.
(*b*) *control type*   (Mnemonic)
    (i) jump   JMP, Jc, PCHL
    (ii) jump to subroutine   CALL, Cc, RST
    (iii) return from subroutine   RET, Rc.

The mnemonics are shown for unconditional operations JMP, CALL, RET, and conditional operations Jc, Cc, Rc, where c represents the condition type. The indirect jump, PCHL, has its own mnemonic as does the special jump-to-subroutine RST, which allows for 8 different destination addresses.

(*c*) *condition type*

All conditions of Fig. 3.5 may be specified with the conditional form of the control types, namely Jc, Cc, and Rc.

The complete instructions are detailed in Figs 3.6 and 3.7. The figures show the action performed, the symbolic form the instruction takes and the octal machine code interpreted by the 8080/85 processor.

Control type/ Destination address	Unconditional		Conditional	
	Mnemonic and description	Machine code (octal)	Mnemonic and description	Machine code (octal)
Jump/direct	JMP X (PC) ← X	3 0 3 XL8 XH8	Jc X if c = true then (PC) ← X else (PC) ← (PC) + 3	3 C 2 XL8 XH8
Jump/indirect	PCHL (PC) ← (H.L)	3 5 1		
Jump to subroutine/ direct	CALL X Store ← (PC) (PC) ← X	3 1 5 XL8 XH8	Cc X if c = true then store ← (PC) (PC) ← X else (PC) ← (PC) + 3	3 C 4 XL8 XH8
	RST N Store ← (PC) (PC) ← 000.0N0	3 N 7		
Return from subroutine	RET (PC) ← store	3 1 1	Rc if c = true then (PC) ← store else (PC) ← (PC) + 1	3 C 0

Fig. 3.6 Control orders of 8080/85

X	jump destination, 16 bits
XL8	lower 8 bits of address in octal
XH8	higher 8 bits of address in octal
c	condition mnemonic } see Fig. 3.5
C	condition code
N	jump destination for restart, 3 bits
Store	return address storage area

Fig. 3.7 Key to Fig. 3.6

As can be seen, the jump and call instructions require 3 words of memory. The return, restart (RST) and indirect jump only use 1 instruction word since the destination address is either stored elsewhere (RET, Rc and PCHL) or specified by a short 3-bit address in the instruction (RST).

Example

A simple example of 4 control orders is illustrared in the program in Chapter 4. Here it is shown in a simplified form in Fig. 3.8. As the program is executed the first control action to break the normal flow causes control to be transferred to the subroutine CLK (1) by use of the CALL instruction. The program then loops (2) due to the JNZ order until the zero flag is set, which makes the program execute the RET (3), returning control to the main program. The actions are repeated, (4) and (5), at the next CALL instruction. The program then loops back to the start (6) by the action of the JMP instruction. More detail can be found in Chapter 4.

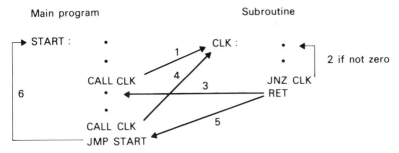

Fig. 3.8 Basic control structure of the example in Chapter 4

Input/output transfers

The input and output routes to the peripherals connected to a computer are treated like registers by the programmer. These registers may reside at memory locations, in which case they are memory mapped, or they may be located in a dedicated memory. In the former case all the memory reference instructions may be used to perform I/O transfers. In the latter case special I/O instructions must be provided to execute transfers between the processor registers and the input/output ports.

The 8080/85 is in the latter category. It supports input and output instructions, the details of which are shown in Fig. 3.9. Both have direct addressing modes, and the input/output register address is part of the instruction. The address is 8 bits long allowing for up to 256 input and output ports. Register A is the source for output instructions and the destination for input instructions.

The input instruction copies the value of the input port into register A. The output instruction copies the contents of A into the output port. The output register will store the value of the data output while the input will just read the instantaneous value of the signals connected to the input port.

Instruction	Type and function	Mnemonic	Machine code (octal)
1-address:			
	Register A implied		3 3 3
3.9A	Input	IN W	W_8
	(A) ← I(W)		
3.9B	Output	OUT W	3 2 3
	O(W) ← (A)		W_8
Key:	W — port address		
	W_8 — port address expressed in base 8		
	I(W) — input port W		
	O(W) — output port W		

Fig. 3.9. Input/output instructions of 8080/85

Halt and no-operation

There are two special instructions which do not fit into the previous categories. Halt causes the processor to idle until released. This order is only of limited value and not used very often. The no-operation instruction does nothing to the processor state, except to increment the program counter. It is used to 'waste' time in program-controlled time loops and to replace redundant instructions while debugging a machine code program. See Fig. 3.10 for details of these orders.

Instruction function and description	Mnemonic	Machine code (octal)
Halt Stop the processor	HLT	1 6 6
No-operation Do nothing	NOP	0 0 0

Fig. 3.10 'Halt' and 'no-operation' instructions of 8080/85

Input/output control

The 8080/85 includes control instructions for input/output operations. The function of these instructions is fully explained in Chapters 6 and 7 and only the form of the instruction will be given here.

Both the 8080 and the 8085 have instructions to enable and disable interrupt, EI and DI, respectively. The 8085 provides facilities for reading interrupt masks and interrupt bits (RIM) and setting the interrupt masks (SIM). These instructions are shown in Fig. 3.11.

Instruction execution times

All instructions are executed in a finite time which is an integral number of machine clock cycles. The times depend on the number of memory accesses required to execute the instruction-fetch and operand-fetch cycles and the number of internal clock cycles required to execute the operations specified.

The times are given in an appendix in terms of clock cycles. The times for the 8080 and 8085 differ for certain instructions. For convenience a clock cycle of 500 ns will be assumed for all calculations, although both processors are capable of much faster operation. More details will be given in Chapter 6.

Summary

The instruction set of the 8080/85 has been briefly described. The basic 8-bit orders, mostly those in the earlier 8008, provide an introduction to the ideas of instruction sets. The more advanced orders can then be added at a later stage when the basic set is understood. The basic orders are well structured and therefore easier to remember and simpler to code. To aid in the description of these orders octal machine code is used. Figures 3.1–3.11

Instruction function and description	Mnemonic	Machine code (octal)
Enable interrupt INTEN = 1	EI	3 7 3
Disable interrupt INTEN = 0	DI	3 6 3
Read interrupt mask (A) ← IMASK	RIM	0 4 0
Set interrupt mask IMASK ← (A)	SIM	0 6 0

Fig. 3.11 Input/output control instructions of 8080/85 (RIM + SIM—8085 only)

and Table 3.1 summarize the instructions in a compact, usable form. The chapter stresses the form the instructions take rather than providing a complete operational description. There are, therefore, minor details omitted for reasons of clarity, such as what flags are affected. These can be found in the instruction set given in Appendix 3. The machine code is also given in hexadecimal form, which is more commonly used in the kits and development systems now available.

Problems

Blank sheets showing a sub-set of the computer state may be used to answer some of these questions.

Operation orders

P3.1 The operands of the 8080 are

    (i) 8-bit A, B, C, D, E, H, L, M, INPORT, OUTPORT.
    (ii) 16-bit B, D, H, SP, PSW, STACK

The operation instructions are shown in Figs. 3.1, 3.2 and 3.9 with a number notation 3.1C–3.1J, 3.2A–3.2N, 3.9A and 3.9B. Draw two tables, one for 8-bit the other for 16-bit operands, showing which operations may be used with each operand.

    (e.g. C–3.1C; 3.1E; 3.2A; 3.2B, etc.)

Distinguish between source and destination operands.

P3.2 Comment on the tables of P3.1. What can you say about the combinations of operations and operands and the freedom of choice offered to the programmer?

P3.3 What functions do the following orders perform:

    XRA A; XRI 377Q; ADD A, DAD H

What do the last two perform that the rotate orders cannot do?

P3.4 Table 3.1 shows the initial values of the registers, memory and input/output ports. Write out the values of the registers that change when executing the following orders.

(Do not forget the program counter. Assume each order is executed at location 000.000).

(i) ADD A; (ii) SUB D; (iii) MVI L, 252Q; (iv) ORA E; (v) OUT 3; (vi) IN 3; (vii) XRI 352Q; (viii) DCR H; (ix) MOV M, L; (x) SHLD 013.015Q; (xi) LXI SP, 250.000Q; (xii) LDA 013.005Q; (xiii) SPHL; (xiv) STAX B; (xv) DAD B; (xvi) PUSH D (note the high byte is loaded to the stack first and the stack pointer value is decremented); (xvii) XTHL.

Program control

P3.5 What are program control orders for? Illustrate your answer with simple examples of three types of control order.

P3.6 Repeat P3.4 for the following orders. In this case the flags are as follows: C = 1; Z = 0; S = 1; P = 1.

(i) JMP 23; (ii) JP M; (iii) JNZ 1.003Q; (iv) JPE 0; (v) CALL 13.000; (vi) RP; (vii) RET; (viii) PCHL

P3.7 Compare the CALL and RST instructions and itemize the differences. What would be the benefit of RST if used for a frequently used sub-routine?

Simple programs

P3.8 There are basically four ways to move operands from memory to processor registers, i.e. MOV RI, M; LDA ADDR; LDAX B; SHLD ADDR. Write sections of code to move

(*a*) an 8-bit operand into register D
(*b*) a 16-bit operand into register pair D.E.

(all registers used must be loaded correctly).

P3.9 Describe what happens at the output ports when the following program is executed:

START:	MVI	B, 0	**Begin**	COUNT: = 0
	MVI	A, 1		
	OUT	1		PORT1: = 1
	XRA			
	OUT	1		PORT1: = 0
LOOP:	DCR	B	**Repeat**	COUNT: = COUNT-1
	MOV	A, B		
	OUT	2		PORT2: = COUNT
	CMA			
	OUT	3		PORT2 = *NOT* COUNT
	JNZ	LOOP	**Forever**	
			End	

Draw a timing diagram of the first 2 cycles of the loop showing the time relationships for each output action. (Assume the output actually occurs at the end of the output instruction cycle.)

P3.10 Figure P3.2 shows the program that has been loaded into the memory shown in Fig. P3.1. Write out on charts as provided in Appendix 3 the state of the computer when execution reaches points Ⓐ, Ⓑ, Ⓒ and Ⓓ. The processor is started from location zero and the charts should be drawn *before* executing the instructions at the points specified. If any of the points are passed more than once then a chart for the first and last time should be produced.

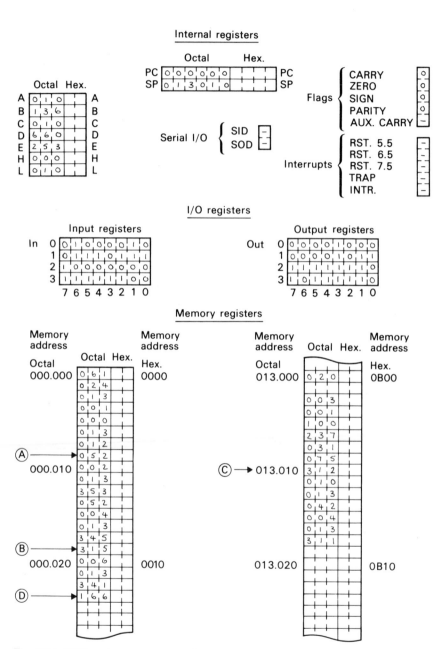

Fig. P3.1 8080 register map example

Label definitions

A1	EQU	013.024	STACK POINTER
A2	EQU	013.000	VAR1 POINTER
A3	EQU	013.002	VAR2 POINTER
A4	EQU	013.004	VAR3 POINTER

Program

			Begin
START:	LXI	SP, A1	SP: = A1
	LXI	B, A2	
	LDAX	B	A: = VAR1
	LHLD	A3	
	XCHG		D.E: = VAR2
	LHLD	A4	H.L: = VAR3
	PUSH	H	STORE: = H.L
	CALL	MULT	VAR3: = VAR3 + VAR2 * VAR1
	POP	H	H.L: = STORE
	HLT		**End**

Subroutine

MULT:	DAD	D	**Repeat** VAR3: = VAR3 + VAR2
	DCR	A	VAR1: = VAR1 − 1
	JNZ	MULT	**Until** VAR1: = 0
	SHLD	A4	VAR3: = VAR3 + VAR2 * VAR1
	RET		**Return**

Fig. P3.2 Program for problem P3.10

P3.11 Why are the operations 'add with carry' and 'subtract with borrow' provided in the instruction set of 8-bit processors?

Write a program to add the contents of registers B, C, D to 3 consecutive locations at 013.000. The 24-bit result should be deposited in memory at 013.010, 013.011, 013.012.

What changes are needed in the specification to make the program a loop?

P3.12 Write the programs which generate the sum of three 8-bit numbers stored in consecutive locations at 013.010. The programs should be as follows:

(a) in-line code (no loops)
(b) a loop not using INX, INR, DCX or DCR
(c) a loop using the orders in (b) as necessary.

(Ignore overflow—assume it never occurs).

What benefits are obtained when using loops if the sum of 100 numbers is required? What benefits accrue when using solution (c) instead of (b)? How many locations are saved and how much faster is the program when summing 100 terms?

P3.13 A table located at address 0100H which is 100 bytes long is to be moved to a new location at 3000H. Write a program using the basic set of instructions (i.e. 3.1C–3.1F; 3.2A–3.2B and the control orders). Write a second program using the full instruction set. Compare the size, performance and ease of writing of the two programs.

P3.14 Explain in detail the operation of the program below:

```
START:  IN    SWITCH      Input value of 4 switches
        ANI   0FH         n bit 0–3 and mask off top bits
        RCL               and shift left
        MOV   E, A        Move this number to D.E ready
        MVI   D, 0        to perform indexing
        LXI   H, ADDTBL
        DAD   D           Add index to table base
        MOV   E, M
        INX   H
        MOV   D, M        Fetch address from table to D.E
        LXI   H, START
        PUSH  H           Place re-entry point on stack
        XCHG
        SHLD  CURSUB      Store current routine entry point
        PCHL              Jump to routine selected
```

Draw a diagram showing the table structures listing the relevant parameters. What happens when the return instruction is executed at the end of the subroutine? Write out the values of all relevant registers when entering the subroutines.

4 Applications (1)

The user of a large computing system can remain totally isolated from the machine and most of its peripherals, both in a literal sense and in that he need have little or no knowledge of the hardware. Lower down the size scale, at the minicomputer level, it is possible, though often not essential, for the user to become involved with the hardware, even if this means just becoming familiar with more of the peripherals, such as analog-to-digital converters. Nonetheless, it is probably true to say that at this level also most users are software orientated, and program their computers without really becoming involved with the hardware.

At the bottom of the computer size scale comes the microcomputer, and here the situation is somewhat different. While the larger machines are commonly in general-purpose, time-shared configurations, the microcomputer tends to serve a more specialized role—often the heart of an instrument performing some sequence control or simple signal processing. In this respect, there is clearly an area of overlap in applications with the minicomputer, just as the minicomputers themselves overlap with larger machines. Fundamental to the successful design of a computer-based instrument is the balance between the hardware and the software and the synchronization of the computer to the outside world via its peripherals. This, of course, implies that the designer should have a knowledge of both disciplines.

Every microcomputer—or every computer for that matter—has an instruction set which, when in its mnemonic form, is called the assembly code. Application programs can be written in this assembly language, or maybe in a higher-level language, such as FORTRAN, BASIC or PASCAL. The choice between high or low will depend on a number of factors: the availability of a high-level language (one may not exist for the computer in question), the complexity of the application and the overall design criteria. The reader is referred to Chapters 9 and 10 for amplification of these ideas. Two simple examples are now treated in some detail; the aim here is to introduce programming in assembly language, and to demonstrate in a very elementary way important principles of design philosophy, problem representation, and matching the hardware to the software. These topics will receive further coverage in later chapters.

Example 1: Square-wave generator

Specification: Write a program to output from a microcomputer a periodic 2-level waveform with the time interval of each level independently controlled in units of 10 μs. The two amplitudes are to be zero and TTL logic 1 ($\approx$ 3 V); the time for zero (ZT) is to be preset using a datum in memory, and the high time (HT) is to be under continual control with thumb-wheel switches.

The first step in producing a program is to identify an overall strategy and the essential ingredients; in other words, produce an algorithm for the overall solution. Too much attention to detail is usually a mistake, for it is important to concentrate on understanding the problem and identifying a 'correct' algorithm. The example here is rather simple, but nonetheless it is worth proceeding step-by-step. The hardware is shown in block diagram form in Fig. 4.1.

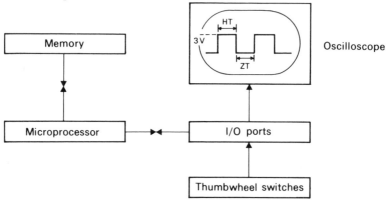

Fig. 4.1 Hardware for waveform generator

The essential ingredients of the solution are shown in Fig. 4.2, and if the 4 tasks (or sub-tasks) are executed sequentially within a continuous loop, then the required waveform will be generated continuously until the processor is halted by some external action. In a more complicated example, each of the 4 tasks in this first level of design would be divided as necessary into more units or sub-tasks, each in turn incorporating additional detail. In this way the first *abstract* design is transformed step-by-step, eventually arriving at the assembly code. But here the example is sufficiently simple to produce the assembly code for each of the four sub-tasks directly.

It would seem appropriate to use a subroutine for the IDLE sections. A subroutine is a section of code separate from the main program and is executed whenever an appropriate CALL statement is encountered. The specification for the subroutine is drawn up, as with any other program section, but in addition an interface between the calling program and the

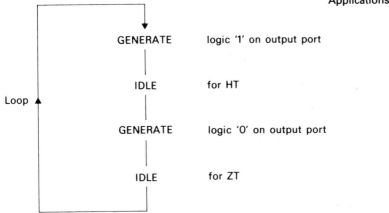

Fig. 4.2 Basic solution for the example

subroutine must be established. Without the interface, neither the main program nor subroutine can be completed, whereas with this knowledge the program and the subroutine can be developed independently—even by different people. The interface must include the location of the subroutine, i.e. its start address, and any common memory area or registers used to transfer parameters. In this example the start address is identified by the label CLK, and register B is used to transfer to the subroutine the number of 10 μs units, i.e. the value of HT or ZT.

Each of the 4 tasks is now expanded into the assembly code mnemonics of the 8080/85:

GENERATE	logic '1'	→ MVI	A, 001
		OUT	W1
IDLE	for HT	→ IN	W2
		MOV	B,A
		CALL	CLK
GENERATE	logic '0'	→ MVI	A, 000
		OUT	W1
IDLE	for ZT	→ MVI	H, XXX
		MVI	L, 200
		MOV	B, M
		CALL	CLK

Output port W1 (Bit 0) is connected to the oscilloscope, and input port W2 is connected to the thumb-wheel switches. It is assumed that a value for the zero time has been loaded previously into memory location XXX.200.

Now the subroutine CLK is to idle an integer number of 10 μs units governed by the contents of register B, so a suitable subroutine is:

IDLE subroutine	→ CLK:	'Idle'
		DCR B
		JNZ CLK
		RET

As mentioned above, CLK is a label serving as a reference point in the assembly code. It represents a specific address which is referenced by control instructions—in this case, the conditional jump within the subroutine and the two unconditional calls in the main program. CLK is not an instruction, and will not appear in the machine code. 'Idle' is necessary to give the loop an execution time of 10 μs. Suitable dummy instructions must now be inserted to make up the 10 μs. Assuming a 500 ns clock, the existing instructions have times:

DCR B   5 clock cycles—2.5 μs
JNZ CLK 10 clock cycles—5 μs

and hence 'Idle' must increase the loop time from 7.5 up to 10 μs. A simple way to do this is to insert an instruction such as MOV A, A. For although the 8080 does have a 'no-operation' instruction (NOP), it takes only 4 cycles, and hence is unsuitable.

The complete subroutine then becomes:

IDLE subroutine CLK: MOV   A, A
                            DCR   B
                            JNZ   CLK
                            RET

It now remains to join together the above sections, allocate the I/O ports and memory space, and assemble the mnemonic form of the instructions into machine code. Figure 4.3 shows the final assembly code, allocated

	Assembly code		Adress: page.line	Machine code	Clock cycles
	LXI	SP, YYY.377	XXX.000	061 377 YYY	10
START:	MVI	A, 001	.003	076 001	7
	OUT	8	.005	323 010	10
	IN	12	.007	333 014	10
	MOV	B, A	.011	107	5
	CALL	CLK	.012	315 050 XXX	17
	MVI	A, 000	.015	076 000	7
	OUT	8	.017	323 010	10
	MVI	H, XXX	.021	046 XXX	7
	MVI	L, 200	.023	056 200	7
	MOV	B, M	.025	106	7
	CALL	CLK	.026	315 050 XXX	17
	JMP	START	.031	303 003 XXX	10
* Subroutine					
CLK:	MOV	A, A	XXX.050	177	5
	DCR	B	.051	005	5
	JNZ	CLK	.052	302 050 XXX	10
	RET		.055	311	10

Fig. 4.3 Example program (octal used throughout, except for I/O port numbers)

memory for the program (page XXX, line 000 up to line 031, and line 050 up to 056 for the subroutine), and the machine code which is to be loaded into the microcomputer. The assembly code form of the program is *assembled* into the machine code—almost a one-to-one transformation; for this process, a table of instructions and their corresponding machine code representations is used (see Appendix 3).

The program may now be loaded into a development system, tested, and corrected as necessary—that is, 'debugged'. Clearly, the page allocation, XXX for the program and YYY for the stack, will depend on the memory available in any given system—the full complement is unlikely to be available. This is true also of input/output ports, and it is assumed that the specific development system in mind uses the I/O instructions, rather than a memory mapped arrangement, and that the port numbers—8 for output, and 12 for input—are available. This information is reflected in the memory map (Fig. 4.4).

Allocation	Function
Memory	
Page YYY (top of page)	Stack
Page XXX (bottom of page)	Program and subroutine
Register	
B	Subroutine control
I/O	
Port 8	Waveform to oscilloscope
Port 12	HT from thumbwheels

Fig. 4.4 Memory map

With a working program in the development system, it remains just to calibrate the square-wave generator. Clearly, this may be done by reading values of time from the oscilloscope and then comparing these with predictions from the clock cycle count. Results from the latter are given in Fig. 4.5.

Example 2: Sinewave generator

Specification: Write a program to generate a sinewave of fixed amplitude but variable frequency, 0.1 Hz $< f < 1$ kHz.

The sinewave is to be generated from a series of discrete samples passing through a digital-to-analog converter at regular intervals; the hardware

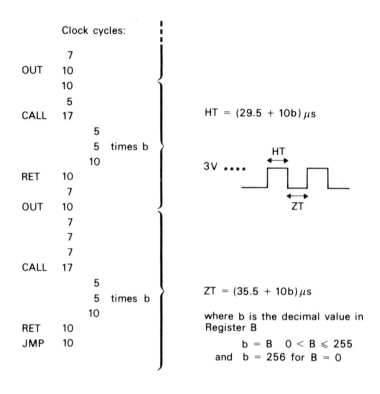

Fig. 4.5 Calibration for clock cycle count

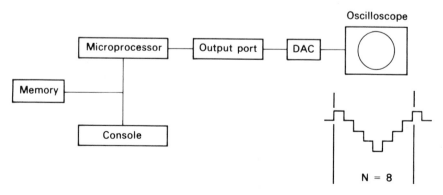

Fig. 4.6 Hardware layout for sinewave generator

layout is shown in Fig. 4.6. The principal components of the program are thus:

Loop continuously
    Calculate sin(ωt)
    O/P to DAC
    Time interval
End of loop

The time interval controls the frequency of the sinewave, and could be implemented along similar lines to the CLK subroutine in Example 1. But how is the instantaneous amplitude of sin(ωt) to be calculated? Two possibilities are a look-up table where a block of memory contains samples of the sinewave, or a routine to calculate the values as they are required. Where a particularly high resolution is demanded it might even be worth considering a combination of these two, interpolating between two successive values in the table. In general a decision should be made in the light of:

ease of programming
time specification
accuracy
memory requirements

Here, primarily because of the first criterion, a look-up table approach is adopted, and the programming strategy is to step through the table at an appropriate rate. The calculation part thus reduces to a look-up:

Calculate sin(ωt) → Fetch next sample

Consider first a table containing samples spanning one complete cycle. This keeps the algorithm as simple as possible, for the operation is merely to step through the table until the end-point is detected, reset the pointer to the beginning, and repeat continuously. So the 'Fetch next sample' can be expanded into assembly code as:

```
Fetch next
    sample → Increment pointer        INX   H
                                       MVI   A, 000
    If end of cycle/table then         CMP   M
         reset pointer                 CZ    SETPOINTER
    Fetch sample                       MOV   A, M
```

A point of interest here is the way in which the end of the table is detected. The end-address can be determined from the start address plus table size, so that the 'end of cycle/table' could be detected by comparing the pointer value with the end-address; or, as in the code above, a specific value in the table (zero in this case) can serve as an indicator; while this is slightly simpler than using the address approach, care must be taken in creating the table: the check parameter must not be duplicated in the table contents.

The complete program is:

```
              LXI   SP, YYY.377
              MVI   C, VVV
              CALL  SETPOINTER
        FRWD: INX   H
              MVI   A, 0
              CMP   M
              CZ    SETPOINTER
              MOV   A, M
              OUT   W
              CALL  CLK
              JMP   FRWD
```

Sub-routines are:

```
         CLK: MOV   A, C
        LOOP: DCR   A
              JNZ   LOOP
              RET
  SETPOINTER: LXI   H,ZZZ.000
              RET
```

Notice the frequency control, register C, has not been made a run-time variable; it is preset to 'VVV' in the initializing section of the program. A full memory map is given in Fig. 4.7.

Allocation	Function
Memory	
Page YYY	Stack
Page XXX	Program and subroutines
Page ZZZ	Sinewave table
Registers	
B	Sign flag—second solution only
C	Frequency control
I/O	
Port W	Output to DAC

Fig. 4.7 Memory map for sinewave generator

A second solution

Clearly it is unnecessary to store a complete cycle of the sinewave, since samples spanning just one quadrant would contain all the information. A sinewave could then be generated by stepping forwards and backwards through the single quadrant table, with the negative half-cycles being realized by simply negating the table values prior to output. A flow diagram representation is given in Fig. 4.8. Notice that two separate loops

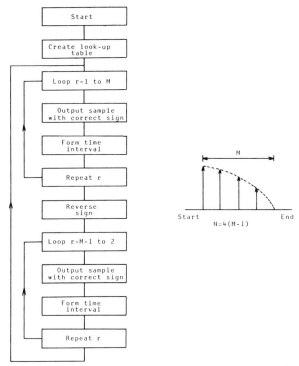

Fig. 4.8 Sinewave generator with single quadrant table

have been used, one stepping forwards and the other backwards through the table; while this is by no means essential (one loop could be adapted to traverse the two directions) it does make the solution easier to understand and to expand into assembly code. It is necessary to have an indicator (i.e. a flag) to record whether the present half-cycle is positive or negative; and this flag is reversed every time a zero-crossing is encountered. The algorithm may also be described in textual form:

```
Loop continuously
      Forward: Do Fetch sample
                  O/P with correct sign
                  Time interval
                  Increment pointer
            Until End of table
                  Reverse sign flag
      Backward: Do Fetch sample
                  O/P with correct sign
                  Time interval
                  Decrement pointer
            Until Start of table
      End of loop.
```

The information conveyed by this description is very similar, if not identical, to that conveyed by the flow diagram, and the choice between such textual and graphical descriptions is very much a personal one. The graphical forms tend to become unwieldy as more detail gets added, but they can be very useful during the initial phases of algorithm formulation; and again when identifying the execution times for the various program paths—see Chapter 10.

Returning to the sineware generator, the single quadrant means that the traversing of the table is first forwards and then backwards, with increments and decrements of the pointer, respectively. Clearly these should balance, so there is no need to reset the pointer to the start address. The other important difference between this and the first solution is the need for the sign flag. As mentioned earlier, this flag is to be reversed at every zero-crossing, and this coincides with the end of the table, assuming a first quadrant cosine is used.

A second flow diagram, merely an expansion of the first, is given in Fig.

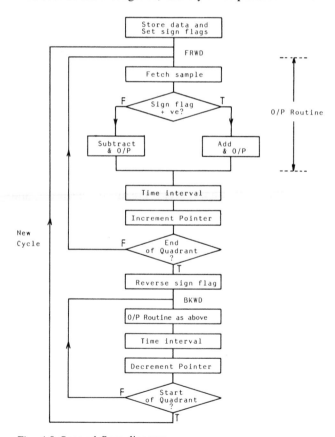

Fig. 4.9 Second flow diagram

4.9, and this closely reflects the assembly code programs for the 8080 in
Fig. 4.10 and for the 6800 in Fig. 4.11. Notice that the two limits of the
table, the start and the end, are both detected by testing for specific
amplitudes, unity and zero, respectively. While care must be taken that
these are unique values in the table, the advantage of this approach is the
ease with which the table can be relocated or its size changed.

The two examples above have served as an introduction to program
design and programming in assembly code. Both generate a time-varying
waveform, and as such are the simplest possible examples of real-time
programming, where it is important to synchronize the computer to the
outside world. The characteristics of the waveforms are dependent on the

	Assembly code		Comment
	LXI	SP, 000.377	Set stack pointer
	MVI	B, 000	Set sign flag
	MVI	C, 001	Set clock time interval
	LXI	H, 001.000	Load data base address
FRWD:	CALL	OUT	**Forward** through table: Call output routine
	CALL	CLK	Form time interval
	INX	H	Increment table pointer
	MVI	A, 000	Acc. A ← zero
	CMP	M	Test for zero (end of table)
	JNZ	FRWD	Cycle until zero
	MOV	A,B	Acc. A ← B
	CMA		Complement (reverse) sign flag
	MOV	B,A	Replace sign flag to B
BKWD:	CALL	OUT	**Backward** through table
	CALL	CLK	Form time interval
	DCX	H	Decrement table pointer
	MVI	A, 037	Acc. A ← peak amplitude[1]
	CMP	M	Test for peak (beginning of table)
	JNZ	BKWD	Cycle until peak reached
	JMP	FRWD	Restart new cycle
*Subroutines			
OUT:	MVI	A, 000	Test sign flag for zero
	CMP	B	(+ve half cycle)
	JZ	PSVE	Jump with zero
	SUB	M	Negate sample value
	OUT	10	Output to port 10
	RET		Return from subroutine
PSVE:	MOV	A,M	Acc. A ← sample value
	OUT	10	Output to port 10
	RET		Return from subroutine
CLK:	MOV	A,C	Timing subroutine
LOOP: DCRA			Loop for interval
	JNZ	LOOP	Count C
	RET		Return from subroutine

Note: Octal used throughout   [1] 6 bit 2's complement bipolar DAC

Fig. 4.10 8080 version of sinewave generator

Address	Machine code			Assembly code			Comment
0140				ORG		0140H	Define origin
0140	1F			FCB		IFH,17H,00	Look-up table
0141	17						
0142	00						
			* *				
0240				ORG		0240H	Define origin
0240	00			FCB		00,01	Set sign flag and clock
0241	01						
	0100		SETPIA:	EQU		0100H	Define address of 'SETPIA'
0250				ORG		0250H	
0250	8E	00FF		LDS		#00FFH	Initialize stack pointer
0253	BD	0100		JSR		SETPIA	Set up I/O ports
0256	CE	0140		LDX		#0140H	
0259	01		EQ:	NOP			Start of cycle
025A	01			NOP			Sample time equalization
025B	01			NOP			
025C	BD	0300	FRWD:	JSR		OUT	Forward through table
025F	08			INX			
0260	BD	0317		JSR		CLK	Form time interval
0263	8C	0142		CPX		#0142H	End of look-up table?
0266	27	03		BEQ		SB	
0268	01			NOP			
0269	20	F1		BRA		FRWD	
026B	73	0240	SB:	COM		240H	Reverse sign flag
026E	BD	0300	BKWD:	JSR		OUT	Backward through table
0271	09			DEX			
0272	BD	0317		JSR		CLK	
0275	8C	0140		CPX		#140H	Start of table?
0278	27	DF		BEQ		EQ	
027A	01			NOP			Sample time equalization
027B	20	F1		BRA		BKWD	
			*	Locate subroutines			
0300				ORG		0300H	Define origin
0300	86	00	OUT:	LDA	A	#0	
0302	B1	0240		CMP	A	0240H	Check sign flag
0305	27	08		BEQ		PSVE	Jump when zero (+ve half-cycle)
0307	A0	00		SUB	A	00,X	Negate sample value
0309	8B	20		ADD	A	#20H	Offset for unipolar DAC
030B	B7	800A		STA	A	800AH	Output
030E	39			RTS			Return from subroutine
030F	AB	00	PSVE:	ADD	A	00,X	Time equalization with SUB
0311	8B	20		ADD	A	#20H	Offset for unipolar DAC
0313	B7	800A		STA	A	800AH	Output
0316	39			RTS			Return from subroutine
0317	B6	0241	CLK:	LDA	A	0241H	Interval forming subroutine
031A	4A		LOOP:	DEC	A		
031B	26	FD		BNE		LOOP	Loop for interval count
031D	39			RTS			
				END			

SETPIA	0100	
EQ	0259	Symbol table
FRWD	025C	
SB	026B	Addresses of symbols used
BKWD	026E	
OUT	0300	
PSVE	030F	
CLK	0317	
LOOP	031A	Hexadecimal used throughout

Fig. 4.11 6800 version of sinewave generator

rate of the output, which in turn is controlled by the program. Usually the synchronization has to contend with inputs as well, and this makes the problem more difficult than indicated by these two examples. Aspects of real-time programming are discussed in Chapter 10.

Problems

P4.1 What are the limits of the page values 'XXX'?

For a development system with 32K of memory (addressed from zero upwards) what would be the largest value of 'YYY'?

What are the limits of the port numbers W1 and W2?

P4.2 The example program uses 'move immediate' instructions to set the accumulator to 001 and 000. How else might this be achieved? Modify the program so that A is set initially outside the main program loop, and then complemented at the appropriate point.

P4.3 Remove the 'move-immediate' instructions which load registers H and L to the beginning of the program—and again outside the main loop. What are the effects of this and the second half of P4.2 on the calibration shown in Fig. 4.5?

P4.4 Explain the limits of b and B in Fig. 4.5.

P4.5 Explain the modifications you would make for increased time units from 10 μs to (*a*) 20 μs and (*b*) 100 μs.

P4.6 Change just one instruction in the program in Fig. 4.2 so that both the amplitude and the period HT are controlled by the thumbwheel switches.

What hardware must be added to the system to display this variation on the oscilloscope?

P4.7 Change the example program so that both HT and ZT are preset and stored in successive memory locations and the amplitude for HT is controlled by the thumbwheel switches.

5 Addressing modes

Instruction word format

Each instruction word in a program provides essential information for the central processing unit (CPU) to carry out its functions. As each instruction is obeyed, the processor needs to identify the location of the operands Z, X, Y and the type of operator, b, in the expression:

$$Z \leftarrow X.b.Y$$

where Z is the destination operand and X and Y are the first and second source operands, respectively. In addition, the processor must be able to identify the location of the next instruction.

All of this information could be contained within the instruction word itself. The information required to identify Z, X, Y and the address of the next instruction could be encoded as $\log_2 m$, where m is equal to the number of words in memory. For example, if m is equal to 64K words, then $\log_2$ 64K, i.e. 16, bits would be required to locate each operand.

Hence, a total of 64 bits would be required for the 3 operands and the address of the next instruction. To this must be added the number of bits required to identify the operator. The instruction word would therefore be very long and this would increase the cost of the memory significantly.

It is usual to restrict the amount of information within the instruction word by providing part of the information by alternative means. It is normal practice, for example, to provide the address of the next instruction by a register within the CPU called a *program counter*. Because instructions are normally required to be obeyed in sequence, the contents of the program counter need only be incremented to provide the next instruction address. If an instruction is required that is out of sequence, then a special jump instruction must be used to load the program counter with the relevant instruction address.

Hence, the penalty for removing the next instruction address information from the instruction word is that special jump instructions must be added to the range of orders, with a possible increase in the number of bits required to define the orders.

By providing a fixed initial destination (an accumulator) for all operands, then destination operand information could be removed from the instruction word. A special operator would then be required to permit the transfer of the contents of the accumulator to a specified memory location.

If the source of the second source operand were always taken to be the accumulator, then information regarding this operand could also be removed from the instruction word.

Thus, the initial universal instruction word containing five types of information, and known as a 3-address format, may be reduced to a 1-address format. Some examples of instruction word formats are shown in Fig. 5.1.

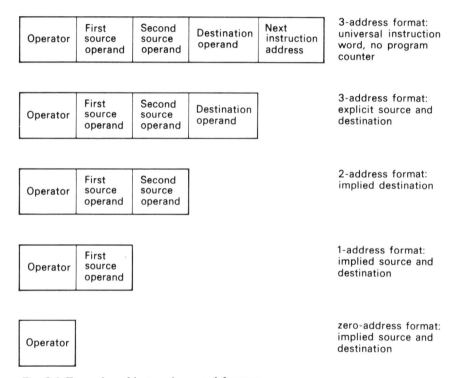

Fig. 5.1 Examples of instruction word formats

In general, a greater range of operators is required to compensate for the lack of generality, and usually more instructions are required to complete a given operation, when a restricted address format is used.

It is possible to reduce the instruction word format to the ultimate of zero-address, in which case the operands are to be found in fixed locations. The most frequently used formats are the 1-address and 2-address, and it is usual to find a mixture of different formats in one processor. Figure 5.2 shows a summary of operation statements using various instruction word formats.

3-address:	$Z \leftarrow X.b.Y$
2-address:	$X \leftarrow X.b.Y$
	$(A) \leftarrow X.b.Y$
1-address:	$(A) \leftarrow X.b.(A)$
	$X \leftarrow (A).u$
	$(A) \leftarrow X.u$
	$X \leftarrow X.u$
Zero-address:	$(A) \leftarrow (A).u$
	$(A) \leftarrow (A).b.(st)$
	$(st) \leftarrow (st).b.(st)$

Key: st—Operand at top of stack
     b—Binary operator
     u—Unary operator
     A—Implied general register (accumulator)

Fig. 5.2 Summary of operation statements

Although it has been assumed so far that each operand field of the instruction word contains information about the location of the operand, this information need not be the actual address in memory of the operand. Indeed, as will be shown later, it is desirable that the operand field information be capable of specifying the location of the operand in a number of different ways. These different ways of specifying the location of the operand are known as addressing modes, and it is the range of addressing modes, together with the range of operators provided in a particular microprocessor, which will largely determine the power or usefulness of that microprocessor.

The need for addressing modes

Data structures

In order to understand the necessity for a microprocessor to have a range of addressing modes, and thus a variety of ways of accessing operands, it is first necessary to examine the different ways in which these operands may be stored.

Operands may be generated as intermediate results in a series of calculations or they may represent data which have been input to the microprocessor and stored, perhaps to be sorted into some special order at a later time.

Operands may be stored in memory in a number of different ways. These are usually referred to as data structures, and some of the more commonly used ones will now be described.

Constants

Operands whose values are fixed when the program is designed and remain constant for the duration of execution of the program are called constants or literals. They can be stored in read-only memories either as parts of instructions in the program or adjacent to the program as single items or organized in tables.

Constants are useful for defining fixed parameters, e.g. masks for bit manipulation, timing parameters, messages displayed on VDUs etc.

Variables

Operands which change during the execution of the program are called variables and must reside in a read/write memory or be input/output operands. Variables can be single items of information or they can be organized in data structures, in which case an item will have some implicit relationship with adjacent items.

The table

In the simplest case the binary words comprising the operands may be stored in consecutive locations, forming a table or sequential list. The data may represent successive amplitude samples of a waveform, in which case the data is time-ordered, or the data may represent the sizes of different samples of a particular item or product, in which case the data may be ordered by magnitude.

Data stored in this way are easy to visualize and are also easy to access. Any operand in the table may be accessed randomly in order to use it or to change it.

A table is characterized by three parameters:

(i) The *base address* is the memory address of the start of the table.
(ii) The *index* or *offset* is the distance of any element from the base of the table. The offset is a function of the structure of the table and is independent of the location of the table.
(iii) The *table length* is the maximum value of the offset or index. Before accessing the table the index can be compared to the length to ensure that a valid access is being performed. This is usually executed by program and is often omitted for simplicity and faster operation.

To access a table element the index is added to the base before accessing the memory.

Tables of constants are useful for defining unchanging data that have some implicit relationship. For example, a table of powers of 10 in binary form is useful for a binary to decimal conversion program, or vice versa. A table of decreasing time periods can be used to define the acceleration and deceleration values for a stepper motor.

Tables of variables are used for storing ordered data that change while the computation proceeds.

A table structure does have some disadvantages. Firstly, if the operands are arranged in order of magnitude, then if another operand is required to be inserted in the table, several other operands must be moved to create just one vacant space. This is illustrated in Fig. 5.3. A similar problem occurs when an operand is to be deleted from the table. Therefore, while the addressing of any operand in the table is straightforward, the actual insertion or deletion of an operand is not so easy.

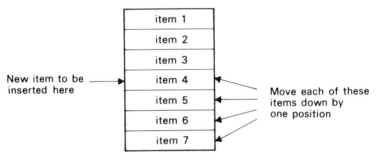

Fig. 5.3 Insertion of an item in a table

Secondly, it is not always possible to know in advance the maximum size of the table required. A section of memory must be allocated for the table, but a problem clearly will arise if the space allocation turns out to be too small, while a wasteful use of memory will occur if the space allocated turns out to be too big.

The linked list

Instead of storing data sequentially in a table, they may be stored randomly throughout memory. Each data word must now contain a pointer field as well as an operand field. The pointer field enables the next data word in the list to be found. This is illustrated in Figs. 5.4(*a*) and 5.4(*b*).

The advantage is that operands may be inserted or deleted easily just by changing the appropriate pointer field. Figure 5.5 shows the deletion of an operand from a linked list.

A linked list is also more efficient in the use of memory space because data words may be stored anywhere as single items, thereby taking up unused spaces within memory. However, a disadvantage here is that a record of usable spaces must be kept. The additional memory space

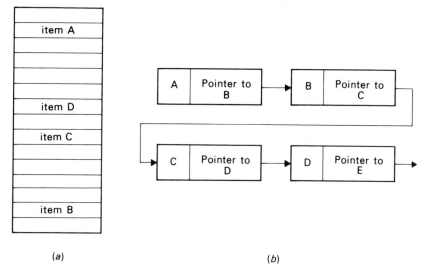

Fig. 5.4 Linked list structure

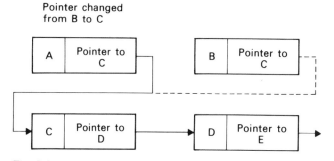

Fig. 5.5 Deletion from a linked list

required to store the pointer field is usually less than the memory space saved by not having to allocate a predetermined space.

However, while the insertion or deletion of operands in a linked list is easier than in a table, an operand in a linked list can only be accessed by sequential scanning of the operands, starting at one end of the list.

The disadvantages of sequential and linked lists can be avoided if access is only allowed to the operands at the ends of a list.

The stack

The stack consists of a number of registers, usually in the main memory. The stack is accessed at one end only, normally referred to as the 'top' of the stack. Items are therefore inserted and deleted in time order. When information is stored in the stack in a certain sequence, it is retrieved from the stack on the basis of 'last in—first out' (LIFO). A stack pointer is used to address the next register to be used in the stack.

The mechanism for a stack operation is one of the following:

	Writing–Storing	*Reading–Retrieving*
(*a*)	Increment–Write	Read–Decrement
(*b*)	Write–Increment	Decrement–Read
(*c*)	Decrement–Write	Read–Increment
(*d*)	Write–Decrement	Increment–Read

where the operation increment/decrement is performed on the stack pointer, and the read/write operation is performed on the memory.

Operations (*a*) and (*b*) will cause the stack to grow upwards towards the high address end starting from the low address end, while operations (*c*) and (*d*) will make the stack grow downwards from the high address end to the low address end.

Operations (*b*) and (*d*) will leave the stack pointer pointing to a vacant location, while operations (*a*) and (*c*) leave the stack pointer pointing to the last occupied location.

Figure 5.6 shows the four versions available. The most common arrangements found in microcomputers are (*c*) and (*d*); the reason seems to be that the stack can be placed at the top of memory and grow downwards while the program is placed at the bottom and grows upwards, thereby minimizing the probability of corruption of one by the other.

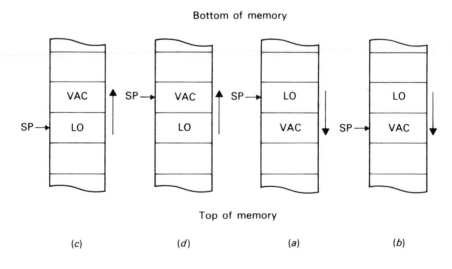

LO – last operand written onto stack;   VAC – vacant location

Fig. 5.6 Various types of stack operation

Most microprocessors have a system stack, in which case the stack pointer register will be part of the CPU as will be the special control logic used for maintaining the stack. Different microprocessors have different ways of maintaining the stack. The 6800 uses method (*d*), but the 8080, 8085, 8086 and Z80 use a stack pointer which contains the address of the last item of information in the stack (*c*).

Usually, special operators are provided for manipulating the stack pointer, in which case any item of data on the stack may be accessed. Also, it is important that the programmer ensures that the stack pointer is initialized before the execution of the first instruction involving the stack.

Other operators effect the storage and retrieval of information in the stack. The decrementing and incrementing of the stack pointer is performed automatically as part of the operator function in the case of the system stack. It is possible to create a separate stack from the system stack by using software to maintain its correct operation. Separate stacks are usually used to store operands, while the system stack may be used to store subroutine return addresses, as described in the following sections.

Subroutines

The stack provides an orderly method of storing a subroutine return address in order to return from a subroutine to the correct point in the main program. This is probably the most common use of the system stack. A return address is saved on the stack automatically when a subroutine call is executed. The return address is that corresponding to the next instruction after the subroutine call. Subroutines are terminated by a return instruction. Upon execution of this instruction, the return address is obtained from the stack and loaded into the program counter.

The 'last in—first out' procedure used with the stack allows a subroutine call to be made within another subroutine by providing the return addresses in the correct sequence.

Operand stack

Operands may be stored on the system stack or on a separate stack. The use of a stack to store operands can be demonstrated in connection with subroutines. Immediately before a subroutine call, the general registers of the CPU may contain data to be used after the return from the subroutine. However, the subroutine itself may require the use of the general registers. In order not to corrupt the data in the general registers, their contents may be saved on the stack immediately before/after calling the subroutine.

Immediately after/before returning from the subroutine, the initial contents of the general registers may be retrieved from the stack. This is particularly useful when a subroutine is called from within a subroutine.

Although the system stack uses consecutive memory locations, a separately created stack may use either consecutive or random locations. A separate stack may therefore either be implemented as a table or as a linked list, the latter being useful when operands of different lengths are required to be stored. The normal disadvantage of a linked list, that it has to be scanned sequentially, does not apply when it is used as a stack.

The queue

A queue is a structure where the first item of data to be stored is also the first item to be retrieved. The data are therefore stored in time order, like the stack, but unlike the stack the data are retrieved on the basis of 'first in—first out' (FIFO).

Access to a queue is therefore made at the ends of the structure. An insertion is made at one end (the tail) and a deletion at the other end (the head). This is shown in Fig. 5.7.

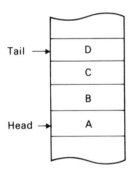

Fig. 5.7 Representation of a queue

A queue structure can be created by allocating an area of memory for the queue and using software to maintain correct operation. Unlike a stack, where one end remains stationary, both ends of a queue are dynamic. Two pointers are therefore required, one for the head and the other for the tail. When a fixed area of memory is allocated for the queue, then a pointer on reaching the last location should jump to the other end of the memory area, thus forming a continuous or cyclic queue of defined maximum length. A queue may also be implemented as a linked list.

Summary of operations on data structures

All data structures must allow operands to be added to, or deleted from, the total list of items. However, from the description of the properties of just 4 data structures, it is clear that the procedure for doing this will depend on the particular data structure being accessed.

Consider the table structure. In order to add an item of data of a specific value to the list, then the numerical value of that item must be specified within the instruction, i.e. the operand field of the instruction word must contain the operand itself.

However, if the item to be added is in a general register, it may be more convenient to specify the identification of the general register, i.e. the operand location within the operand field of the instruction word, rather than the operand itself.

When items in a table have to be moved to create space for a new item, again it is convenient to refer to these items by their addresses, rather than by value.

When the contents of a general register are to be saved on the stack it is the identification of that general register, not the operand itself, which will be specified within the instruction word. However, when the stack pointer is initialized to a particular value, that value must be specified in the instruction word.

Thus it can be seen that in order to perform operations on data structures, operand information needs to be able to be specified in different ways. The most frequently encountered ways of operand addressing are discussed in the next section.

Common addressing modes

In this section, definitions of the various addressing modes will also be given using the Instruction Set Processor language (ISP) (see Bell and Newell, 1971). Single-byte immediate operands are designated by n, while double-byte immediate operands are designated by m.

Implied

Many instructions use operands that are implicit in the operation and they cannot be changed by the programmer. These operands are therefore implied operands and are often not apparent to the programmer.

Example:
8080/85   ADD   M   ;   add memory location pointed to by H,L to
the A register
In ISP
$(A) \leftarrow (A) + M (G(H \cdot L))$

This instruction has two implied operands, A and M(H,L), but neither is apparent in the instruction mnemonic.

Example:
8080/85   RRC   ;   rotate A register right by 1 bit.

Many instructions have implied operands and these instructions must be remembered by the programmer. An instruction set with many implied operands is undesirable for this reason and makes the machine very restrictive in its use.

Immediate

In the previous section it was seen that it was necessary to provide the facility for loading the numerical value of the operand into a memory location or into one of the general registers (see Fig. 5.8).

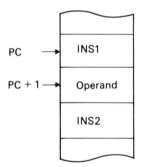

Fig. 5.8 Immediate mode

This facility is provided by the immediate addressing mode, where the operand field of the instruction word contains the numerical value of the operand.

In the case of a multi-byte instruction word, the first byte may contain the definition of the type of instruction and the operator, while the second byte would represent the value of an 8-bit operand, or the second and third bytes may be concatenated to represent the value of a 16-bit operand.

Example:
6800:   LDA A,   23H; Load $\left(\begin{array}{c} \text{register} \\ \text{accumulator} \end{array} \right)$ A with the number 23 hexadecimal

8080/85: MVI A, 23H;

In ISP:
G(A) ← n ; n = 23H or decimal 35
where G represents the array of general registers.

Direct

In direct addressing the operand field of the instruction word contains the address of the operand. This enables operands to be moved from one location to another, not by referring to the operands themselves, but by referring to the locations of the operands, e.g. moving operands down by one location in a table to create space for the insertion in the table of a new operand.

Direct addressing is used to access single operands, either constants or variables, which define a single item of information. For example, width of paper in a printer, speed parameter for motor controller, time-out parameter for an analog-to-digital converter, the timer input port, etc.

Direct addressing may be sub-divided into three types:

(a) General-register direct
In this type the operand field represents the location of the value of the operand in an array of general registers on the microprocessor chip. The location of a register in the array is designated by g (see Fig. 5.9(*a*)). This

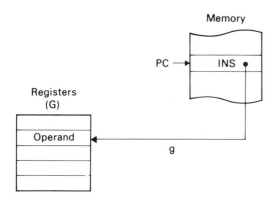

Fig. 5.9(a) Direct register mode

makes the instruction more compact since g only requires a few bits of the instruction field.

Example:
8080/85 : MOV B,C ; move the contents of register C to register B.
In ISP: $G(g_1) \leftarrow G(g_2)$ or specifically $G(B) \leftarrow G(C)$

(b) Main-memory direct
In this type the operand field represents the location of the operand in the main memory. The size of main memory which is addressable depends on

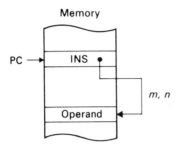

Fig. 5.9(b) Direct memory mode

whether a single (8 bits) or double (16 bits)-byte address is used (see Fig. 5.9(*b*)).

Example:
6800   : LDA A, 23H; load register A with contents of memory
                             location 23 hexadecimal
8080/85: LDA   23H
In ISP:
    $G(g) \leftarrow M(m)$
    $G(A) \leftarrow M(23)$

8080/85: LHLD 23H; load registers L and H with contents of
                       memory at 23H and 24H, respectively
In ISP:
    $(H) \leftarrow M(m + 1)$: $(H) \leftarrow M(24)$
    $(L) \leftarrow M(m)$: $(L) \leftarrow M(23)$

(c) Input/output direct
When a microcomputer has the facility for dedicated I/O hardware, then

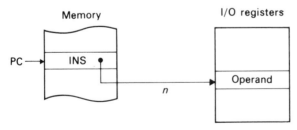

Fig. 5.9(c) Direct input/output mode

the instructions that address the I/O normally have direct addressing modes (see Fig. 5.9(*c*)).

Example:
8080/85: IN W; move the contents of port W to the A register (A is
implied).
In ISP: (A) ← I(W)

Indirect

In indirect addressing the operand field of the instruction word represents
the address of the location (in the general registers, G, or memory, M) of
the address which points to the location (in the main memory, M) of the
operand, i.e. the operand field contains the address of the address of the
operand (see Fig. 5.10 (*a* and *b*)).

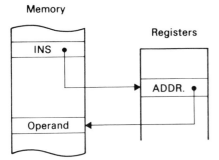

Fig. 5.10(a) Indirect register mode

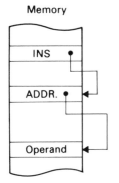

Fig. 5.10(b) Indirect memory mode

Indirect addressing provides an efficient method of accessing single
operands. The instruction may only contain a few bits of information which
identifies the location containing a large address field. It provides an
expansion of the addressing range without wasting instruction codes. The

disadvantage is that the register that contains the address must be loaded with the correct address prior to accessing the memory.

Indirect addressing provides access to linked lists particularly if memory indirect access is provided (see 5065 microprocessor).

Example:
8080: ADD M; add the contents of the memory location whose address is in the register pair H,L to the A register (implied),

STAX B; the contents of register A are stored in the memory location whose address is in register pair BC (see Fig. 5.11).

In ISP: $G(g) \leftarrow M(G(rp))$
$G(A) \leftarrow M(G(BC))$

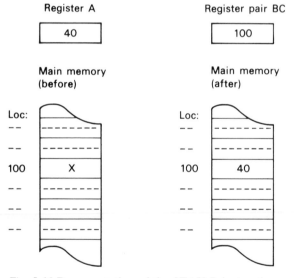

Fig. 5.11 Representation of the STAX B instruction

Indirect addressing is often used to sequence through a table of operands. The address of the first operand in the table is placed in a register pair and the first operand is accessed by indirect addressing of that register pair. The register pair contents need only be incremented or decremented for the same instruction to access the next operand in the table. In some processors, the incrementing/decrementing of the register pair contents is done automatically when an operand is accessed, thus removing the need for a separate increment/decrement instruction. This extra facility is known as auto-increment/auto-decrement.

Indirect addressing is also useful when a program contains a number of instructions referring to single operands. If the operands had to be relocated to another part of memory, then all instructions referring to those operands would have to be modified so that the new operand addresses would be changed for the old ones if direct addressing had been used.

If, however, indirect addressing had been used, the program itself would not need to be altered. The only alteration would be to a table which lists the relationship between the actual operand address and the operand field used in the instruction. The amount of effort involved in the modification is thus greatly reduced.

Indexed

In this operand addressing mode the operand address provided in the operand field of the instruction word is added to the contents of a register to determine the address of the location of the operand in main memory (see Fig. 5.12). Indexed addressing is effectively a special form of indirect addressing.

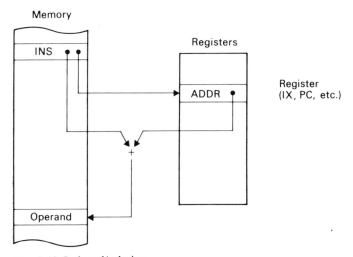

Fig. 5.12 Indexed/relative

The indexed addressing mode provides a direct implementation of the table accessing process described earlier. One of the addresses is the base address, while the other is regarded as the index. The latter will usually change frequently compared with the base, so operation orders which manipulate the index are more common than those for the base. The base should have the full addressing range capability, whereas the index can be 8 or 16 bits long.

The 6800 has a 16-bit index and only an 8-bit base address.

Example:
    6800: LDAA 4,X ; the contents of the memory location, whose
                    address is formed by adding 4 to the contents of
                    the index register, are moved to register A (see
                    Fig. 5.13).
    In ISP: G(g) ← M(G(IX) + n)
            G(A) ← M(G(IX) + 4)

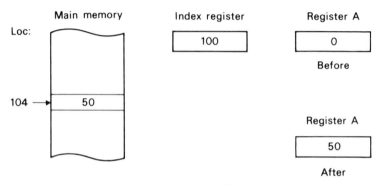

Fig. 5.13 Representation of the LDAA 4,X instruction

The indexed mode of addressing is very convenient when accessing operands arranged in separate tables, especially when the same calculations, or sequence of calculations, are to be performed on the separate tables of operands. The number in the operand field (base address) will be added to the contents of the index register to form the required address for the first table. On completion of the calculation on the operands in the first table, the index register contents are changed to form the required address for the next table, when added to the base address in the instruction word.

In microprocessors which have an index register it is desirable to have operators which allow the direct addition or subtraction of numbers to the index register contents.

Although some microprocessors may not have an index register as such, e.g. the 8080, a form of indexed mode addressing can be used because arithmetic operations can be performed on register pairs BC, DE and HL, which are also used for memory addressing.

Relative

In relative addressing, the operand address is determined by adding the address specified within the operand field (the offset) to the program counter. Relative addressing is therefore a form of indexed addressing.

In many microprocessors, relative addressing applies only to branch instructions. The offset in this case is usually a single byte having a decimal value in the range of -128 to $+127$. It can be calculated as:

offset = destination address $-$ program counter $- 2$

In the source statement the absolute address of the destination of a branch instruction, either as a numerical value or as a name, is specified. The assembler then determines the offset.

Branch instructions are generally used when a test has been performed and it is required to return to the beginning of a loop. The number of instructions in the program over which branching is required is usually quite limited.

Example:
6800: PC value (hex)   Example program
    0200   LOOP   – – –

                                     – – –
    0250   BNE   LOOP
Thus, offset = 0200 $-$ 0250 $- 2$ = AE hexadecimal.

The programmer need not be concerned with calculating the offset unless programming directly in machine code.

When it is required to branch over a range outside the limits of the offset field, it is usual to branch to a near location containing a jump instruction which has a two-byte absolute address field.

In some applications the facility to locate a program anywhere in memory is desirable. Relative addressing enables this to be achieved without modification to the program.

Stack

A stack is accessed at one end only and operands are stored or retrieved from the stack at an address in main memory determined by the contents of the stack pointer (SP). Stack operations are usually implied since there is often only one stack in the system, this being the system stack referred to earlier.

Example:
8080: PUSH B; push (store) the contents of register pair BC on to the stack.
In ISP: M $((SP) - 1) \leftarrow G(B)$
         M $((SP) - 2) \leftarrow G(C)$

Problems

P5.1 Cite two examples of information that might be stored as (i) constants, (ii) variables, (iii) tables, (iv) linked list. Briefly explain why.
(Hint: The temperature of a fermentation vat would be stored as a variable in a computer-controlled system.)

P5.2 For binary to decimal conversion, and vice versa, the powers of ten, in binary form, are needed. Discuss the advantages and disadvantages of storing the values in tables compared with calculating them using a program.

P5.3 A square-law power series is required with 10, 100, 10,000 points. Compare the merits of tables and code for the generation of these.

P5.4 Describe in detail the operation of the stack during the following sequence of operations:

    (i) Stack write (STWR)
    (ii) Stack read (STRD)
    (iii) STWR
    (iv) STWR
    (v) STRD
    (vi) STWR
    (vii) STRD
    (viii) STRD
    (ix) STRD

The method of stack control should be method (c) in the text. Comment on the (ix) access to the stack.

P5.5 Draw a nested diagram showing the subroutine structure if the stack operations of P5.4 are call and return for write and read, respectively. What happens at the last access?

P5.6 Constants can be loaded into registers using both immediate and direct addressing modes. Compare and contrast the two methods in the 8080/85 microprocessor for both 8-bit and 16-bit operands.

P5.7 Tabulate the number of bits in the operand field of the instruction and the number of operands available for the following schemes of operand addressing:

(a) immediate 8 bits
(b) direct register 15 registers
(c) register indirect, with 2 registers of 16 bits
(d) memory direct 8 bits
(e) indexed register, 4 registers of 16 bits added to 16-bit offset in instruction.

P5.8 Describe the actions of an incrementing, indirect addressing mode which adds 1 after accessing the memory. What value is such an instruction? How does this compare with an instruction which increments before reading and decrements after writing?

P5.9 Indexing can be performed between many address types. Describe the action of instructions in a processor that has 4 16-bit index registers using offsets as follows:

  (i) 16-bit literal

 (ii) 8 direct registers each 8 bits long

(iii) Direct memory word (16 bits), offset of 16 bits

(iv) 4 registers indirect (2 bytes each), offset of 8 bits.

Assume the memory is 8 bits wide. State the number of instruction bits required in the operand field and the maximum size of table that can be accessed.

P5.10 Discuss the merits of relative addressing when 8-bit and 16-bit offsets are used. Why is operand addressing using relative addressing not particularly useful in microcomputer systems?

Six The processor–memory system

Introduction

The main components of a microcomputer system were shown in Fig. 2.1 and described in Chapter 2. They are the *processor*, its *program* and *operand memory* and the *peripheral image memory* which connects the processor to the external devices with which it interacts. The input–output system, or image memory, is treated here like the main memory, as an array of registers which are accessed by the processor. The paths or routes that connect the memories to the processor are described and alternative methods compared. The signalling requirements are briefly considered.

The image memory is then examined in more detail to explore the special requirements that the control of peripheral devices demand. This chapter considers the logical and physical features of the hardware, and some aspects of large-scale integration of the input–output system. The following chapter considers the interaction of program and hardware when controlling many peripherals which are active simultaneously.

Background and conventions

In the first section no distinction is made between the memory that connects peripherals to the processor and the main memory; they are all assumed to be in the address space of the processor while considering the data routes needed to effect a transfer between them. There are special cases, as in the TMS 9900, which cannot be generalized in this way, but by far the majority of systems is included. The differences between main memory and image memory will be developed in the second section of this chapter.

To describe the routes, symbols are required for the functions inherent in the structure. These elements are the *register*, the *bus driver* and the *multiplexer*. The register stores data until overwritten by a control action which loads the register (see Fig. 6.1). The output of a register is static and valid for the time interval between successive load operations. The driver is able to transmit (drive) data on one input onto a bi-directional route or read data from the bi-directional route onto an output. There is no storage

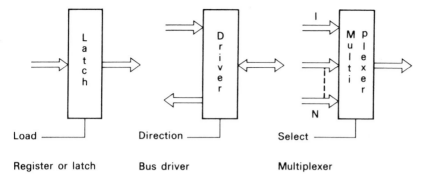

Register or latch   Bus driver   Multiplexer

Fig. 6.1 Elements for data route descriptions

in a driver and a single direction control is required. A multiplexer allows 1 of N inputs to be routed to a single output, and is controlled by a selection signal. In the data paths to follow the presence of the control signals referred to above is implied and will be omitted for clarity. They will be explicitly described in the section on signalling and timing.

The processor is considered as a source of memory addresses and a source or destination for memory data for WRITE and READ, respectively. For this discussion it is not necessary to distinguish exactly from where the information originates; however, it will be contained in a register and therefore is assumed to be a static value. The memory address may originate from the program counter, the stack pointer, an index register, input–output address, or any other possible source of addresses. The destination of memory READ operations may be the instruction register, the ALU registers, or any other operand destination register (e.g. A, PSW, HL, SP in 8085). A source register for a memory WRITE will be any operand register in the processor. The processor may be simplified to a block containing a memory address register and a memory data register (see Fig. 6.2).

The memory may be similarly simplified. In this case a SELECT input provides the address of the location required. The location contains a register which holds a static value when being read or a register which will be loaded for a WRITE operation. The memory requires a WRITE data route for the value to be written and a READ data route for the value being obtained from the selected location. READ and WRITE control signals are needed to define the function the memory must perform. Usually this is encoded onto a single signal indicating READ when logic '1', say, and WRITE when logic '0'. The basic routes between processor and memory are shown in Fig. 6.2. The basic activity implied by the diagram is as follows. A memory address is presented to the memory by the processor control circuit. For a WRITE operation the memory data is presented at a similar time. The memory will then load the contents of the

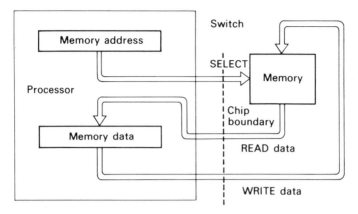

Fig. 6.2 Basic routes between processor and memory

WRITE route into the selected register. For a READ operation the memory will present the contents of the location selected on the READ route and the processor will load the value into the memory data register. The timing activity implicit in this transaction is controlled by the processor and will be briefly elaborated later.

To emphasize the importance of the chip boundary of the processor a broken line is drawn on this and subsequent diagrams. The tables that follow will summarize the pin count at this boundary for comparison.

Processor–memory routes

Since the memory can only be either reading or writing, the two data routes can be merged to one to produce the bi-directional data route shown in Fig. 6.3. Two drivers (one each side of the chip boundary) provide a

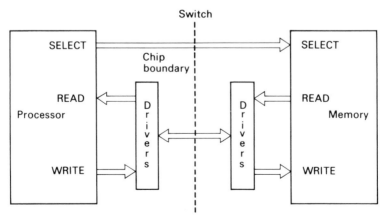

Fig. 6.3 Bi-directional data—direct address

bi-directional drive capability, one receiving while the other transmits, and vice versa when the direction of flow changes. Since both have the ability to transmit, the drivers must be of the open-collector or 3-state type so the receiving device can have its transmitters disabled. The processor must generate a signal (usually READ (RD) because it enables a memory read) which crosses the chip boundary, and enables or disables the external driver without enabling both drivers together. Table 6.1 shows the processors with this basic arrangement and the column for pin count (Npn) is given by $Npn = Na + Nw + 1$, where Na is the length of the address in bits, and Nw the word length and the extra pin is required for the READ signal.

Table 6.1. Bidirectional data—direct address

Processor	Word length (Nw)	Address length (Na)	Memory size (K words)	Pin count (Npn)
8080	8	16	64	25
6800	8	16	64	25
6501/2	8	16	64	25
6504	8	13	8	22
6503/5	8	12	4	21
EA9002	8	12	4	21
PPS–8	8	14	16	23
Z80	8	16	64	25
2650	8	15	32	24
TMS9900	16	16	32*	33

* Byte addressing allowed.

The pin count can be reduced further by multiplexing the information by transferring it across the chip boundary in consecutive time intervals. All the data routes are combined inside the chip by a multiplexer–driver combination, and externally these are demultiplexed by the appropriate latch circuits and control signals. Two situations are shown in Fig. 6.4. If $Na = Nw = Np$, where Np is the width of the data port (normally equal to Nw), two beats will complete the transfer of the address and the data. The arrangement of Fig. 6.4(a) illustrates this and the pin count is given by: $Npn = Np + 2$; one of the control signals is for READ and a further one is required to load the latch. A variation on this (Fig. 6.4(b)) is required if $Na > Np$, because the memory address must be transmitted in two beats. The pin count is now $Npn = Np + 3$, the extra control signal being required to load the second address latch. Processors with a single multiplexed bus are shown in Table 6.2.

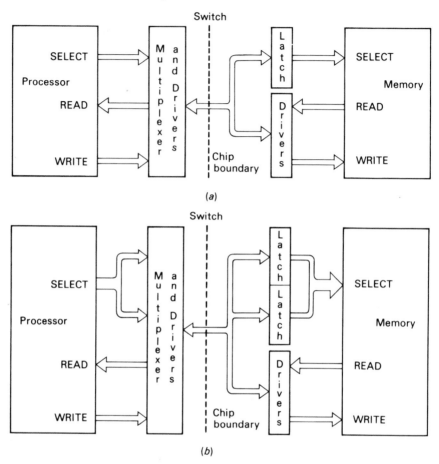

Fig. 6.4 Single multiplexed route (a) Address and data words of equal length
(b) Address word length greater than data word length

Table 6.2. Single multiplexed route

Processor	Word length $(Nw = Np)$	Address length (Na)	Latch length (Nl)	Memory size (K words)	Pin count (Npn)
GI-1600	16	16	16(a)	64	18
PACE	16	16	16(a)	64	18
MPS-1600	16	16	16(a)	64	18
CRD-8	8	16	8 + 8(b)	64	11
8008	8	14	8 + 6(b)	16	11
IM 1600	12	12	12(a)	4	14
8048 (DATA)	8	8	8(a)	1/4	(14)
F 100	16	15	15(a)	32	18

When $Na > Nw$, an intermediate solution is possible which improves on the speed of Fig. 6.4, but needs extra pins. One of the two data routes of Fig. 6.3 is used to multiplex part of the memory address; the multiplexed data route is shown in Fig. 6.5(a), while the multiplexed address route is

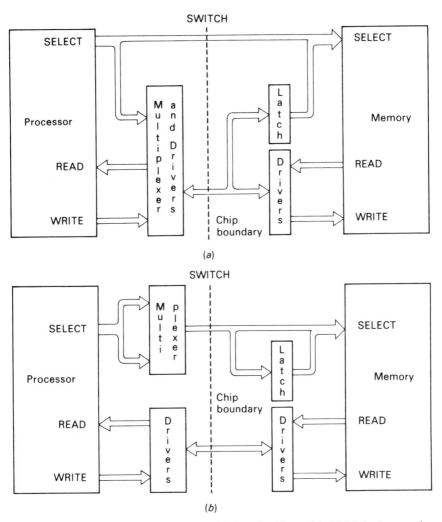

Fig. 6.5 Bi-directional data route—multiplexed address (a) Multiplexing on the data route (b) Multiplexing on the address route

shown in Fig. 6.5(b). Both require a single latch of length Nl and one extra control signal to load the latch. The pin count for both solutions is $Na - Nl + Nw + 2$, provided $Nl \leqslant Nw$ for (a) and $2Nl \leqslant Nw$ for (b). The processors using this switching method are shown in Table 6.3.

Table 6.3. Bidirectional data route—multiplexed address

Processor	Word length (Nw)	Address length (Na)	Multiplexing Latch length (Nl)	Multiplexing Route A or D	Memory size (K words)	Pin count (Npn)
8085	8	16	8	D	64	18
8048 (PROG)*	8	12	8	D	4	14
COSMAC	8	16	8	A	64	18
MK5065	8	15	8	D	32	17

* Bank switch internally.

Bank switching

Bank switching is a method of extending the basic addressing capability of a processor to provide a larger memory, which some processors have as an inbuilt switch function. The address issued by the processor is concatenated with Nb bits of the bank register (Fig. 6.6) to produce the full memory

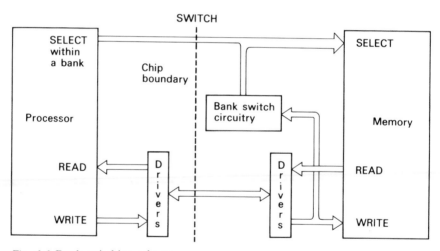

Fig. 6.6 Bank switching scheme

address. A special bank switch instruction is used to load the bank registers. Difficulties arise in maintaining program continuity when switching banks, and so the method is not used frequently; those that do are shown in Table 6.4, and the pin count is $Npn = Na - Nb + Nw + 2$, where the extra control signal loads the bank register.

Bank switching can be used with any processor configuration to enlarge the memory of a processor, but the user must provide the bank switch mechanism.

The 8048 uses bank switching internally (the user is unaware of it) to

Table 6.4. Bank switching in microprocessors

Processor	Word length (Nw)	Address length		Memory size			Pin count (Npn)
		Total (Na)	Bank (Nb)	Banks	Bank size (K words)	Total	
SC/MP	8	16	4	16	4	64K	22
CDP1801	8	16	8	256	1/4	64K	18

extend the program address range from 2 to 4K words. However, the technique has been cleverly applied so that the bank switch change can be programmed at any time but it only occurs on the next jump instruction. The processor also stores the full address, including bank switch bit, when storing a subroutine return address.

It is becoming less necessary to find ways of extending the addressing range of machines, as machines like the Z8000, 8086 and 68000 appear with 20-bit and more addressing capability.

Summary of processor–memory routes

The tables and diagrams show the main features of the P–S–M organizations found on most microprocessors. The 8048 appears in two because the program memory and data memory are separate and use different arrangements for each. The popularity of the arrangement of Fig. 6.3 is obvious, the fast memory access it offers is appealing (all the accepted industry standards are in this class) and the memory interface is simple. The high speed of this organization is essential for the efficient execution of instructions in the TMS 9900 with its memory-to-memory operations, but the huge 64-pin package may be embarrassing to many users.

Intel's successors to the 8080, the 8085 and the single-chip computer, the 8048, both use the arrangement of Fig. 6.5(a), with no apparent loss of speed and the gain of 7 extra pins, although the status information provided in the 8080 is no longer available. With a simple latch, the 8085 can be matched to the memory interface of the 8080.

Except for TMS9900, all the 16- and 12-bit word machines use the single bi-directional route (the intermediate of Fig. 6.5 is of no benefit here), requiring a large address latch outside the chip and operating at the lower speed expected of this organization.

The pin count proposed for each organization may be hypothetical because many pins have multiple functions, and although the signal functions described must be present they may, in fact, be provided indirectly. For example, in Table 6.2 the 8008 has a 6-bit latch on an 8-bit route; the other two bits provide the READ/WRITE information.

Additional switch information

Many processors provide additional switching information to indicate INSTRUCTION FETCH (usually the first word of a multi-word instruction and the most common), DATA READ, DATA WRITE and STACK access either READ or WRITE (pop or push). A further distinction can occur between program and data memories in some processors (8048 for example), which differs from the instruction fetch mentioned earlier. The status information is usually provided early in the memory cycle to provide a 'look ahead' for the switch, which can be useful in multiple processor configurations or where memory access checking is performed by the switch prior to requesting a memory cycle. Because of the exclusive nature of these signals they can be optimally coded; i.e. 2 pins could provide 4 signals, so the overhead is not large.

Signalling

Signals are supplied by the processor which dictate or indicate when valid transactions must or can occur. These control or signalling lines are essential features of interfaces but are often omitted in block diagrams for clarity, or combined into a single 'control bus'. These signals define a protocol for information interchange between processor and memory. The timing and sequence of signalling information is crucial and requires careful examination before designing the appropriate matching hardware.

The signals between memory and processor may be divided into two classes: those which define the function required (what) and those which define the timing (when).

Function signals

READ and WRITE are the main function signals between memory and processor. They define the action the memory will perform. In processors that provide for a dedicated image memory (see next section), another important function signal is one to distinguish a memory transfer from an input–output transfer.

With routes that multiplex address and data, signals are needed to define which latch or register to load.

Timing

Timing information is always related to the clock that controls the state machine in the control unit of the central processor. Such systems are called synchronous because the activity has to be synchronized to some defined 'tick' of a central clock. To economize on pins on the processor package and to simplify external hardware designs, the timing information (when) is often encoded with the function signal (what). An obvious example is the latching signal for demultiplexing (see Fig. 6.5); where only one latch is required the two elements are more economically encoded into a single signal that defines both time and function (e.g. *load* latch *now*).

The WRITE signal is another that frequently conveys both time and function; it is designed to drive the WRITE pulse line of semiconductor memories directly. When studying data sheets it is crucial to distinguish the dual nature of such signals. A truly timing-only signal is a memory-ready signal used to cause the processor to idle to synchronize the slow memory device to the faster processor. The 6800 microprocessor is a good example of a machine that separates function and timing in the signals at the processor memory interface. Table 6.5 shows the signals for the 8080, 8085, 6800 and Z80. The table indicates clearly the alternative approaches available but also stresses the variety of solutions possible where signalling is concerned.

Table 6.5. Signalling conventions for four processors

8085	
ALE	Load address from data route
IO/$\overline{\text{M}}$	I/O transfer if active—memory transfer inactive
$\overline{\text{RD}}$	Read function and data route timing
$\overline{\text{WR}}$	Write function and memory write timing
RDY	Synchronization for slow memory

8080*	
$\overline{\text{MEMR}}$	Memory read function and data route timing
$\overline{\text{MEMW}}$	Memory write function and memory write timing
$\overline{\text{IOR}}$	I/O read function and data route timing
$\overline{\text{IOW}}$	I/O write function and register load timing
RDY	Synchronization for slow memory

6800	
VMA	Address valid for memory cycle function
R/W	Read or write function
CLK2	Data and address route timing

(Note 6800 has no special I/O function)

Z80	
$\overline{\text{MREQ}}$	Memory access function
$\overline{\text{IORQ}}$	I/O access function
$\overline{\text{RD}}$	Read function and data route timing
$\overline{\text{WR}}$	Write function and register load timing
$\overline{\text{WAIT}}$	Synchronization for slow memory

* 8080 signals are for a standard 3-chip set.

The following section describes the timing of one, the Z80, to illustrate the basic principles of memory–processor signalling.

Processor READ cycle

Figure 6.7 shows the signalling cycle for a memory read on the Z80 processor. The machine cycle is the interval between one memory access and the next. The time t_{cyc} depends on the clock frequency and the instruction type, the one shown being typical. The address (SELECT)

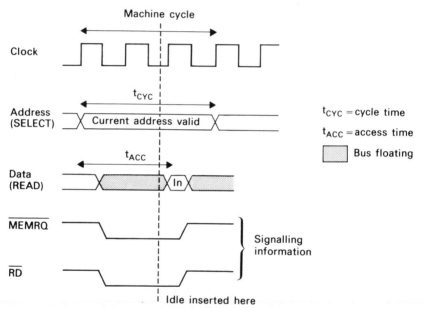

Fig. 6.7 Memory READ cycle for Z80

information is generated and a memory request (MEMRQ) issued indicating that the address is valid. The READ signal (RD) becomes active when the internal drivers on the processor have reached the high-impedance state (3 state outputs) and is used to enable the drivers of the selected memory block. The memory has a time of t_{ACC} seconds to get the data ready for the critical period shown. The data must be held by the memory until RD and MEMRQ terminate the cycle. If the memory is unable to perform an access in the time t_{ACC} then the processor must be prevented from reaching the critical point by making it idle. Most processors provide an input, called WAIT on the Z80 or READY in the 8080/85, which if inactive makes the processor idle. When the memory is ready it makes 'ready' active and the machine cycle continues. Some processors also generate a 'wait' status on entering the idle state, and by connecting this to the 'ready' signal a single idle period can be generated for every memory access. Except for exceptionally slow memories this would normally be adequate.

Processor WRITE cycle

The write cycle is illustrated in Fig. 6.8, the only difference being that the processor now generates the data for the memory, the memory drivers being disabled by RD being inactive. After a time the WRITE active signal is generated which is normally used to load the memory on the rising edge. The delay from the data valid time to the active WRITE signal is to allow for the setting up of the data in the memory. Many processors provide this type of signal to simplify memory circuits. For slower memories an idle state can be generated.

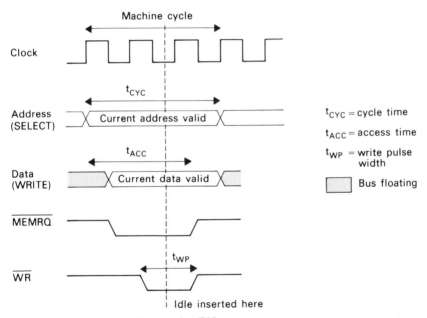

t_{CYC} = cycle time

t_{ACC} = access time

t_{WP} = write pulse width

Bus floating

Fig. 6.8 Memory WRITE cycle for Z80

Route sharing

To economize on wires it is common to share the routes between processor and memory to provide alternative connection paths. The data route is an example where sharing between READ and WRITE cycles is performed. Often, however, external devices require access to the address route, data route and the signal lines to perform transfers to or from the memory independent of the processor; this is called direct memory access, or

DMA, which is described in the next chapter. The processor must be capable of releasing the routes for use by the other device and, since memory accesses are impossible, idle until released. The typical solution is for the external device to request the routes and for the processor to acknowledge once they have been released. The signals used for this function on the Z80, 6800, 8080 and 8085 are shown in Table 6.6.

Table 6.6. Bus-sharing control lines

	Z80	6800	8080	8085
Request release of address route	BUSRQ	TSC	HOLD	HOLD
Request release of data route	"	DBE	"	"
Acknowledge release	$\overline{\text{BUSAK}}$	BA·	HOLDA	HOLDA

Loading of processor signals

The outputs of microprocessors can normally drive 1 or 2 standard TTL loads, and for small systems this may be adequate. But when the capacitance, signal line lengths or loading become larger, all the signals from the processor need buffering to increase the drive. This decreases the available access time for memories because the outward and inward signals are delayed by one gate each at the processor. These factors must be considered when designing the system and calculating the performance.

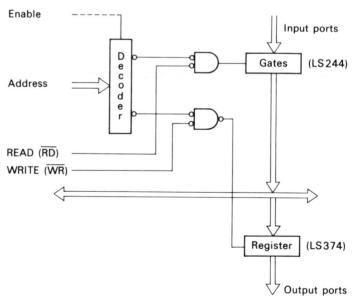

Fig. 6.9 Basic image memory design

Peripheral image memory

The data and address routes for image memory (input–output) are usually shared by the main memory and have been treated in this way so far. The basic structure of the image memory is shown in Fig. 6.9. The address is decoded to select an input register for READ and an output latch for a WRITE operation. The gates on the input port allow the digital information to be applied to the data route during the READ cycle. The latch retains the output data until updated by a subsequent output operation. The READ and WRITE control lines also define the timing of reading and loading. The circuit shown will operate on Z80, 8080 and 8085 processor routes, although minor variations are required.

Input/output register access

The system designer has two choices for the location of the image memory: either memory-mapped or dedicated memory.

With memory-mapped image memory the registers are decoded in the main address space of the processor, in which case, the dotted line may be omitted from Fig. 6.9, since the locations are defined solely by the address decoder and must be unique. Memory-mapping fragments the main memory, provides a rich set of I/O instructions (all the normal memory reference orders are available) and requires large decoding circuits. All processors may operate with memory-mapped input/output.

Many processors have a dedicated memory function for input/output registers. A special small memory is selected by extra control signals (e.g. $\overline{\text{IORQ}}$, IO/$\overline{\text{M}}$, etc. from Table 6.5), which disable normal memory operations on the data route and enable image memory transfers. The relevant control signal would be connected, as shown dotted in Fig. 6.9. This approach requires special input–output instructions which activate the control lines via the control unit of the processor. Smaller decoders are usual because the memory space is smaller and only processors with the appropriate hardware can support dedicated image memory (e.g. the 6800 has to have memory-mapped I/O). Table 6.7 shows processors with dedicated memories, the address range, and number of instructions supported.

Special input/output circuits

A large range of peripheral circuits are available now and only a limited number can be examined here. Three types that are widely available will be described; the programmable parallel I/O device, serial I/O device or (USART) and timers.

The programmable parallel input/output port circuits provide both input and output circuits at the same pin of the package. The direction, or I/O circuit, required is selected by programming an appropriate register. A simplified circuit is shown in Fig. 6.10. The direction signal is programmed

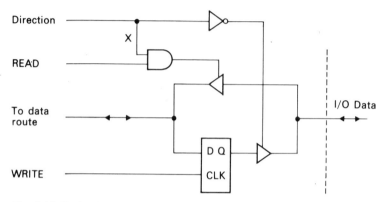

Fig. 6.10 Basic circuit of programmable I/O bit

'0' for output, '1' for input, using a conventional output register. This would be contained inside the I/O circuit chip. If programmed for input then a READ operation would enable the I/O data onto the data route. If programmed for output then a WRITE operation would load the D type register and the data presented to the I/O data signal. If the direction control line is disconnected from the input buffer control signal at point X, then an input (READ operation) when programmed for output would read the contents of the output port. Some devices allow this, others do not.

Serial input/output devices

The earliest LSI circuit made from random logic gates was the serial–parallel, parallel–serial converter for asynchronous or synchronous transmission of characters; the UART or USART. These devices predated microprocessors so they were obvious candidates for peripheral interface products. Many are available and all have very similar features and characteristics. Control words are used to set up the transmitted and received format, to select synchronous or asynchronous mode and many other functions. The status word indicates character sent, character received and any error conditions. Some have full V.24 standard* compatibility, and these signals are available through the control and status words.

* V.24 is a CCITT communications standard for serial interfaces.

A limited selection of these products is listed in Table 6.7. Few devices generate the voltage and current levels needed for transmission along lines, so buffering circuits are usually needed on the serial input and output lines.

Table 6.7. Processors with dedicated image memory

Processor	Width (bits)	Number of ports		Number of instructions
		I	O	
8008	8	8	32	1
8080	8	256	256	2
8085 EXT	8	256	256	2
8085 INT	1	1	1	2
Z80	8	256	256	12
8048 INT	8	2		4
8048 EXT	4	16		3
9900 INT	1	1	1	5
CDP 1802	8	7	7	2
MK 5065	8	16	16	4
2650	8	256	256	2
IM 6100	12	64	64	6
F8	8	256	256	4

INT – Internal: Registers on the chip
EXT – External

Timing input–output devices

In real-time applications, time information is required for a variety of reasons. Timing with a program is extremely tedious and never very accurate. The timer is a counter, driven by an external clock, usually the processor's, which is read or written by the processor for setting programmable time intervals. A selection of circuits is shown in Table 6.8 and see Appendix 5 for further details.

Summary of special input/output devices

Table 6.8 lists some of the wide range of products presently offered. Most are designed for specific processors, but where they may have more general use this is indicated. The TMS 5501 has an appealing specification but is inflexible because it is closely tied to the 8080 processor, so much so that it is not compatible to the 8085 or the Z80, both very close relatives of the 8080. Processors and memories with integral input/output are included.

Table 6.8. Parallel, serial and timer devices

Device no.	Parallel ports				Processor family	General-purpose
	Width	In	Out	I/O		
Z80–PI0	8			2	Z80	Y
6820/6821	8			2	6800	Y
8155 (RWM)	8,8,6			3	8085	N
8755 (ROM)	8			2	8085	N
8255	8			3	8080	Y
8243	4			4	8048	N
TMS 5501	8	1	1		8080	N
F8 (3850)	8			2	F8	—
3851 (ROM)	8			2	F8	N
8048	8			2	8048	—

	Serial Ports				
	No.	Syn	Asyn		
Z80–SI0	2	*	*	Z80	Y
8251	1	*	*	8080	Y
TMS 5501	1		*	8080	N
6850	1		*	6800	Y
6852	1	*		6800	Y
6854	1	*		6800	Y

	Timers			
	No.	Length (bits)		
8155	1	14	8085	N
8253	3	16	8080	Y
TMS 5501	5	8	8080	N
8048	1	8	8048	—
6840	3	16	6800	Y

Problems

P6.1 Figure 6.1 shows the latch, driver and multiplexer as functional units for route construction. Describe each in turn giving a simple logic circuit for one bit of each element.

P6.2 Two additional elements are introduced in Fig. 6.9, the decoder and gates. What are decoders required for? Show a circuit for a 2–4-line decoder. The gate circuit drives onto a bi-directional data route. What are the special output requirements for this function?

P6.3 A memory address register is illustrated in Fig. 6.2. Name four possible sources of the memory address in the 8085 when accessing memory operands. Explain when the following 8085 registers are used as memory data registers:

Register A, program counter, instruction register, flag register, Register H.

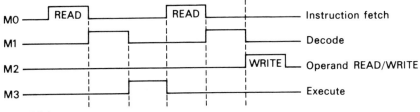

Fig. P6.1

P6.4 Figure P6.1 shows the timing waveforms M0 to M3 for the instructions MOV A,D; MOV M,A, when executed in sequence. Explain the actions during each active phase. (Hint: the internal move operation does not need an operand fetch, while the move to memory phase does not require an execute cycle.)

P6.5 Explain the waveforms in Fig. P6.2 for the following instruction sequence. MVI, A,11: ADD M: JMP 2.

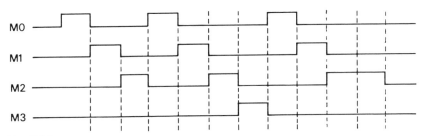

Fig. P6.2

Identify the READ and WRITE memory cycles.

P6.6 Because the decode and execute cycles are internal they are often invisible, so they may be omitted. Draw just M0 and M2 for the following sequence of instructions (assume M1 and M2 take zero time).
ORI 24: MOV M,A: INR L: MOV A,M: JZ Z: RRC.
(Note the value of L is such that the jump does not occur, but the processor still fetches the jump address.)

For the following questions the program counter (PC) is 2832H, H is 1BH, L is 6CH and the memory locations contain the value XM, at the start of each sequence. The processor is an 8085.

P6.7 For problem P6.4 the address route and data route would contain the following for the M0 and M2 cycles, for an 8080 processor.

Cycle type	Address route (16)	Data route (8)	Read/Write
M0	2832	7A	R
M0	2833	77	R
M2	1B6C	XA	W

(where XA is the contents of the A register, all numbers in hex.).
Explain the contents of the table.

P6.8 Write out tables for P6.5 and P6.6 assuming a bi-directional data route and separate address route (Fig. 6.3) as for the 8080 processor.

P6.9 The 8085 multiplexes the low address onto the data route during the memory access (see Fig. 6.5(a)). Thus the M0 cycle must be divided into 2 beats. The example of P6.7 would appear as follows:

Cycle type	Address route (8)	Data/Address route (8)	Read/Write
M0/0	28	32	—
M0/1	28	7A	R
M0/0	28	33	—
M0/1	28	77	R
M2/0	1B	6C	—
M2/1	1B	XA	W

Repeat P6.8 for the 8085 processor.

P6.10 It is possible to make the hypothetical assumption that processors exist with the 8085 instruction set but with the processor–memory routes of Fig. 6.4(b) and 6.5(b). Repeat question P6.8.

(a) using routes of Fig. 6.4(b)
(b) using routes of Fig. 6.5(b)

P6.11 If a bi-directional route has to be buffered to achieve power gain and reduce loading, what circuit is required? How would it be controlled using any of the signalling conventions of Table 6.5?

P6.12 Describe with the aid of diagrams the READ and WRITE memory cycles for the 8085 and 6800 based on information in Figs 6.7 and 6.8 and Table 6.5. (Do not look up details in data books; deduce the operation from the information given and your own mind.)

P6.13 The image memory circuit of Fig. 6.9 is not designed for any specific processor. Describe with diagrams as necessary how the circuit would be connected to:

(a) Z80   memory mapped
(b) 8085   dedicated memory
(c) 6800   memory mapped
(d) Z80   dedicated memory.

P6.14 Compare and contrast memory-mapped image memory and dedicated image memory for the 8085. Highlight the instructions available for I/O transfers.

7 Concurrency

Timing within main frame

The flow of data within the processor and between the processor and the memory of the main frame is controlled by signals at times related to a basic clock. A sequence of clock pulses is required to order the actions within the basic series of machine operations to 'fetch instruction', 'decode instruction', 'fetch operand', 'obey operation', 'determine next instruction', as each instruction of the program is interpreted by the circuits of the processor–memory pair in the main frame. The number of clock pulses required by an instruction will depend on the complexity of its operation within the processor and on the number of accesses to memory required to fetch the instruction and to transfer operands and results between the processor and the memory. The time required to execute an instruction will depend on the instruction, but will be equal to a multiple of the basic clock period.

The list of instructions which comprises the program is traversed one instruction at a time by the processor. The program counter within the processor points to the instruction currently being interpreted, and the processor will dwell on this instruction in the list for a time sufficient to execute its interpretation. The dwell time will vary, hence the rate at which the pointer moves through the list of instructions will vary, but each dwell time is a strict multiple of the clock period. Every action is synchronized to the basic clock. The strict synchronous regime within the processor–memory pair is an essential basis for the design of the main frame and ensures reliable and predictable operation.

Concurrent regimes

The total system comprises the main frame and the peripheral equipment. Some of the peripheral equipment, such as indicators and solenoids, can be within the synchronous regime of the main frame. Other peripheral equipment, such as a keyboard, an analog to digital converter (ADC) a paper tape reader or a disk have their own timing regimes. Some regimes will be asynchronous. The keyboard changes state when a key is pressed by an operator. Though a skilled typist may develop a rhythm which has a semblance of a synchronous regime, the key strokes will be asynchronous and occur at random times relative to both the human heart beat and the basic clock of the main frame.

Electromechanical devices such as the tape reader or disk will have a synchronous regime with a rhythm or clock period related to the motor which is at the heart of the device. Electronic devices, such as modems and ADCs, will have their own synchronous regimes determined by the system to which they belong.

The total system may be viewed as a set of concurrent regimes, each with its own rhythm, either synchronous or asynchronous. The different regimes are required to communicate with each other, usually through the main frame, as shown in Fig. 7.1. A regime will not be in synchronism with any of the others. It is therefore necessary to establish a procedure for signalling and transferring data between the mutually asynchronous regimes. In any such transfer one regime will act as a sender while the other is a receiver.

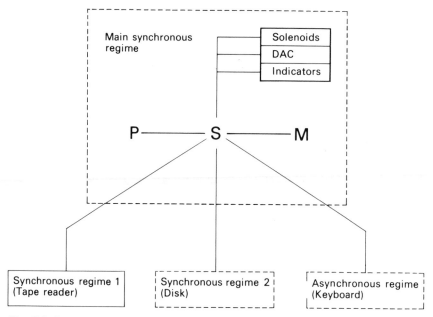

Fig. 7.1 Concurrent regimes of a microprocessor system

Both the sender and the receiver will be executing a regular sequence of operations as ordained by the design of their individual circuits or programs. The time allotted to each operation will be determined by the local clock. Within the sender, one of these operations will be to generate the message to be transmitted to the receiver, while within the receiver there will be an operation to accept a transmitted message. It is unlikely that the time interval, within the sender, to transmit the message will coincide with the time interval within the receiver to accept a transmitted message. It is necessary to provide an intermediate buffer register to hold the message at the time it is generated until the accept action of the receiver occurs.

The receiver may be able to accept a message more often than the sender can generate one, thus the sender must provide an extra intermediate FLAG flip-flop to indicate when a new message is set into the buffer register. The receiver will interrogate this flag at fixed intervals to determine whether a new message has been buffered and is ready to be accepted. The flag will be reset during the execution of the transmission. There are many protocols which have been established to provide rules of etiquette which ensure the safe transmission of messages between two mutually asynchronous regimes. It is beyond the scope of this chapter to develop these in more detail except to present two fundamental problems. The first is often termed the 'glitch', while the second is termed the 'crisis time'.

The glitch

The FLAG flip-flop is set by a pulse, or edge, timed with respect to the clock of the sender regime, when the buffer register is set with a new message, as shown in Fig. 7.2(a). The FLAG output is connected across the boundary between the sender and receiver regimes and is gated with a pulse timed with respect to the clock of the receiver regime. The resultant pulse, SET ACCEPT, is staticized on the ACCEPT flip-flop, the output of which acts as input to the combinatorial logic which decides on the next action to be executed within the receiver regime. If the ACCEPT flip-flop is set to the 1 state then this logic will choose to execute the transfer of the message from the buffer into the receiver. The waveforms for the ideal synchronization of the interaction between the two mutually asynchronous regimes are shown in Fig. 7.2(b).

In practice, because of the mutual asynchronism, the receiver clock waveform will shift with respect to the sender clock, and there is a finite probability that the receiver clock will overlap the setting of the FLAG, as shown in Fig. 7.3. The SET ACCEPT pulse will be narrow. This is the glitch, not to be confused with the race hazard of logic circuits which can be eliminated by careful design. The glitch cannot be designed out of a system and we must learn to accept its inevitability. The consequence of the glitch is that the energy delivered by the SET ACCEPT signal is insufficient to cause a normal transition of the ACCEPT flip-flop from the 0 to 1 state. The energy is sufficient to begin this transition, but only to the point where the flip-flop is left in a metastable state somewhere between 1 and 0. It will

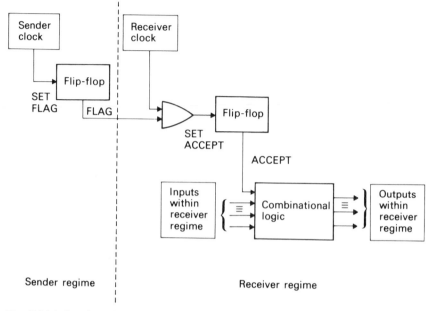

Fig. 7.2(a) Synchronization circuit

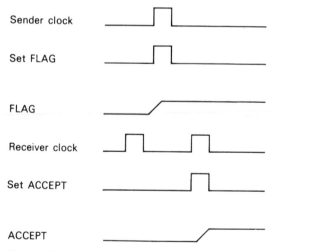

Fig. 7.2(b) Ideal synchronized waveforms

linger in this uncertain state until some random perturbation causes it either to return to the 0 state or to move up to the 1 state. The net effect is that the settling time of the ACCEPT flip-flop in response to a SET ACCEPT signal is much longer than the normal settling time. The consequence for the combinatorial logic, which is processing the ACCEPT

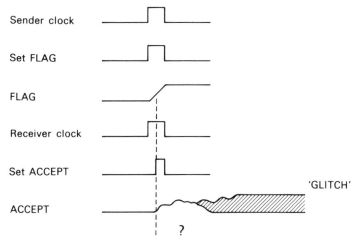

Sender clock

Set FLAG

FLAG

Receiver clock

Set ACCEPT

'GLITCH'

ACCEPT

?

Fig. 7.3 The 'glitch'

flip-flop output, is uncertain. At best it will not interpret the ACCEPT flip-flop as being set and will wait until the next receiver clock pulse to confirm the status of the FLAG flip-flop, but it is possible for this combinatorial logic to give an indeterminate output because some of its gates will interpret the metastable state of the ACCEPT flip-flop as a 1 and others will interpret it as a 0. An erroneous output can occur which will cause a fault in the receiver.

The probability of the occurrence of this glitch fault is low but finite. The mean time between failures may be hours or weeks, similar to the MTBF of electronic components. The procedure when any fault occurs is to remove the equipment from service and then test the equipment to isolate the source before replacing the failed component. If the fault is due to a glitch the tests are unlikely to reveal the cause and there are no faulty components to replace.

This failure mode cannot be eliminated. The designer must endeavour to ensure that its probability is as low as possible and that the consequences of its occurrence are not dangerous.

Crisis time

In a synchronous regime which is acting as a sender the sequence of operations may generate messages to be transmitted at regular time intervals. There is a strict minimum time between the generation of each message and thus between consecutive attempts to load the buffer and set the FLAG. This time is termed the 'crisis time'.

If the receiver does not recognize the FLAG and accept the message from the buffer within this crisis time, then erroneous operation occurs.

A crisis time also exists within an asynchronous regime. Though the time between consecutive buffer loading may vary, there will be a known minimum time interval, the crisis time. In some situations the sending regime may wish to transmit only one message which may be an alarm indicator. In this case the crisis time is determined by other factors which are left to your imagination.

In any system involving a sender and a receiver it is necessary to establish the crisis time of the peripheral regime and take due note of this in the design of the system.

Transfers within a microprocessor system

A typical microprocessor system is shown in Fig. 7.1. The registers of the peripheral devices will have allocated locations within the image memory, as indicated in the previous chapter, and the sequence of instructions of the procedure to effect the transfer between device and memory can be written. The problems which remain are to determine the time at which the procedure becomes an active process and how the process can be fitted into the main process which is active in the processor–memory pair.

A basic information-processing task involves three separate processes:

Process 1: Input transfer of data from peripherals into memory.
Process 2: Main process to turn these data into results in memory.
Process 3: Output transfer of results data from memory to peripherals.

In a simple system each process can be allowed to occur once in the sequence; 1 then 2 then 3. Thus the three processes do not occur concurrently but sequentially. Each of the transfer processes can be affected either solely by a procedure in the processor–memory pair or by a combination of such a procedure plus assistance from an active process in the peripheral device.

A basic transfer procedure is shown in Fig. 7.4(a), which repeats a procedure TR_p until the string of input data has been transferred. The procedure TR_p is shown in Fig. 7.4(b). The first action is to copy the value of the FLAG flip-flop into a convenient location in the processor. This is equivalent to gating the FLAG flip-flop output with the clock of the main regime and attempting to set the ACCEPT flip-flop (see Fig. 7.2(a)). The copy of the FLAG flip-flop is tested to determine the status of the buffer register in the peripheral regime. If the copy is zero then no action takes place except to exit from TR_p. If the copy is true then the transfer of the contents of the buffer register to the memory is executed by a sequence which involves an initial transfer from buffer register to accumulator, then from accumulator to the memory location determined by the contents of central register B_p. Register B_p is acting as an index register and must be

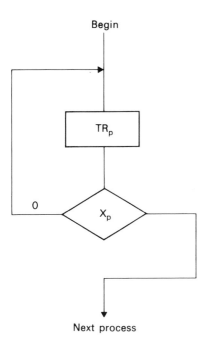

Begin

TR_p

0

X_p

Next process

X_p - qualifier SET by TR_p when string
of data has been transferred.

Fig. 7.4(a) Basic transfer procedure

incremented by 1 ready for the next transfer. The FLAG flip-flop is reset to 0 prior to the final action, which tests whether the transfer of the string of information from the peripheral devices has ended. There may be several test criteria which apply. If the transfer just executed was the last of the string, then the qualifier bit X_p is set, prior to exiting from the TR_p procedure.

Management of concurrent peripheral transfer

If more than one peripheral device is transferring concurrently then the basic transfer procedure of Fig. 7.4(a) must be modified to that of Fig. 7.4(c), which is able to accommodate n concurrent peripheral transfers. Each individual peripheral (P) is managed by a concurrent transfer routine CTR_p, which is also shown in Fig. 7.4(d). The qualifier X_p is set within each procedure TR_p when the peripheral string has ended. All the n qualifiers $(X_0, \ldots, X_{n-1})$ are processed to set the final qualifier Y, when all n string transfers have ended.

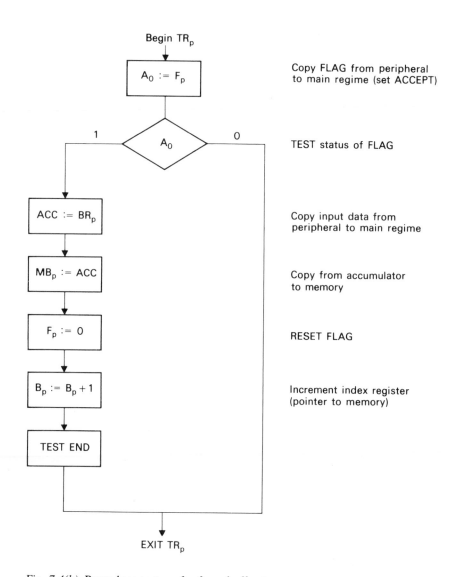

Fig. 7.4(b) Procedure to transfer from buffer to memory

A   := ACCUMULATOR REGISTER IN PROCESSOR
A_0 := Bit 0 of A
F_p := FLAG flip-flop in peripheral regime
BR_p := Buffer register in peripheral regime
MB_p := Memory location given by value of B_p
B_p := Index register in processor
TEST END := Procedure to test end of string transfer.—Sets X_p when all data has
               been transferred

Begin concurrent transfer procedures

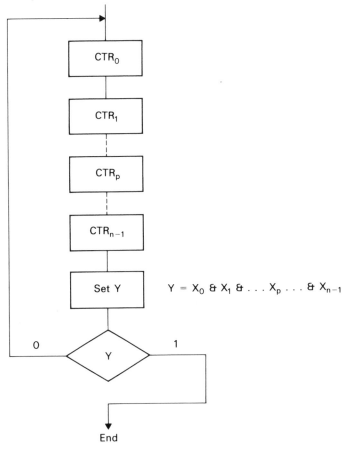

$$Y = X_0 \mathrel{\&} X_1 \mathrel{\&} \ldots X_p \ldots \mathrel{\&} X_{n-1}$$

Fig. 7.4(c) Basic concurrent transfer procedure

The time to execute a procedure CTR_p will depend on whether or not the peripheral p is transferring:

T_p max when $X_p = 0$
T_p min when $X_p = 1$

The time to execute the sequence set Y, then test Y, is equal to T_t.

The maximum time between examining a FLAG flip-flop and next examining it and finding it set, and then completing the transfer, is approximately equal to

$$\sum_{p=0}^{n-1} T_p \text{ max} + T_t$$

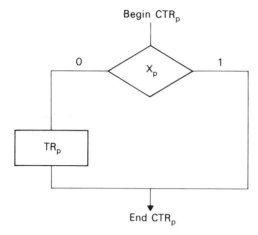

Fig. 7.4(d) Procedure for transfer within concurrent procedure
TR_p:= Procedure to transfer from peripheral to memory
X_p := Set to 1 when all data have been transferred

.

This time must be less than the crisis time of the peripheral regime P:

$$\text{Crisis time}_p > \sum_{p=0}^{n-1} T_p \max + T_t$$

Before such a concurrent transfer procedure is entered there must be an initial process which initiates the peripheral devices by giving appropriate start commands and which sets the appropriate qualifier bits (X_p) to zero. This action allows the concurrent procedure to identify those peripherals which are active and require the process TR_p until the individual string transfer has ended. No other peripheral devices can be activated once the concurrent transfer process has begun, until it has ended.

Implementation by program

The procedures to manage the transfer of data between peripherals and the main memory may be implemented entirely as programs within the main processor–memory pair. The basic sequence of input-transfer–main-process–output-transfer may be written as one complete program using the normal disciplines of program development. This simple sequence may be tested as three separate procedures which are linked during the final development phase. The result is a single program to execute the total task which becomes an active process that is predictable, and which may be relied on during the diagnosis of hardware faults that will arise in the developed system.

Concurrency by polling

In some systems it may be necessary for the three processes, 'input transfer', 'output transfer' and 'main process' to be concurrent. Such concurrency may be implemented entirely as a program which polls between the three processes in a regular manner. The polling procedure is constructed out of the procedures for the three separate processes as follows.

The main procedure A is partitioned into a series of sub-procedures, A_0, A_1, A_2, . . ., A_{n-1}. The length of each sub-procedure is chosen so that the time it requires as an active process does not exceed a time t_a. In the case of a single-input peripheral and a single-output peripheral, it is possible to implement each transfer by a separate procedure. Let the input procedure be C, which requires up to time t_c as an active process, and let the output procedure be B, which requires up to time t_b as an active process. The polling timing diagram is shown in Fig. 7.5. The time to execute the sequence $A_i \rightarrow B \rightarrow C$ ($t_a + t_b + t_c$) must be less than the crisis time T of the more urgent peripheral transfer.

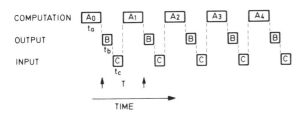

Fig. 7.5 Polling timing diagram

The three procedures are linked to form the program as shown in Fig. 7.6. At the end of each sub-procedure A_i there is a DUMP procedure which stores in memory the processor state vector of the A process. This includes all the registers and flip-flops within the processor which contain information necessary for subsequent sub-procedures A_{i+1} etc. This frees all the facilities of the processor to be used by the transfer processes. The two transfer procedures are similar to that shown in Fig. 7.4(*d*). On leaving the second transfer procedure there is a restore procedure which transfers the processor state vector of A from the memory to re-establish the status of A to that which obtained when the sub-process A_i ended. The sub-process A_{i+1} may then begin.

The polling cycle time T will be less than or equal to $t_a + t_b + t_c$ depending on the state of the FLAG flip-flops and the time needed to execute the processes B and C. In systems which involve several concurrent peripherals the polling scheme may be employed, provided care is exercised to ensure that the crisis times are met. The peripherals with the

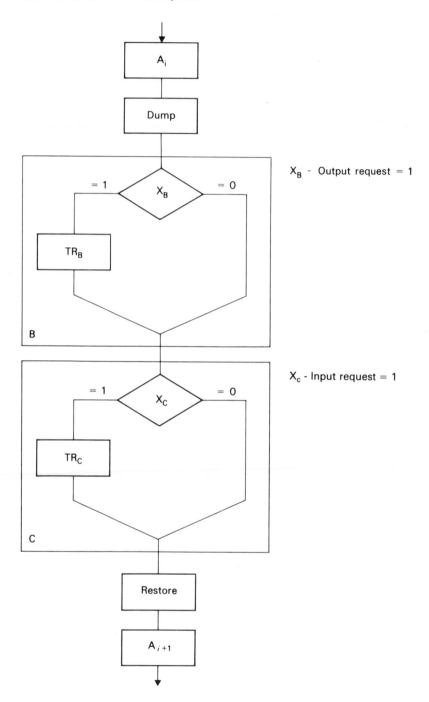

Fig. 7.6 Polling program

short crisis time may be polled more frequently than those with long crisis times. By preparing timing diagrams similar to that shown in Fig. 7.5, it is possible for the designer to guarantee the reliable operation of the total system.

A feature of the polling system is that the main process A is in control. The actual partitions between the sub-procedures A_i may be placed at convenient points of the main procedure. These break points are known by the programmer and can be used during program development to advantage. Furthermore the main process ensures that the processor state vector is correctly preserved after it has been set by the sub-process and before it permits the processor to be used for the peripheral processes. This is a further aid to program development and provides for easier fault diagnosis during operation of the developed system.

In many microprocessor applications the time to execute the main process is very short compared with the time to transfer each string of information between the peripheral devices and the memory. There will be times when the main sub-process A_i approximates to zero and the processor–memory pair is fully occupied in polling the peripheral devices. In these cases the polling scheme would seem to be the natural method of managing the peripheral transfers since it has many virtues during program design and development and during the operation of the finished product or system.

Summary of the strategies

The microprocessor application is viewed by the designer as a complete entity. The specification of the complete product or system includes all the information necessary to design the hardware and the software. The hardware design requires the correct disposition of processor and memory and the assignment of the peripheral registers and flags to locations within the addressable memory space. The memory map is available to the programmer of the software. The program for the product may be partitioned into the three tasks of main process, input and output. When the program is assembled the programmer has control *a priori* of the actions within the processor–memory pair. The programmer controls the times at which the processor switches between the three processes and should be able to analyze and predict the operation of the system during development of both the hardware and the software and their interworking, and during the diagnosis of faults in a finished product.

Management of peripheral transfer by interrupt

An alternative strategy to that outlined in the previous section is to partition the three processes into separate procedures. The main procedure is written on the assumption that its input data will be deposited in an input well in the memory by the input process and the output data will be removed from an output well in the memory by the output processes, the use of these wells by the main process being governed by suitable protocols.

The main procedure is written without any concern for the detailed operation or timing of the peripheral transfers. After it has been developed and assembled the following selection clause is inserted between each instruction:

    if   Peripheral flag set
    then Interrupt process
    else Continue

The interrupt process involves the suspension of the main process to allow the transfer requested by the peripheral flag. When the transfer has been executed, and the flag has been reset, the next instruction of the main process is executed, and so on.

The instance at which control of the processor passes from the main process to the interrupt peripheral process is not known at the time the system is being designed, it is known only *a posteriori* when the system is in operation. The responsibility for ensuring reliable concurrent operation of the system passes to the designer of the interrupt procedure.

It is too cumbersome to implement the above selection clause as a machine instruction which is inserted between each instruction of the main procedure. It is implemented by a hardware mechanism within the processor which initiates a call to the interrupt procedure, which itself is a program of instructions.

The basic hardware mechanism requires the FLAG flip-flop of the peripheral regime to be brought into the processor where it is gated into an ACCEPT flip-flop (cf. Fig. 7.2(a)). An attempt is made to set the ACCEPT flip-flop once during each instruction cycle. The test of the value of the ACCEPT flip-flop is made before the fetch-instruction operation of the instruction cycle. If the ACCEPT flip-flop is not set, the next instruction of the active process is fetched in the normal way, or else the INTERRUPT process is initiated.

The FLAG flip-flop and ACCEPT flip-flop must be reset to 0 before the time at which the attempt is made to set the ACCEPT flip-flop in the instruction cycle, or else the processor will continue to repeat the entry to the interrupt process and it will not make any progress. The processor hardware automatically prevents further interruption by disabling the ACCEPT flip-flop. The peripheral regime must remove the interrupt request (FLAG) when the processor acknowledges recognition of the interrupt signal, to avoid multiple interrupts on a single request.

The first step is to store the processor state vector. In some processors this is facilitated by providing separate banks of registers for the state vector internally, e.g. 5065 (3 banks), Z80 (2 banks), 8048 (2 banks), 9900 (2K banks). The 6800 stores the state vector automatically on interrupt and restores it on return from the interrupt routine by a special order.

The next problem is to find the first instruction of the interrupt routine. The fetch instruction operation is allowed to proceed but the program counter is not incremented. The instruction is not read from memory but its value is forced onto the data port of the processor at the appropriate time. The value is provided by the peripheral regime. The instruction is then decoded and operated on in the normal way. Special instructions are usually provided for this purpose. In the case of the 8080 (8085), the RST instruction is similar to a call instruction in that the contents of the program counter are placed on the stack. The program counter is then forced to a value which is equal to the start address of the interrupt routine in memory. The next machine cycle will cause the instruction to be fetched from this address.

Once the interrupt routine has been entered, the process must first ensure that all of the processor state vector is safely stored and the processor is free to be used to bring about the peripheral transfer. After the transfer process the interrupt routine must restore the processor state vector and 'enable' the interrupt before executing the return order which caused the program counter to be loaded, with the address of the next instruction of the interrupted process.

Management of concurrent peripheral transfers by interrupt

The interrupt mechanism can be extended to deal with several concurrent peripheral regimes. There are two main problems:

(1) Identification of the peripheral regime which is trying to cause an interrupt.
(2) A peripheral regime of short crisis time may need to interrupt the interrupt process of a peripheral regime of longer crisis time.

In certain microprocessors, such as the 8080, there is only one pin on the package (interrupt) to allow the connection of the FLAG flip-flop from the peripheral regime into the circuits of the processor. In this case it is necessary to provide an OR gate external to the microprocessor which collects the FLAG flip-flop from all the peripheral regimes. Each FLAG flip-flop must be assigned to a location in the peripheral image memory so that the interrupt process can scan the FLAG flip-flops to determine the one which caused the interrupt. The order in which the scan occurs is determined by the crisis time of the peripheral regime. Those of shortest crisis time are scanned first, so that when two or more FLAG flip-flops are set the more urgent regime is dealt with first. When the most critical FLAG flip-flop has been found the interrupt process must enter the transfer procedure which deals with it.

In some microprocessors (8008, 8080, 8085, Z80) a signal, interrupt acknowledge, is generated during the instruction cycle following the detection of the interrupt. This signal may be used to find the highest priority FLAG flip-flop which is set, force the appropriate interrupt start-address code as part of the RST instruction and then reset the highest priority FLAG flip-flop. Special modules are provided to implement this mechanism. This is often termed 'vectored interrupt'.

Some microprocessors (e.g., 8085) offer several interrupt connections which carry with them an implied priority ranking and automatically arrange for the forcing of the appropriate start-address code.

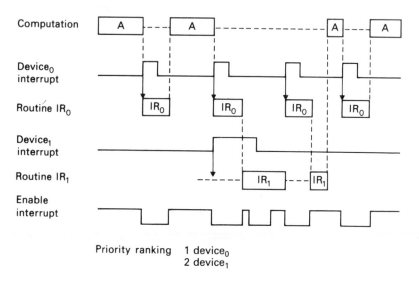

Fig. 7.7 Interrupt timing sequence

The interrupt process will disable interrupts so that it may run to completion before it returns control to the interrupted process. If a peripheral of higher priority should try to interrupt then it will have to wait, unless the interrupt process of low priority enables the interrupt before it has terminated. In this case there is a probability that an interrupt will occur while the low-priority interrupt process is active. The return address of the interrupted interrupt processes will be saved in the same way that nested subroutine return addresses are saved. The stack mechanism allows several interrupt routines to be nested. Figure 7.7 shows the timing for a 2-level interrupt driven system.

It is desirable to be selective in the enabling of interrupts. This can be achieved by masking flags of lower priority and unmasking flags of higher priority. This facility is available in special peripheral interface modules.

The 8085 has an overriding interrupt connection TRAP which cannot be disabled and which is used for interruptions of utmost urgency.

Direct memory access (DMA)

So far in the discussion the transfer of data between the peripheral regime and the memory has been managed by a process within the main processor–memory pair based on a procedure which involves two machine instructions:

(1) Move data between peripheral and processor
(2) Move data between processor and memory.

The direction of each move instruction and the ordering of the sequence depends on the direction of data flow between peripheral device and memory.

The direct memory-access controller is a processing element containing a process which manages the transfer as one step: move data between peripheral and memory. The buffer register which holds the data in the peripheral regime is connected through a direct route to the switch of the processor–memory pair, as shown in Fig. 7.8. The FLAG flip-flop is connected to the DMA controller. The process within the DMA controller accepts the flag signal and presents the address of the memory location involved in the transfer. It also increments the address and carries out the test for end of string.

The address generation by the DMA controller may be concurrent with address generation by the processor. The DMA controller must cause the processor to halt so that the peripheral memory transfer may take place in preference to a processor–memory transfer. The memory locations involved in the peripheral transfer will be pre-determined by the programmer to ensure that these do not correspond to memory locations used by the concurrent main process. Before the peripheral string can be transferred the main process must indicate to the DMA controller by assigning to it the start address of the block of memory locations designated for the transfer and also the limit to the size of this block to be used by the DMA controller in determining the end of the string and the termination of the transfer.

Thus a main process can initiate a peripheral transfer managed by the DMA controller before it proceeds with its own processing task. This task will then run at the normal processing rate until the DMA controller begins to steal memory cycles. The main process will hesitate as each peripheral–memory transfer occurs leading to a slight reduction in its processing rate.

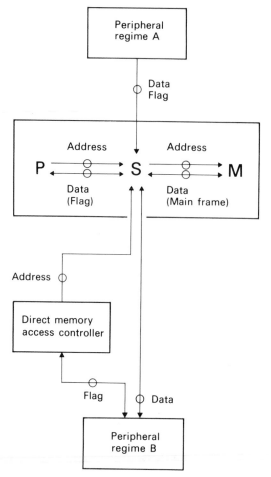

Fig. 7.8 Direct memory access controller

Each hesitation causes a minimum of disturbance to the main process since it is not required to manage the peripheral transfer, merely to wait for the DMA controller to act.

Problems

P7.1 Estimate the crisis time for byte transfers between the processor–memory pair and each of the following peripherals:
Paper-tape reader
Paper-tape punch
Single density floppy disk

Keyboard and copy typist

Sine wave of 500 Hz.

P7.2 Estimate the time interval between the copying of the FLAG flip-flop to the accumulator and testing the accumulator within the procedure shown in Fig. 7.4(b) for a typical microprocessor.

P7.3 Estimate the time interval between examining the FLAG flip-flop and testing for interrupt for the same microprocessor example used in P7.2.

P7.4 Comment on the susceptibility to glitch faults in each example used in P7.2 and P7.3.

P7.5 Code the equivalent procedure to that shown in Fig. 7.4(b) for the transfer of data from the processor–memory pair to an output peripheral.

P7.6 Discuss the criteria which may be applied to determine the end of the transfer of a string of bytes.

8 Support software

Before considering specific software aids for microprocessor systems, it is worthwhile reviewing the lessons learnt by the mainframe and minicomputer manufacturers over the past 20 years. From a software viewpoint there is little difference between a microprocessor and a mainframe processor, apart from the complexity of the instruction set, and even this difference may disappear in the future. The mainframe manufacturers have learnt to solve several problems by experience over a number of years and there is a danger that the users of microprocessors will not learn from this experience. Three main points which are now widely accepted by the mainframe and minicomputer manufacturers and which are pertinent to micro-computer systems are:

(1) software costs are high;
(2) system software should be written in a high-level language wherever possible;
(3) programs should be written with portability in mind.

The cost of software production, a labour-intensive activity, has been rising while the cost of hardware has been falling. This has led to the manufacturers 'unbundling' (paying separately for) their hardware and software; forcing users to pay for the software they require and also for its maintenance. In microcomputer systems this means that the software is assuming increasing importance and appropriate techniques have to be used to attempt to contain the software costs. One of these techniques is to write the software in as high level a language as possible, that is, in as concise a form as possible. For example, a typical statement in a high-level language is equivalent to 5–10 statements in assembly code (see Fig. 8.2). Since programmer productivity, measured by the number of statements produced, is approximately the same for all languages, the higher the level of the language the lower the cost of software production for a given program. One of the drawbacks, however, is that it is frequently the case that programs written in a high-level language require more memory space than the equivalent program written by a competent programmer in a low-level language. This leads to the situation of a high-level language being used for products with short production runs and low-level languages being used for products with long production runs, since for the latter the total extra memory costs will outweigh the one-off software cost. Other language considerations are discussed later in this chapter.

A further method of reducing software cost is to make the software portable so that it does not need to be rewritten for new hardware. This means that the cost can be spread over a greater number of systems. Using a high-level language aids portability since this makes the program less machine-dependent. Other techniques, such as using an interpreter, as described later, can also help. With microcomputers portability can be very important, especially for large systems, since the hardware is changing so rapidly that current hardware may not be available for the life of a product. The economics of making a program portable or rewriting it if necessary depend on the ratio of the hardware to software costs. Small programs can quickly be rewritten at small cost whereas large programs could be prohibitively expensive to rewrite.

The software aids which need to be provided for microcomputers have themselves to be implemented on some computer system. The user can provide this microcomputer software support by one of two methods. If he has a mini or mainframe computer available to him, then the software support system can be provided on that machine in the form of crosstranslators which produce code to be loaded into the particular microcomputer. An alternative method provided for those who do not have access to another computer is either to buy a development system from the particular microprocessor manufacturer, or to buy a general-purpose development system such as the Tektronix 8002. Both these development systems consist of a general-purpose computer based on the particular microprocessor with the relevant software development aids. This has the disadvantage from the user's point of view that it is specifically aimed at a particular microprocessor and, if he wishes to use a different one, then he will probably have to buy another development system, or another hardware module. It does have the advantage, however, that the micro-computer software developed will run on the development system; there is no need to transfer it to another computer for testing. Where the software support is provided on a different processor system, there is a need to simulate the action of the microprocessor, so that the software can be tested and debugged before being loaded into the target microcomputer. This can lead to problems as discussed later.

Since the cost of development systems is still falling the current trend is for users to purchase their own development system for the particular microprocessor they are using, rather than using larger computers.

Assemblers

An assembly language is one in which there is normally a small ratio, frequently 1:1, between statements in the language and machine-code instructions. The assembler, which translates from assembly code to machine code, is therefore comparatively simple to produce. Assembly code is a mnemonic form of machine code (binary) with symbols replacing bit patterns. It is a low-level language because of its closeness to the actual bit pattern the computer understands. In fact, since the instruction set for a particular processor is unique, there is a different assembly language for every different microprocessor. The programmer is able to utilize the special features of the processor, but this means that the programmer has to be experienced and competent to produce an efficient program. The chances of producing an error-free program decrease exponentially with the length and complexity of the program: assembly code is therefore not suitable for producing large programs, especially with inexperienced programmers. Typical figures for debugged code production are 5 instructions/programmer day for assembler code in a large-scale project. For a smaller project the figures would be correspondingly higher.

Until recently it has not been feasible to run an assembler efficiently on a microcomputer, since the process of translation requires a high-speed input/output (I/O) device and a medium in which to keep the intermediate code for several passes of the translation. If these facilities are not available on the microcomputer, a large computer is used with a cross assembler that produces code to run on the target microcomputer. It is worth while noting here that while processor and memory costs are relatively low, the prices of most I/O devices are not. Thus it is not usually feasible to run an assembler on the production system, since it will not normally have the expensive software-development peripherals that are required. This is why a development system or another computer is used to provide software support.

An assembly-code instruction normally consists of an operation code (opcode) and possibly some address fields (operands). Examples are shown in Appendix 6 and in the programs throughout this book. The number of address fields depends on the instruction, e.g.

HLT the halt instruction requires no address field;
DCR C this instruction requires one address field.

The address fields may usually be expressions. Typically expressions are evaluated from right to left and can contain operators such as $+$, $-$, AND and OR.

All assemblers allow a label to be attached to an instruction or a data item so that reference may be made to that item symbolically from elsewhere in the program. The label will be separated from the rest of the instruction by a delimiter; the exact form of the delimiter depending on the details of the particular assembler being used. Some assemblers, based on paper-tape or terminal input, accept free-format input in which the various fields are separated by delimiters, while card-based ones tend to use a fixed-field format with particular fields having to occupy particular card positions. Most microcomputer assemblers fall into the former category.

All assemblers allow the programmer to intersperse assembly directives or pseudo-operations with the code to be translated. These assembly directives allow the programmer to control the operation of the assembler. Two of the most common pseudo-operations are those that tell the assembler the starting address of the assembled code (or sub-section of code), and those that tell the assembler that the end of the code to be assembled has been reached. Neither of these directives generates any code; they just control the assembler. Other types of assembler directives do generate code. A typical example is the 'define' directive which allows the user to load constants or expressions into the next location in the code output. This directive would normally be labelled so that its associated data can be referred to symbolically in the program. Normally, the user can also associate a symbol with a value and some assemblers even allow macro facilities.

Macros

A macro facility (Fig. 8.1) gives the user a method of performing simple text substitution at assembly time. For example, if the programmer wishes

	Macro name		Macro parameters
MACRO	SWAP		'X, 'Y, 'Z
	MOV	'Z, 'X	
	MOV	'X, 'Y	code to be substituted
	MOV	'Y, 'Z	on macro call
ENDMACRO			

Fig. 8.1(a) A macro definition to produce code to exchange the contents of its first two parameters using the third as workspace

—			—	
—			—	
—			—	
—			—	
SWAP	B, C, A	Exchange B and C	MOV	A, B
—			MOV	B, C
—			MOV	C, A
			—	
			—	
SWAP	D, E, B	Exchange D and E	MOV	B, D
—			MOV	D, E
—			MOV	E, B
—			—	
			—	

Fig. 8.1(b) A typical example of the use of a macro and the code produced

to insert a section of code into his program in several different places the macro facility allows him to define this code once, in the form of a macro, and to insert calls to the macro in the correct places in his code. At assembly time the section of code defined in the macro will be substituted for the macro calls normally as a preliminary to the translation. The macro facility, therefore, gives the programmer a similar facility to subroutines except that the macro substitution happens at assembly time rather than execution time. There are many sophisticated features of some macro systems which allow complicated text substitution but these are outside the scope of this text. The interested reader is referred to the books by Campbell–Kelly and Brown in the bibliography.

Link editors

Another common feature of many assemblers is the facility for the programmer to specify his program as a set of modules or segments. These segments are assembled separately and a further program, normally called a link editor, is used to link the separately assembled segments into one complete program. This allows the user to set up a library of standard segments and to use these in appropriate programs. It also, in some systems, allows the user to write different segments of the program in different languages; for example, a high-level language for the calculation and low-level ones for controlling special peripheral devices. The reason why the extra program, the link editor, is required is to fill in the cross-references between the various segments since, because the assembler only assembles one segment at a time, it cannot know the addresses of symbols defined in another segment. This brings in another problem, which is that if the assembler only deals with one segment at a time then the programmer cannot know where each segment will be loaded into memory since this will depend on the length of the preceding segments. This leads to the requirement that the segments must be written in relocatable code, that is, code which is either position-independent or is able to be easily modified if it is moved. Typically all segments are assumed to be loaded into address 0 onwards by the assembler, and the relocation necessary to make the separate segments of code contiguous is performed by the link editor. The provision of relative, as well as absolute, addressing in the instruction set of the microprocessor facilitates this relocation. A further advantage of using a link editor is that during debugging, only those segments with errors have to be reassembled—not all segments—which reduces the time taken. For large programs this time saving can be significant.

Other features

Many assemblers have more complicated features than those described here, mainly to help the programmer of large systems. The aim is to reduce the programming task by improving the facilities in the language, that is, to move towards a higher-level language while retaining the desirable features of assembly code, that is, closeness to the hardware. Interested readers are referred to the books by Barron and Donovan quoted in the bibliography.

There has to be some method of transferring the assembler or cross-assembler output to the target microcomputer system. Many systems use PROM to store the program; the output must therefore be in a form that can be fed into a PROM programmer. Other systems may require the program in a RWM, in which case a loader is required to input the machine code either through a machine–machine link or by a medium such as paper-tape or floppy disk.

Summary

As can be seen from the foregoing description the main tasks of an assembler are similar for all assemblers; the difference being that the features available in the assembly code depend on the details of the hardware. Since much of an assembler is general-purpose, it is relatively easy to produce a new assembler for a new microprocessor. Assembler generators exist which are programs which take a description of the assembly language and target microcomputer architecture as input and which produce as output an assembler for that language on that microprocessor (Johnson & Mueller, 1976).

Simulators

If the program is to be correct, it must be tested extensively. Again, because the target computer does not have the required facilities, this is best carried out on a development system or on a mini or mainframe computer. In a development system, the same processor as in the target computer is employed, hence the code will execute directly except, perhaps, for the special I/O instructions required by the target system. For example, analog–digital converters would probably not be available on the development system. With the mini or mainframe computer, a different processor is used and so it cannot immediately execute the code for the target machine. The normal method of overcoming this problem is to write a program, usually in a high-level language, to simulate the instruction set and environment of the target microprocessor. In effect, the target microprocessor code is interpreted (see later) on the host computer. Using this method it is comparatively easy to add features to the simulator to help with testing and debugging; in effect to simulate more ideal hardware. For example, if the programmer addresses non-existent memory, then the simulator will print a sensible error message; real hardware might go into a 'wait' state. Also it is easy to trace any required events during execution. This might not be possible with the target system. One of the main drawbacks with using a simulator is that, in general, they do not work in real time. This means that time-dependent errors are difficult or impossible to detect on the simulator.

Just as there are assembler generators there are also simulator generators (Johnson & Mueller, 1976) which, given a definition of the architecture of the microcomputer system, will produce a simulator for that system.

High-level languages

As discussed previously the level of language to be used in developing software for microcomputers depends on a number of factors. Basically, the more complicated the problem, the higher the level of the language which should be used to implement the software, while the higher the production volume the more efficient, in terms of hardware utilization, should the language implementation be. At the present time this latter requirement means that high-level languages, which have not, in general, been efficiently implemented on microcomputers, are restricted to complex products produced in limited quantities. However, the benefits of using a high-level language in terms of such features as programmer productivity and ease of modification and debugging, will lead, in the medium term, to the increased use of high-level languages in these systems.

Since high-level languages are further away from the machine architecture they are less specific to a particular microprocessor. Hence using a high-level language increases the portability of the product. To change from one microprocessor system to another the code generation phase of the translator has to be modified. This is a relatively minor change compared with rewriting a large number of assembly code programs. The high-level language approach gives a high degree of machine independence, so that the software and hardware can be developed in parallel. It also allows major changes in the hardware of the system to have minimal effect on the software.

The question of which high-level language to use to develop software for microcomputers is a difficult one to answer. Common high-level languages, such as FORTRAN, COBOL, and PL/1, are both too large for microcomputer and do not contain the facilities required for micro-processor programming, for example direct control of I/O devices. Be-cause of this there have been a number of smaller languages with more appropriate facilities produced for microprocessors, for example PL/M, which is a subset of PL/1, from Intel. These languages suffer from the drawback that they are usually only applicable to a single manufacturer's product. One exception to this rule is BASIC, which has been im-plemented on most microcomputers. This language suffers from the fact that most microprocessor implementations are interpretive, and therefore slow, and that BASIC, because of its lack of structure, is really only successful in small programs or where its interactive nature is of great help. However, BASIC is used in a number of microcomputers applications because of its simplicity and ease of use.

A number of MOLs (machine-orientated languages) or SILs (system-implementation languages) are suitable for use on microprocessors. Such languages as BCPL and PL360 are intermediate between a high-level language and assembly code and usually allow the user to insert machine or assembly code where facilities are required which are not available in the language. CORAL 66 is similar in this respect and has been used successfully.

As indicated above there is a spectrum of levels of languages to use on microprocessors ranging from such high-level languages as PASCAL at one extreme to assembly code at the other. The choice depends on the nature of the problem and the number of systems to be produced.

Features of a high-level language which are relevant to microcomputers include structured data types, safe pointed variables, abstract data types and powerful control structures. These features are only found in the newer programming languages and it appears from the developments taking place at present that PASCAL or PASCAL-like languages, which contain many of the above features, are likely to be the preferred high-level languages for microcomputers for the foreseeable future.

Implementation

There are two basic methods of implementing a high-level language; interpretation and compilation. The process of compilation translates the high-level language into an equivalent set of machine code instructions which may then be executed directly (Fig. 8.2). Interpretation, on the other hand, simulates the action of the abstract machine defined by the high-level language (Fig. 8.3). This simulator then 'understands', that is, can execute, statements in the high-level language. This implies the existence of a program (interpreter) at run time in the target microcompu-ter system. The basic difference between these two techniques is that an interpreter is usually relatively simple to construct, slow to execute and

IF X > Y   THEN X: = X + 1;

Fig. 8.2(a) Typical high-level language statement

			Comments
	LDA	X	Load Acc with contents of X
	LXI	H, Y	Load address of Y
	CMP	M	Compare X and Y
	JM	L1	Jump if minus or zero
	JZ	L1	
	LXI	H, X	Load address of X
	INR	M	Increment X
L1			

Fig. 8.2(b) Equivalent assembly code for 8080 produced by a compiler

contains good error-detecting facilities, while a compiler is more complex, and produces a more efficient program to execute. Interpreter code is also more compact than compiled code and so requires less memory space, although the interpreter itself requires space, preferably in a ROM. Because of these differing properties some systems, including PASCAL, are normally implemented in several stages, often by different techniques for each stage.

1. Fetch next instruction from memory to register using simulated program counter
2. Increment simulated program counter
3. Go to subroutine for that instruction indirectly via an address table
4. Return to step 1.

Fig. 8.3(a) Typical structure of an interpreter

			simulated program counter = BC
START	LDAX	B	get next instruction
	INX	B	increment simulated PC
	MOV	E, A	
	LXI	H, TABLEADDRESS	get table address
	DAD	D	get position in table
	MOV	E, M	
	INX	H	
	MOV	D, M	get value in table to DE
	XCHG		to HL
	PCHL		to PC i.e. jump

routine for an instruction

.
.
.

JMP START

TABLEADDRESS DATA INS1, INS2, INS3 . . . address table

Fig. 8.3(b) Typical interpreter structure for 8080

Program design

As the complexity of computer systems increases, there is a need for more and more formal design and program structuring methods. This has been noted and action taken by the large computer manufacturers; it will become increasingly important with microprocessor systems as their complexity increases. In this respect, high-level languages are better than low-level languages because they help the designer to produce better structured, better documented programs. As the hardware cost of microcomputer systems is relatively small, there will be situations where the cheapest way to produce a system with more computing power will be to add more processors to the system. There are relatively few multiprocessor and distributed systems in operation, and the software design methods to produce such systems, while known in some detail, are still the subject of a great deal of research. It will take some time to produce formal design methods for these systems, and so at present it is difficult to produce satisfactory dedicated multiprocessor computer systems.

Operating systems

An operating system performs two functions in a computer system: resource management and the provision of a user interface. In its resource management role it provides low-level routines to control the peripheral devices at the hardware level so removing these low-level details from the user's domain. It also provides a resource sharing policy system so that several users may use the system simultaneously. This latter aspect is not normally required in microcomputers since they are usually dedicated to one particular task. In the role of the user interface the operating system provides a language, normally called a job control language, by means of which the user may instruct the system in his job requirements. Typical commands provided by the job control language would include instructions to load and save the contents of memory, to set instruction breakpoints for debugging and to print the contents of any memory location.

Most microcomputers are provided with a simple operating system (monitor), in a PROM, which provides a job control language and a set of simple device driver routines. An example of a simple monitor for a typical microcomputer system is given in the chapter on development systems.

Documentation and debugging

These two topics are considered together since they are both extremely important but they are frequently neglected, especially by the inexperienced software engineer. It is virtually impossible to debug or modify a program which has not been properly documented. Proper documentation does not mean adding comments to every program statement. The aim of proper documentation is to enable someone unfamiliar with the program to understand its structure and implementation in order to be able to modify or debug that program. Adequate documentation of a program, therefore, consists of structure documentation such as flowcharts or structured pseudo-code, together with an explanation of the implementation such as the meaning of variables used and the representation of the data structures. It is also helpful to have comments attached to some statements in the code which supplement the other documentation. Documentation aids exist, for example, FLOCODER (Morris, Kennedy & Last, 1971). These aids are very useful, if not essential, for large projects but for smaller projects they are not essential.

Debugging is very important, especially so in real-time systems. Since this is the area in which many microcomputers are used, debugging techniques should play an important part in microcomputer software projects. For a system to be adequately debugged a good deal of thought has to go into planning the details of the debugging strategy. It is not sufficient simply to run a set of data with known results and if this works to assume that the system is correct. Mathematical techniques for proving programs correct are still not sufficiently developed to be used in practical systems and until they are extensive testing by exercising all the paths through a program is necessary. Some aids are available to the designer to enable him to discover all these paths and the conditions under which they will be executed. The designer still has the problem, however, of choosing the input data and checking the results and, in many cases, deciding which paths to test, since testing of all paths is very time-consuming. Testing, therefore, can never give the user complete confidence in the program. This should be achieved when mathematical program-proving techniques are in wider use.

Conclusion

The software requirements for microcomputers are not different in type from other computer systems but only different in the emphasis given to the various requirements. This means that many of the lessons learnt by other computer manufacturers are equally applicable to microcomputers, especially those concerning the economic aspects since they become more relevant in microcomputer systems owing to the lower cost of hardware. This does not mean that software for microcomputers has to be very expensive, but is is very necessary to invest money in the proper software design and implementation aids for microprocessor systems just as it is for software development on larger computers. The lack of this investment is one of the main reasons for failure of microcomputer projects at the present time.

As to the future, the hardware of microcomputer systems will become more complex as more can be put on a chip. This will lead to better architectures which can better support high-level languages, for example, the 8086. One current trend seems to be towards multiprocessor and distributed architecture. This increases the software problems by at least an order of magnitude and much research work still needs to be done in this area. However, when the changes in hardware technology slow down, as signs indicate is happening at present, the architecture of microcomputers will become less variable and so more software development effort will be put into providing good programming systems. Eventually this will lead to the type of sophisticated software systems now found in the mini and mainframe field.

Problems

P8.1 What is an assembly language and what is its relationship to the bit pattern which it represents?

P8.2 What is an assembler directive? Give examples of some typical directives.

P8.3 How are the addresses required for a jump instruction produced by the assembler?

P8.4 Why do high-level languages lead to greater programmer productivity?

P8.5 Translate the following piece of FORTRAN into 8080 assembly code (assume integer arithmetic).

```
        A = B + 1
        X = A/2
        IF (X.GT.2) GO TO 2
        X = X + 1
    2   WRITE (5, 100) X
  100   FORMAT (I1)
        STOP
```

What assumptions have you made in your translation?

P8.6 What features of a high-level language would you look for to be especially amenable for microcomputer implementation?

P8.7 What is the difference between a simulator and an interpreter?

P8.8 Why are real-time programs more difficult than other types of program with respect to debugging and simulation?

P8.9 What factors influence the cost of software development?

9 Structured programming

Introduction

Structured programming is the name which has been given recently to a methodology of designing computer programs. Many programmers insist that they have been using this technique for a long time and this may well be true, but the recent emergence of this technique has resulted from an attempt to formalize the process of designing programs in the same manner as logic design has been formalized. The techniques used are, in general, not new but the formal basis is.

Structured programming techniques can be classified into two categories, those which deal predominantly with the control structure and those which deal predominantly with the data structure. In this chapter the former technique will be taken as the most suitable for the type of simple control operations in which many microprocessors are used. For applications involving the manipulation of large quantities of different types of data, for example, business applications, the reader is referred to the Jackson technique expounded in the book by Michael Jackson quoted in the bibliography.

Design considerations

The process of designing and writing a program can be subdivided into a number of tasks:

(a) understanding the problem;
(b) producing an algorithm to solve the problem;
(c) coding the algorithm in a particular language;
(d) testing the resulting program;
(e) iterating round the above tasks until the program is correct.

In conventional programming, tasks (a) and (b) are undertaken by the systems analyst and (c) and (d) by the programmer, with (e) shared between them.

This decomposition process can be thought of in a number of ways, but structured programming would suggest that it should be looked at as a top-down analysis, i.e. each stage is an elaboration of the previous stage with a greater degree of detail and complexity. This means that the problem is initially specified at a relatively low level of complexity and detail, and that the problem is gradually elaborated to produce the final program by stepwise refinement.

The nature of the difficulties involved in each step will depend on the problem and on the constraints of its solution, e.g. the resources available. The main difficulty in any problem solving is to contain the complexity of the problem, and it is this complexity which provides the intellectual challenge of programming. In structuring the solution, an attempt is made to simplify the complexity and to aid understanding. This approach is more likely to result in a correct solution.

Structured programming offers a number of benefits to its users:

(*a*) Each step is independent of other steps, hence allowing separate checks at each step.
(*b*) Each step may be checked by checking the elaborations stage by stage.
(*c*) An error may therefore be detected in a systematic manner.
(*d*) At any time only a small amount of information has to be remembered and manipulated.
(*e*) The structure evolved is suitable for a rigorous proof of the correctness of the entire algorithm.

Programming considerations

How do the concepts of structured programming produce 'better' programs? Taking the decomposition of a problem into its programming solution using structured techniques, the programming solution must contain a structure of 'boxes within boxes' in a pictorial representation,

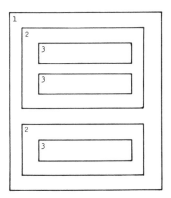

Fig. 9.1 Block structures (the numbers represent the levels)

where boxes within boxes represent the lower level elaboration at the upper level (Fig. 9.1). This exhibits a modular structure, where modules can be tested independently.

It should be pointed out here that this structure looks, in some respects, similar to a *flowchart* which gives a pictorial representation of the program structure. The main difference is that the concepts in structured programming place restraints on the equivalent flowchart representation. The shortcomings of flowcharts are that they are too general and do not constrain the structure to be 'well-formed'. The main problem is the undisciplined use of the 'goto' or 'jump' instructions which can cause convoluted flowcharts.

Turning to the constructs in programming languages which allow structured program to be built up, a number of simple constructions suffice in many cases. In the following, textual constructions are used in the main, rather than graphical constructions, but this is purely a matter of choice.

Simple succession

This is just the normal sequencing method, i.e. the instructions are executed in sequential order.

Repetition

This involves repeating an operation a sufficient number of times until a condition is satisfied:

       repeat* operation
       until   condition

or

       while condition
         do   operation
e.g. **while** $X > Y$
         do   subtract X from Y

Note that this can be decomposed into lower-level statements if necessary:

                                             L1: if not A goto L2
while A is equivalent to   B
  do   B   goto L1
                etc.   L2:

This structure is equivalent to the flowchart of Fig. 9.2. Notice that this flowchart has one entry and one exit. This is one of the constraints of structured programming.

---

* Reserved words are shown in bold type.

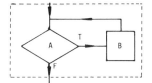

Fig. 9.2 **While—do** construct

Selection

This involves choosing from a set of actions:

If A **then** B **else** C

which is equivalent to the flowchart of Fig. 9.3. Again there is one entry and one exit to the flowchart.

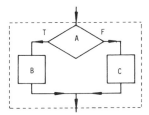

Fig. 9.3 **If—then—else** construct

Sub-programs

Subroutines and functions obey the rules of structured programming, e.g. one entry and one exit; so they may be used in the production of structured programs.

These constructions are just some of the possible primitives from which structured programs may be built. Provided that the rule of one control input and one control output is obeyed, users may design their own primitives, although it is not normally necessary.

The programming constructions elaborated above have been specified in a high-level language, but they could equally well be put as constraints at a lower level.

The task of programming is now reduced to elaborating the structure in layers by using the programming constructs defined above. To comprehend fully the benefits of structured programming, it is essential that a number of examples are worked through. It is not possible to realize the benefits until the method has been used on specific problems. It is strongly recommended that the reader tries the example before consulting the solution.

An example of structured programming

The problem

Suppose that the problem is to design a stepping-motor controller with the following inputs:

(*a*) number of steps;
(*b*) forward or reverse.

The four signals required to drive the motor are shown below.

To run forwards the table is traversed downwards; for reverse it is traversed upwards. Each line steps the motor once and the minimum time for each step is 5 ms:

A	B	C	D
1	0	0	1
1	1	0	0
0	1	1	0
0	0	1	1

The solution

The design of anything is an art as much as a science and involves personal choices and decisions. This example will show the way in which decisions were reached and the reasons for them. These will almost certainly not be identical to those another designer would take in the same design, and other solutions could be equally valid.

Returning to the example, we instinctively look for a pattern, for some order in the table. After a moment's thought it is obvious that the pattern is that the line above is the line below moved one place to the left, with a carry around from A to D. This is a significant step forward, as it now gives us two possible strategies for implementing the solution (two different algorithms). The complete table of values could be stored and the output generated by sequencing through the table in the correct direction, or only one value could be stored and the subsequent values generated by the algorithm just discovered.

At this stage we shall not get involved in deciding which method to adopt; this detail is not relevant until later in the design, and one of the objects of structured programming is to leave the decisions until it is necessary to solve them, i.e. to leave options open until the last possible moment.

Consider now the overall structure of the problem. We shall start the design in high-level programming terminology. Notice that this is a personal choice which has no relevance to structured programming. The problem itself breaks down into two actions, inputting the data specified and producing the required outputs. Hence the first level of the design is:

L0   «input data»
     «generate required sequence»

Each of the actions is enclosed in brackets to show that it is an intermediate step in the solution of the problem. Only the final code will be shown without brackets.

This has split the original problem into two sub-tasks which are to be carried out in sequence. Each of these actions will now be elaborated at a lower level.

What are the sub-actions in «generate required sequence»? Since this involves several sub-actions, write the description as a function:

L1   «generate next sequence» becomes
                               function generatesequence (direction, steps)
                               «function body»
                               end;
                               generatesequence (direction, steps)

     «input data» becomes   «read no. of steps»
                               «read direction»

This has broken down the action into a function which requires two parameters, direction and steps, which are the values obtained by the input action. Notice that we have not attempted to elaborate the algorithm of the function yet. One of the biggest pitfalls is to try to take too many decisions at once. If we make only small changes they are easy to correct if the decision was wrong, and this should tend to isolate the decision-making so that one wrong decision does not mean modification to all the program.

At the next level «function body» needs to be elaborated:

L2   «function body»   becomes   «initialize sequence»
                               while «not finished»
                               do «get next sequence»
                                       «output sequence»
                                       «wait until ready»
                               endwhile;

Notice that we have not yet chosen how to generate the next sequence; we could still use either method elucidated earlier. The above elaboration has produced a loop construction which allows us to generate the sequence of outputs required.

At the next level we wish to elaborate the test for the **while** statement. How do we know when the output sequence is to stop? We want to output 'steps' number of output sequences, and so the test is steps > 0, and we also need to decrease this count inside the **do** body. This is a standard loop construction and we could have incorporated this in a special construction for structured programming, as many people have done, but we will keep to the simple constructions shown earlier in this example:

L3   «not finished»   becomes   steps > 0
       «get next sequence» becomes   «get sequence»
                                              steps $=$ steps $- 1$

It is assumed that we are producing a high-level language program at this stage, and we have translated some parts into a high-level language notation.

At this stage we can really get no further without making a decision on how to generate the sequence required; so we need to make a choice between the two alternatives. At first sight the generation algorithm looks more attractive than the table look-up since it uses less storage space. However, we still need to consider how to do the generation. In a high-level language it is normally difficult to perform bit manipulation (which is what is called for by this example), so in a high-level language approach we will use the table look-up method since this is easier and more efficient to implement. Notice that we have taken into account the target language for this design; we shall see the relevance of this later on.

Having decided on this approach, we can now decide on the relevant program data structure on which to map the table. In the present case the most appropriate would be a circular list if that were available, and we would need a doubly linked list to enable forward and backward traversal of the information as the problem requires. Since we do not wish to deal with the complexities of such data structures here, we will assume that the high-level language has the appropriate routines to create (initlist) and access such a structure.

One more elaboration which we need to do is to elaborate «get sequence»:

L4   «get sequence»   becomes if «forward direction» then fitem (seq)
                                                            else bitem (seq)

where fitem and bitem are standard routines for producing the next forward item and the next backward item in the data structure.

If we now assume that all the actions that have not been elaborated so far are calls to functions already present in the system, we have the complete program as:

```
read (steps);
read (direction);
function generatesequence (direction, steps);
initlist (seq, 11, 14, 6, 3);
while    steps > 0
do       if direction then fitem (seq)
                     else bitem (seq);
         steps = steps − 1;
         output (seq);
         delay (5);
endwhile;
end;
generatesequence (direction, steps);
```

It is assumed here that the function read reads a value of true for forward, and false for backwards into direction.

This solution has been structured for a high-level language. For this type of problem, implementation on a microcomputer might involve using a lower-level language such as PL/M* (see reference) or assembly code. We will first consider how to map the problem solution into PL/M and then to assembly code.

The first point is that PL/M is a lower-level language, but this does *not* mean that the complete design above should be taken and elaborated downwards. To get even a reasonably 'good' program the design decisions taken in the previous design need to be carefully scrutinized. What is necessary is to start at the top level and check each decision made to see if it is applicable in the present situation. When this is done the only major decision which needs reconsidering is the algorithm to be used for generating the sequence. In the high-level language approach we used a doubly linked circular list. This is not an easy structure to provide in PL/M; so it is worth considering the alternative method. The operation to produce the next sequence is a 4-bit rotate operation. Assuming that we are producing code in PL/M then we have to deal with an 8-bit quantity, i.e. our data structure has to be a minimum of 1 byte. How can we map a 4-bit rotate operation onto a PL/M instruction? This is equivalent to asking how we can simulate a 4-bit rotate operation in PL/M. The answer is to notice that if we duplicate the 4-bit pattern to an 8-bit pattern and perform the PL/M rotate function on this pattern we obtain the required result in the bottom 4-bits. To produce the required output pattern to top 4-bits must be masked out of the resulting byte pattern. This appears easier than implementing circular lists; so we shall use this approach to solve the problem in PL/M.

* PL/M is the trade mark of Intel Corporation.

We can start the new phase of the design from the abstract stage of the previous design:

«read number of steps»
«read direction»
«routine generatesequence»
«initialize sequence»
  while «not finished»
    do «get next sequence»
      «output sequence»
      «wait until ready»
  endwhile;
«end of routine»
«call routine with parameters»

Before continuing we must examine this design to see that no false decisions have been taken. It is clearer to put the definition before or after the execution sequence. We shall, therefore, reorganize the design to:

L0 «procedure generatesequence»
    «initialize sequence»
      while «not finished»
        do «get next sequence»
          «output sequence»
          «wait until ready»
      endwhile;
    «end of routine»
    «read number of steps»
    «read direction»
    «call routine with parameters»

Notice that this is not identical to the design we had for the high-level language solution—we have changed function generatesequence into «procedure generatesequence» and end to «end of routine». These changes were necessary because we had made too large a step in the first design and had gone straight to a high-level language. For the present design we need to go back to a more abstract definition.

Before we can write this solution in PL/M the only parts which need further elaboration are «not finished» and «get next sequence».

L1 «not finished»   becomes STEPS > 0
    «get next sequence» becomes «if forward direction
                             then next sequence
                             forwards else next
                             sequence backwards»
                             STEPS = STEPS $- 1$

At this stage it is possible to write down the complete PL/M program:

```
          /*  STEPPING MOTOR SOLUTION IN PL/M */
GENSEQ:   PROCEDURE (STEPS, DIRECTION);
          DECLARE (STEPS, DIRECTION) BYTE;
          DO WHILE STEPS > 0;
              IF DIRECTION = 0 THEN SEQ = ROR (SEQ, 1);
                              ELSE SEQ = ROL (SEQ, 1);
              STEPS = STEPS − 1;
              OUTPUT (8H) = SEQ AND 0FH;
              CALL TIME (50);
          END;
          END GENSEQ;
              DECLARE (STEPS, DIRECTION) BYTE;
              DECLARE SEQ BYTE INITIAL 33H;
              STEPS = INPUT (0);
              DIRECTION = INPUT (1);
              CALL GENSEQ (STEPS, DIRECTION);
          EOF
```

Some comments on this solution are relevant here. Firstly, the port assignments, 0 and 1 for input and 8 (hexadecimal) for output, were chosen simply because this is how the equipment used in this problem was configured. STEPS and DIRECTION were both chosen as bytes since DIRECTION has only 2 values, assumed to be 0 and 1, and the limits of STEPS are undefined in the problem, hence a byte was chosen arbitrarily. ROR and ROL are provided as standard functions in PL/M and provide the simplest method of generating the required pattern. In this solution the DO WHILE construct is used with the statement STEPS = STEPS − 1. These two statements could be combined to the DO statement of PL/M; however, the design method used leads to the given solution. Furthermore, in this example the parameters STEPS and DIRECTION need not have been explicitly used; their declaration outside the procedure could simply have been placed at the front of the program. However, it is not good programming practice to declare all variables as global to all the program; it is better to limit the scope of variables to those parts of the program where they are used. In this simple example there is no difference with either method.

It is interesting to compare the solution in PL/M with that in the higher-level language. There is very little difference in the size of the program and almost certainly the PL/M solution would occupy less memory. This illustrates the good points of PL/M; it is very suitable to these types of simple application. Tackling much larger problems the comparison would not be so favourable to PL/M, especially where complicated data structures are concerned. However, there are many microprocessor applications in this relatively simple area and a language such as PL/M is very suitable.

Now let us turn our attention to producing a solution in assembly code. Again we return to our abstract solution used in the PL/M example. In assembly code we shall also use the technique of generating the sequence using the rotate instructions:

```
L0   «routine generatesequence»
     «initialize sequence»
        while  «not finished»
           do   «get next sequence»
                «output sequence»
                «wait until ready»
        endwhile;
     «end of routine»
     «read number of steps»
     «read direction»
     «call routine with parameters»
```

We can now elaborate this design to a lower level:

```
L1   «initialize sequence»  becomes   «initialize sequence
                                       to first value»
     «not finished»         becomes   «steps > 0 »
     «get next sequence»    becomes   «if forward direction
                                       then next seq. forward
                                       else next seq. backward»
                                      «steps = steps − 1»
```

Notice that this looks very similar to the previous design except that the statements are enclosed in brackets indicating that they are still to be elaborated further.

At this stage certain decisions have to be made concerning the allocation of data to locations in memory. This is handled automatically in a high-level language and PL/M but is one of the designer's tasks at the lower level. In this example we need locations to keep the direction, number of steps and the current sequence. We shall assume that these locations are register B, register C and register D of the 8080:

```
L2   «procedure generatesequence»  becomes   GENSEQ: as a label
     «read number of steps»        becomes   «read no into C»
     «read direction»             becomes   «read no into B»
     «call routine with parameter» becomes   CALL GENSEQ
     «end of routine»             becomes   RET
```

We do not require any explicit parameters since they are in registers:

```
     «initialize sequence»        becomes   MVI      D,33H
```

Assuming as before, that direction is 0 for forwards and 1 for backwards:

L3	if «forward direction» then «next seq.	becomes	MVI	A,00H
	forward» else «next seq. backwards»		ADD	B
			MOV	A,D
			JNZ	L1
			RAR	
			JMP	L2
		L1:	RAL	
		L2:	MOV	D,A

This looks as though we have taken a large step instead of several small steps. What we have done is to translate the **if** . . . **then** . . . **else** construction into assembly code together with translating the operations on the data. Notice that we have now become involved with the intricacies of the 8080. The reason why we need the first two instructions rather than MOV A,B is due to the way in which the 8080 sets its flags. It is this sort of detail which should be left for as long as possible before being inserted into the design.

To keep in mind what we have achieved, here is the complete solution so far:

GENSEQ:	MVI	D,33H
«while»	«steps > 0»	
«do»	MVI	A,00H
	ADD	B
	MOV	A,D
	JNZ	L1
	RAR	
	JMP	L2
L1:	RAL	
L2:	MOV	D,A
	«output sequence»	
	«wait until ready»	
	«steps = steps − 1»	
«endwhile»		
	RET	
	«read no into C»	
	«read no into B»	
	CALL GENSEQ	
	HLT	

Refining further:

L4	«while» «steps > 0»		becomes	L5:	MVI	A,00H
	«do»				ADD	C
	«steps = steps − 1»				JZ	L3
	«endwhile»				JM	L3
					—	
					—	
					DCR	C
					JMP	L5
				L3:		

The next problem is the method of input and output. We shall assume in this example that both number of steps and direction are single digits input from switches connected to ports 0 and 1 and are set up prior to execution. To output the sequence, mask the value and then output it to the correct port which we shall assume is port 8 (hexadecimal).

«output sequence»	becomes	ANI	0FH
		OUT	8H
«read no into C»	becomes	IN	00H
		MOV	C,A
«read no into B»	becomes	IN	01H
		MOV	B,A

The only elaboration left is «wait until ready». We need some code to delay for 5 ms, so we need a loop around a piece of code to generate this delay. In a loop we have to decrement a counter and test to see if it is the end of the loop. This involves a total of 5 cycles for the decrement and 10 cycles for the test. For the 8080 with a cycle time of $0.5\,\mu s$, to get a delay of $5000\,\mu s$ we need to go around this loop approximately 1000 times. We have not used register E so far, so we may use this as the counter, but 1000 exceeds the maximum count of 256 for this register.

We must make the loop bigger. We could insert 6 NOP instructions which makes the loop 24 cycles, or we could insert PUSH H, POP H and NOP, which takes 25 cycles and uses less storage. For the latter, the loop count is 250, i.e. 0FA hexadecimal:

«wait until ready»	becomes	MVI	E,0FAH
	L4:	PUSH	H
		POP	H
		NOP	
		DCR	E
		JNZ	L4

The complete program is therefore:

```
GENSEQ                  D,33H
L5
          ADD     C
          JZ      L3
          JM      L3
          MVI     A,00H
          ADD     B
          MOV     A,D
          JNZ     L1
          RAR
          JMP     L2
L1:       RAL
L2:       MOV     D,A
          ANI     0FH
          OUT     08H
          MVI     E,0FAH
L4:       PUSH    H
          POP     H
          NOP
          DCR     E
          JNZ     L4
          DCR     C
          JMP     L5
L3:       RET
START:    IN      00H
          MOV     C,A
          IN      01H
          MOV     B,A
          CALL    GENSEQ
          HLT
```

This is the program in assembly code although it is still not quite complete. The assembly code which when translated produces the correct machine code has been produced, but it does not contain any assembler directives. There are at least two that are necessary. An END directive must be given end to indicate the end of the program to be translated, and an ORG directive specifying the address in memory from which the assembled code is to be placed has to be inserted at the front of the program.

It might be felt that a lot of effort has been expended on what is essentially a trivial program. This is true, but consider what might happen on a large program. It is essential that the program should be designed properly, whether it is small or large, and attempts to cut short the design process almost invariably end in a badly designed program that is difficult to modify and debug.

The lack of comments in the final program is really a matter of taste. Provided that the initial design is kept, there is no need for extensive comments in the program, but some designers like to keep the design decisions in the program as comments.

Some programmers might be tempted to 'optimize' this program to try and make it more efficient. This is allowable provided that they modify the design accordingly. The program itself should be transparent, in that it should represent as clearly as possible what the programmer intended. This is more important than a saving of a few microseconds in efficiency.

This example has indicated the methods used in structured programming and given the reader an insight into program design. For more detailed information the reader should consult the books given in the bibliography (Dahl *et al.*, 1972, Dijkstra, 1976).

Problems

P9.1 Why can uncontrolled use of a jump instruction lead to unstructured programs?

P9.2 Explain how the **while – do** construct can be implemented in 8080 assembly code.

P9.3 What rules should be obeyed when using subroutines to produce a structured program?

P9.4 Are any other loop constructions needed apart from **while – do** and **repeat – until**, and if so, why?

P9.5 In terms of structured programming and design why are the newer programming languages such as PASCAL to be preferred over the older ones such as FORTRAN?

P9.6 Produce a structured program which will control a set of traffic lights (*see* Appendix 6). Is your program different from that given? If so assess the differences.

P9.7 What basic difference of approach would be taken if a commercial data processing system were being designed rather than a control application? (Hint: Read the book by M Jackson quoted in the bibliography.)

10 Applications (2)

Introduction

The two simple examples in Chapter 4 served as an introduction to programming a microcomputer, illustrating the most fundamental principles of design philosophy, timing constraints, and assembly code programming. In this chapter these themes are continued, with particular emphasis on real-time programming, since this is prominent in many microcomputer applications.

To be able to judge any design activity, it is necessary to establish some criteria, and so in the case of a microcomputer-based design it is worth asking the question: 'What is a good end-product?'. In common with the design of anything functional, the prime criterion must be that it works (it meets the specification) and the costs are reasonable. Other factors depend to a large extent on the product itself. If, for example, it is to be made in very large quantities, then an important factor is the production cost; for while writing software is a labour-intensive activity, the software itself tends to be cheaper to mass produce than hardware. Alternatively, it could be desirable for the program to run as fast as possible, or to design with program portability in mind, to allow for a later up-date in the micro-computer hardware.

A feature often associated with microcomputer-based design is the nature of the hardware and software interdependence; for the hardware, techniques such as logic design are well established and widely practised, but programming is a comparatively young discipline. Structured programming is an attempt to formalize design techniques for software and, of course, applies not specifically to the programming of microprocessors, but to computers in general.

Functional description

The first stage of any practical design is to expand the initial specification into a more complete functional description: what the system is to do, and what it is not to do. This is then checked for completeness and consistency. It is unrealistic to expect the functional description to be complete in every detail, but sufficient information must be given so that in pursuing a top-down approach the designer is able to create a correct overall strategy. The term completeness then refers to the fundamentals rather than the cosmetic details, and at this stage the description should be able to accommodate minor additions or modifications without changing the overall strategy. The description is said to be consistent if there are no contradictions or conflicts. These fall into two categories, the absolute ones—whether for example it is theoretically possible to process the signal in the specified way—and the relative ones which transform into compromises—as cheap as possible and as fast as possible. With a complete and consistent description, the next stage is to sub-divide the problem into tractable sub-systems; and for each of these to be designed in detail, implemented and tested. The return path is the bringing together of these constituent parts, accompanied by further testing, with the eventual realization of a working prototype.

Hardware and software

As said at the beginning, this design approach can apply to almost any practical situation; it is well understood and practised for hardware design but is in its relative infancy for software. However these two usually form important constituent parts of microprocessor applications, and throughout each must be designed with a knowledge of the other so that the two match in terms of the I/O, memory and other requirements. An important feature in testing and de-bugging the hardware is test software: programs written specifically to exercise the hardware in a prescribed manner. A very simple example is a linear ramp function routine to test a digital-to-analog converter (DAC). In most situations it is both practicable and sensible to build the test software into the final system for the purpose of fault finding in later life. These programs form the front-line maintenance for the hardware system. Intelligent designs of test programs allow all hardware wiring and functional units to be tested.

Programming

The design and implementation of a computer program should include the following:

  (i) Study of the problem specification
 (ii) Algorithm design
(iii) Appraisal of the hardware
 (iv) *Coding* the solution in a programming language
  (v) *Translating* the program language into machine code.

Clearly, the first three are closely linked and not serial activities.

The processor, memory and I/O requirements should have a preliminary examination to establish the basic needs. The processor may need special characteristics, e.g. fast multiplication, a 16-bit word, etc. The memory size, both for read/write and read-only storage, should be considered to determine the cost and size of the hardware. Dedicated input/output hardware may be needed, for example, a USART to provide a serial link to VDU or computer, or special-purpose hardware for any other time critical activities. An example later in the chapter illustrates this point.

Items (iv) and (v) may be regarded as links between the machine independent *abstract* design and the lowest-level binary representation of the program. There is a certain amount of inconsistency in the use of the word 'programming'. One interpretation is that indicated by (iv) alone, i.e. the writing of statements in BASIC, FORTRAN or a low-level language assembly code. A much better interpretation includes all of the items (i) to (v), for this implies the design and implementation of a set of actions (by implication to be executed by a computer) to carry out a particular job. (Note in the term 'structured-programming' it assumes this meaning.)

In the first stage of design, the aim is to create a description of the overall strategy: how the problem is to be solved. Later, this description can be elaborated step-by-step, eventually arriving at the machine code program. Many beginners erroneously start the programming exercise at the *coding* stage, and in the total or partial absence of items (i), (ii), and (iii) there is a good chance of failure.

Real-time programming

The two examples in Chapter 4 are 'real-time' programs, for they generate outputs which are functions of time. In general, a real-time system is one where the timing of I/O operations is important. Often the operations must be at a regular rate, as with the outputs for the waveform generators, and the program design must balance execution times of the main tasks with the time-dependent I/O operations. Real-time systems can be switched on and left running for ever, with an equilibrium between inputs, outputs and processing.

Polling and interrupt

These are the two ways that the microcomputer can receive asynchronous requests for service. In a *polling* arrangement, the input ports are checked by the program at designed intervals, and actions taken accordingly; in effect, the inputs are checked to see if they have changed by examining a status bit indicating ready for service. An *interrupt* is invoked by the ready state occurring in the external world being detected directly by the hardware of the microcomputer (see Chapter 7). Polling is very common in microprocessor applications, since these are often orientated around I/O. The software associated with servicing interrupts can be very complex, and for this reason interrupt systems are more common in larger machines than they are in microcomputers. When an interrupt is received, the program presently being executed is *interrupted* and the state of the CPU and all the relevant register contents are stored, to be restored later after the interrupt has been serviced. To do this reliably, and to ensure that the interrupt service program does not overlap (and corrupt) the interrupted program, can prove very difficult.

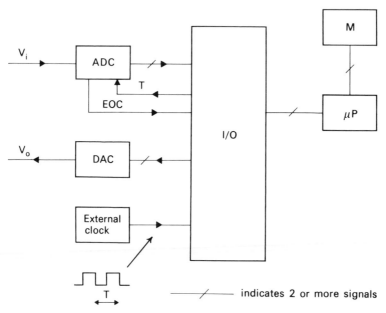

Fig. 10.1 Typical hardware configuration for a real-time system

A common configuration, shown in Fig. 10.1, is an analog-to-digital converter (ADC) and a digital-to-analog converter (DAC), connected to a microcomputer performing a signal processing task. It can be important to ensure that the samples are regularly spaced in time, both at the input and at the output, and therefore the two peripherals must be serviced at a constant frequency. Provided that these two are the only 'real-time' peripherals in use and the computer is dedicated to the signal-processing task and not required to execute other jobs on a time-shared basis, then it is relatively easy to synchronize with the outside world the input and output operations to give a regular sampling rate. Here, the ADC and DAC rates are assumed equal, and of course, if this is not the case, the problem is very much more difficult (see Programmable clock).

The need to implement this sort of synchronism between the microcomputer software and the outside world is a key feature of real-time programming. This example is considered below in a little more detail, but while it is a common configuration, it must be remembered that this is a relatively simple case, and as the number of peripherals increases and the number of possible tasks to be executed increases, the synchronizing problem becomes rapidly complex, demanding equally complex software.

Software controlled timing

One approach to ensure a regular sampling rate for the ADC and DAC is to arrange for all possible program paths that can form a loop between successive inputs (or outputs) to be equal in execution time (see Fig. 10.2). Of course, this begs the question, can all path lengths be predetermined? But for the present, assuming this to be the case, then there will be one or more *critical* paths (see Fig. 10.2(a)) taking the longest time, and all others must be 'padded out' with no-operations (NOP). The critical path gives the *minimum* possible time for regular inputs (and outputs) but, of course, if a slower sampling rate is desired it is easy to increase the loop times by further insertion of NOPs.

This form of software-controlled timing can be easy to implement and give highly consistent results. Time intervals are formed by the accumulation of a fixed number of machine cycles, and the machine cycle time is governed usually by a highly stable crystal oscillator clocking the microprocessor.

A pictorial representation such as a flow diagram is very useful when identifying all the program paths and balancing their execution times. Some processors do not have a specific NOP instruction, but there are pseudo-no-operations such as move register to itself (e.g. MOV A,A) or complementary stack operations (leaving the stack unchanged), or a subroutine call to a return, or a jump to the succeeding location. Large time differences can be balanced by using a timing function similar to the subroutine in the square-wave generator (Chapter 4).

This software approach is satisfactory only in simple cases, and even an apparently harmless second input can give errors in timing. In Fig. 10.2, after triggering the ADC to initiate the conversion process the microcomputer must wait until the conversion is complete (and the data valid) before executing the input. This can be done by monitoring the 'end of conversion' (EOC) signal from the ADC so that the 'wait for conversion' process becomes a 'test-and-loop' arrangement (Fig. 10.2(c)). Now if the conversion time changes (it might be dependent on the converted data

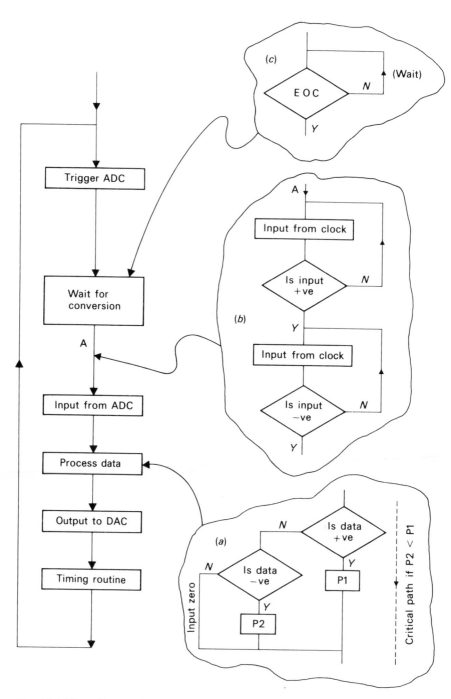

Fig. 10.2 Flow diagram for ADC/DAC example

value), then the loop time, and hence the sampling rate, will be subject to the same changes. This source of error has been introduced by the second input (the EOC control signal) and setting the microcomputer the additional task of effectively measuring the ADC conversion time. Of course, in this case there is a simple alternative which is to have a fixed wait time longer than the maximum conversion time, but the principle is demonstrated: multiple inputs and tasks can make real-time programming very difficult.

An external clock

An alternative to the pure software-controlled timing is to connect an external clock to an input port, and use this to control the timing of critical I/O operations (see Fig. 10.2(b)). The external clock period must be guaranteed longer than the *critical* path, so that cycles are not lost. Immediately prior to the I/P from the ADC the external clock is monitored—waiting, for example, for a falling edge. (Note: if the output to the DAC is to be at a regular rate also, then this operation must be placed adjacent to the input operation).

This arrangement is more flexible than the pure software approach, and does not require each sub-section of the sampling loop to be of a fixed time. Only a maximum or critical time need be known. Also, a variable external clock results immediately in a variable sampling rate at run time. The obvious disadvantage is the small amount of 'jitter' due to the clock monitor, the extremes of the jitter being given by the interval between samples from the external clock. The jitter can be effectively removed by triggering the ADC directly from the external clock, while still monitoring the clock as before.

Programmable clock

A popular method of realizing an external clock is to use a programmable timer, like the one referred to in Chapter 6. For example, the 8155/56 (see Appendix 5) READ/WRITE memory and I/O circuit contains a 14-bit timer which is usually fed with the microprocessor clock giving a high resolution and stable timing component.

The program loads the time value and then starts the timer; a loop program can then examine the status word in the timer to determine when the specified time has elapsed. (An example is given in the problems at the end of this chapter.)

If two times are used, one for the ADC and one for the DAC, provided the requests are not too fast, the microprocessor can simply look for the timers to signal an end-of-time period and then perform the appropriate action. Therefore the ADC and DAC can operate at independent sampling rates—a condition which is difficult to achieve with a purely software solution. This is an example of polling: for the two asynchronous peripherals—the timers—need to be synchronized by the program.

The addition of the external clock is a simple example of an important fundamental design principle: the hardware versus software trade-off. Triggering the ADC and waiting for the conversion can be done by software alone or with the help of some external hardware, which in turn makes the software easier. This is generally the case; additional hardware can be added to reduce the software complexity with the prime aim of reducing execution time (in a time-critical system) or development time. Of course, for the latter, the designer must equate the relevant costs. Once the software has been developed, its reproduction tends to be very cheap, but the hardware equivalents tend to be cheaper to develop; hence the total number of systems to be built must be borne in mind.

External program control

Consider a real-time system whose function at any given time is externally controlled. A very simple example might be a general-purpose waveform generator that produces either a square-wave, or a sinewave, or a ramp function according to the setting of an external 3-position switch. A suitable program structure would be:

> Loop continuously:
> **begin** input from switch and decode
>   **if** position 1 **then** square-wave routine
>   **if** position 2 **then** sinewave routine
>   **if** position 3 **then** ramp function routine
> **end** of loop

or, alternatively, with nested conditions using *else*:

> Loop continuously:
> **begin** input from switch and decode
>   **if** position 1 **then** square-wave routine
>   **else if** position 2 **then** sinewave routine
>   **else if** position 3
>   **then** ramp function routine
> **end** of loop

Each routine could be designed to generate just one cycle of the waveform before returning to check the switch, and the routines could be based on the individual programs discussed in Chapter 4.

The merits of these two forms are that they are concise and easy to understand. But direct implementation of either would result in a 'hiccup' at the end of each cycle, whether or not a new waveform had been selected. It may be important (in the case of the sinewave, for example) to ensure that the rate of the output to the DAC is constant, and so allowance would have to be made for the extra instructions at the end of each cycle. A regular rate can be achieved by padding the time-wasting instructions within each of the routines, or by an external clock, as described above.

The nested **if–then–else** is equivalent to the **case–of** structure, and an efficient approach to its programming in assembly code is to use a table-driven arrangement (Fig. 10.3). An address table comprises a set of

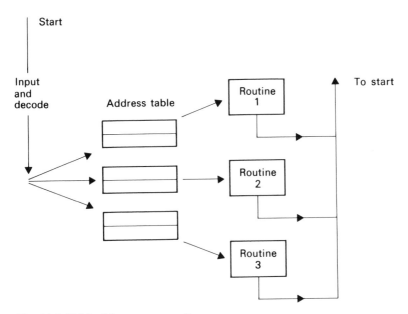

Fig. 10.3 Table-driven program flow

start addresses—one for each routine—and the decoding of the input condition identifies the appropriate location in the table, which in turn contains the appropriate start address. At the end of each routine the program flow returns to the 'input and decode' sections, rather than fruitlessly testing the other conditions as in the first structure.

Note that the routines are not subroutines, for they do not *return* to the point in the program from which they were entered but jump back to the start.

Worked example

Consider the general-purpose waveform generator postulated above with the specification changed slightly to read: three 'ON–OFF' switches, appropriately labelled 'square', 'sine' and 'ramp', are connected to bits 0, 1 and 2, of port W, and when one (and only one) switch is ON, the specified function is generated. The switches are continually monitored to check any change of request. No waveform is to be generated if no (or more than one) switch is on.

An assembly code program for the 8080 is shown in Fig. 10.4. TABLE specifies the location of the first start address, that of the square-wave routine which has been allocated page 1. Each routine is assumed to start at line 0, and the first two cannot occupy more than 256 bytes.

	Assembly code		Comments
START:	IN	W	Only bits 0, 1, 2, can be set by the
	ANI	07	switches. TABLE labels start of address
	LXI	H, (TABLE-2)	list
	MVI	C, 03	Set bit count
TESTBIT:	DCR	C	Test only first three bits, otherwise
	JM	START	TESTBIT loop could be infinite;
	INX	H	jump after three iterations;
	INX	H	each start address occupies 2 bytes
	RAR		
	JNC	TESTBIT	
	ORA	A	Test number of bits set and jump if
	JZ	ADDRESS	only carry bit set
	JMP	START	More than one bit set, i.e. more than one switch 'ON'
ADDRESS:	MOV	E, M	D,E ← start address of routine
	INX	H	defined by the one'1' at port W
	MOV	D,M	
	XCHG		D,E ← → H,L
	PCHL		Jump to routine
			Address list:
TABLE:	00	01	Page 1: start address for square-wave
	00	02	Page 2: start address for sinewave
	00	03	Page 3: start address for ramp function

Fig. 10.4 Assembly code for the table-driven program control

Note that there are two tests to be carried out on the input data— the first finds which, if any, bit is set; and the second checks whether more than one is set. The example illustrates the use of the two instructions XCHG and PCHL to effect a JUMP to the address held in the register pair H,L.

Clearly the output rate within each of the routines will be affected when the program transfers to the 'input and decode' section, and with the program in Fig. 10.4 it is possible to calculate the execution times for this section. In general, another important consideration is the execution time for the routines, for if this is too long, data will be lost at the input.

Problems

P10.1 Software timing is used to give a regular output rate to the DAC for the sinewave generator in Chapter 4. Balance the loop times for the 8080 program in Fig. 4.10.

The next three problems refer to the ADC, DAC, and microcomputer configuration shown in Fig. 10.1 and 10.2.

P10.2 Three methods of achieving a regular sampling rate for the ADC and DAC have been described; one is purely software, and two use an external clock. What job does the clock do and how does it reduce the software requirement? In general, what must the designer consider in the hardware/software trade-off?

P10.3 Write, in 8080 assembly code, a program for the external clock monitor shown in Fig. 10.2(b). Assume the clock is connected to bit '0' of input port W. Assemble your program for page 2 of memory.

P10.4 What is the maximum 'jitter' on the ADC sampling rate when using the external clock in the configuration shown in Fig. 10.2(b)? Calculate the value from your program of P10.3.

P10.5 The timer on the 8155 has the functional description shown in Appendix 5. Write a program to control the timer to make the ADC sample every 1.000 ms. What is the jitter on this solution?

P10.6 Assemble the program in Fig. 10.4 for page 0 of memory. Use hexadecimal representation, and assign the label TABLE the value F0H.

P10.7 How can the program of Fig. 10.4 be modified so that the function programs can finish with a RET instruction instead of a JMP?

P10.8 The program in Fig. 10.4 is to include the control of three lights connected to bits 0, 1 and 2, of output port W1, which correspond to the three switches. A light is to be lit only when the corresponding waveform is being generated (remember the outputs are latched). Redefine the sequence of operations to be performed by this program and suitably modify the program of Fig. 10.4.

11 Development environment

The design of a microcomputer-based product contains many inter-related activities demanding widely differing skills, both technical and managerial.

As well as the process of program design and implementation, the hardware must be designed, constructed and tested. Test and diagnostic facilities must be developed and, finally, the whole system must be integrated and tested. Development systems provide the facilities to pursue these activities efficiently and quickly. To understand the nature of the development aids the design process needs to be elaborated.

Design process

The process of designing a microprocessor-based solution starts, as all methods do, with a specification for the product. From the specification the designer must identify the method of solution and specify the major functional units required to produce a solution. The functional units may be implemented in hardware (electronic and logic circuits only), software (on a large computer system) or with a combination of both. The latter is likely to be a microprocessor-based solution which would exploit the benefits of LSI technology, although a minicomputer might also be used.

When a microprocessor-based solution is selected which achieves the operational and performance requirements, further elaboration of the solution follows. The most difficult aspect is to distinguish between the hardware and software components. Here, as has been stressed earlier, there are no clear-cut rules and in many cases both approaches may be possible. If hardware is used then that hardware must be constructed and tested in every product produced, whereas a program once tested (if tested exhaustively and well) is easy to replicate in either PROM or ROM. Thus in a large-volume application the aim will be to use software, or highly integrated hardware, wherever possible. However, for low-volume production it may be quicker to build special hardware which makes the software easier to construct, reducing the overall design costs.

A microcomputer-based product

To obtain an insight into the development process a microcomputer-based product will be examined and the process of designing and commissioning it will be discussed. Figure 11.1 shows a typical product which comprises a processor and its memory, input/output and the peripheral devices being controlled.

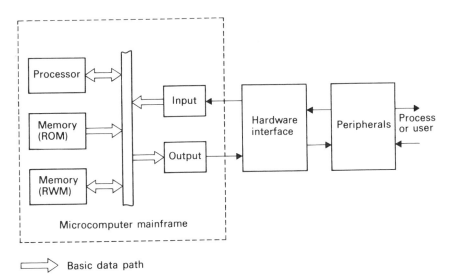

Basic data path

Fig. 11.1 Microcomputer product

The peripheral units may communicate with the user, i.e. keyboards, display etc., or they may be part of a process which is being controlled or monitored. Although the process plant can be large the discussion here will be confined to a small self-contained product that might have stepper motors, photosensors and solenoid controls which are manufactured as part of the product.

The hardware interface contains the circuits which convert the digital information at the output ports into a form suitable to drive the peripherals. There could be power amplifiers and isolators to drive solenoids, drive electronics for stepper motors, and many other forms of output transformation.

The input signals, from sensors, would be conditioned, possibly amplified, and then digitized if necessary ready to feed into the input ports.

A company converting to microcomputer-based control from relay or standard logic systems would already have the skills to assemble the peripheral and hardware interface requirements of the new product line.

The rest of the product, the microcomputer mainframe, is conventional.

The memory is composed of read-only sections which store the program and permanent data (constants), and read/write memory areas storing working variables, the stack and other changing data. The memory sizes must be selected to accommodate the information to be stored, but an excess of memory should be avoided if an economic product is to be produced. Predicting memory sizes can be a 'black art' especially before any code has been written.

The input/output section may contain a variety of LSI circuits which perform part of the systems functions. These are usually selected to simplify or save program effort. This hardware/software trade-off is a complex business, requiring many years of experience of both hardware and software system design.

The ultimate objective of the development process is to build the hardware depicted in Fig. 11.1, install a fully tested program and check out the performance of the product prior to delivery to the customer. The rest of this chapter will briefly describe the processes involved and the tools available.

Development process

The two major activities in making a prototype microcomputer-based product are the development of the hardware system and the programs. These two activities may be treated independently provided a precise definition of both parts is produced prior to starting. This definition should then be considered sacrosanct and only altered if major difficulties arise in either the hardware or software solution. The most important definition is the interface between the hardware and software systems. The hardware provides an environment which supports the execution of the software and its definition must be accurate and fixed, otherwise the software cannot possibly perform correctly.

The most obvious interface is the input/output definition. This describes where in the address space the peripheral resources reside and specifies the bit patterns for controlling and monitoring the peripheral actions. This interface definition is part of the specification of the hardware system and defines what the programmer expects to see in the hardware.

Hardware system

The hardware system comprises all the units shown in Fig. 11.1. Much of it may be purchased directly from a manufacturer in the form of computer boards and peripheral and memory expansion boards. Alternatively the complete system can be produced from basic component parts. In the latter case much more thought must be put into test methods and debugging aids, whereas purchased boards will be tested before despatch. The tools required for the initial testing are conventional; logic analyzer, oscilloscope, test probes. In-circuit emulation (ICE) may prove valuable for prototype testing but is probably not appropriate for production checkout.

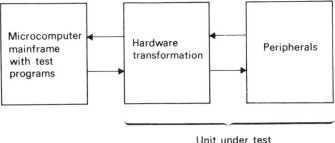

Unit under test

Fig. 11.2 Testing the external hardware

Figure 11.2 shows a scheme for testing the peripheral hardware, where the microcomputer has been replaced by another that contains testing programs and debugging aids. The objective is to ensure that the peripherals operate as expected without complicating the problem by using unproven computer hardware.

The microcomputer often may be a standard prototyping system that is eventually replaced by the target or product microcomputer. The test programs are made as simple as possible. They must check out the wiring and the basic functions of the peripherals. For example, ensure photosensors work, stepper motor rotates, etc. The objective is to demonstrate the basic integrity of the hardware system and establish the basic functional characteristics are correct. These tests may form a valuable front-line maintenance tool in the end product.

Only when all the hardware tests seem satisfactory and the basic definition of the hardware/software interface is satisfied should the applications program be submitted to the hardware for testing.

Software system

Two basic types of program exist; those that interact with peripheral hardware, often called peripheral handlers, and those that perform a computational task on information that resides within the memory of the machine. The latter type can be tested in any computing environment that can execute the program and accomodate all the necessary information in its memory. These purely software orientated programs should be tested in a safe, clean environment free of the constraints of peripheral hardware. The only I/O necessary is a terminal or printer to which the results can be passed. A microcomputer development system, or MDS, is a typical environment for such testing.

Programs that operate with peripherals are more difficult to check out—especially ones that perform interactively in real-time. As much testing as possible should be done in an MDS type environment by simulating the I/O transfers from the terminal. However, ultimately the program will have to be executed in the target system with full peripheral support. The hardware and software activities now merge together and the full integrated system is put under test.

Development tools

In the brief description above reference was made to the tools required to carry out the development process. These and others are now described.

The microcomputer development system (MDS) is the usual tool for program support and development. Most development systems support assemblers, compilers, editors and an operating system to provided disk file storage, library facilities, etc. (see Chapter 8). Programs are stored on a backing store medium like floppy disk and may be edited, translated and tested. The testing would be without application peripheral support. Any general-purpose computer system could support these facilities.

For pure program testing the MDS must be able to execute the object code or simulate execution. The former is preferable, in which case the MDS contains the particular microcomputer to execute the program. This is done either by using the same microcomputer or by inserting a second, of the appropriate type, which executes under control of the main MDS processor. The latter method is called in-circuit emulation. Thus a standard MDS, like MDS-800, can support 8080, 8085, 8048, 8086 by the insertion of appropriate boards. The systems from Tektronix and Hewlett–Packard support an even wider range, encompassing different manufacturers' processors, using the same basic method.

The emulating processor acts like a special peripheral of the main MDS processor: options include using the main MDS memory for the user program, use of the MDS peripherals as well as connecting to the target-product hardware. It is this that makes ICE such a powerful tool. The processor in the target hardware can be replaced by the emulation processor using an 'umbilical cord connection'. The hardware surrounding the emulation machine can then detect errors in the target hardware. Programs can be executed from the target memory or the MDS memory, and more significantly, the target peripherals may be accessed under control of the emulation processor but with the full range of powerful aids the MDS supports.

Having successfully tested the programs by placing them in the MDS read/write memory, PROMs can be programmed and located in the target hardware and still executed under control of the MDS in-circuit emulator.

Separate target hardware

Often the development system cannot support direct execution of the target machine and so a separate target machine is used which has the full application peripheral support. This method may also be desirable to reduce the debugging time on more expensive microcomputer development systems, enabling more efficient utilization of costly resources. The target testing system has a few extra components added to the basic product hardware of Fig. 11.1. A typical arrangement is shown in Fig. 11.3,

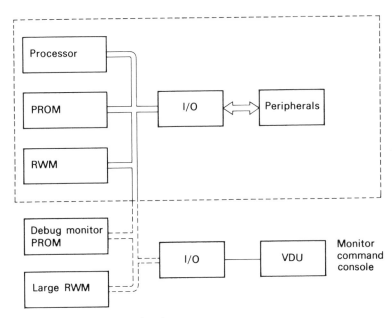

Fig. 11.3 Target testing hardware system

where a debug monitor PROM, a large read/write memory and a VDU have been added to the basic scheme. The debug monitor provides basic debugging commands, a typical selection being:

I(N)	Insert code at address N
S(N)	Substitute data at address N
X	Examine/substitute register values
G(N)	Execute program from address N
D(N,M)	Display memory contents from N to M
M(N,M,L)	Move contents between N and M to L

P(N)	Examine/insert data at port N
N	Single step program
G(N,M)	Execute program from N and break at M

If a small backing store on cassette or paper-tape is available then commands for reading and writing would be provided. Memory test programs could be included for checking new memory hardware. These facilities are provided in most prototyping and kit microcomputer systems.

The next ingredient of the system is a medium for transporting the object program from the MDS, where the program is developed, to the target hardware where it is tested. If backing store peripherals are available these may be used. If another serial link is provided the program could be down-line-loaded from the MDS over a wire link. For successful use of this method a multi-user MDS is really needed to avoid interrupting other users of the MDS.

A third alternative which has been used successfully in project development is to use PROMs to transport the program. The cost is minimal and the method is fast. The target system must already accommodate sufficient space for PROMs which will contain the program. The program is assembled on the MDS as if located in the extra read/write memory, and then loaded into PROMs. The PROMs are inserted in the microcomputer hardware. The contents of the PROMs are then transferred to RWM using a move-memory-block command. The program can now be executed.

This method has a few distinct advantages but requires careful recording of any modifications. If the program gets corrupted it can be compared with the original (a new monitor command) or easily reloaded. As changes are made these must be recorded in a 'mod' book so they can be inserted after reloading. After about 10–20 simple corrections have been made and recorded on the program listing, the designer returns to the MDS and updates the source program, clears out the PROMs and starts the cycle again.

The extra hardware used for target testing costs about £1000 per station in the UK. This compares with £12 000 or more for an MDS that can perform the same functions. If three or four engineers can share one MDS the initial cost is £16 000 compared with £48 000 if they had an MDS each. The four engineers would spend most of the time working on the target hardware system so occupancy of the MDS is optimized but not overloaded. The ICE system would be used for the more difficult 'bugs' that cannot be located on the target equipment. The method relies on the microcomputer hardware being operational. If hardware development and testing proceeds as described earlier, then this will be achieved.

Summary

Microcomputer product development introduces a completely new range of design and development tools without which only poor quality and late delivered systems would be produced. The tools are, however, expensive and a realistic compromise between investment in tools and development time must be reached. A brief description of methods used to produce a range of products has been given and the attributes of typical tools described.

Problems

P11.1 Describe in your own words the process of developing a microcomputer-based product.

P11.2 Highlight factors you consider relevant at the hardware/software interface. Comment on the following in this respect:

    (i) Size of read-only memory
    (ii) Size of read/write memory
    (iii) Instruction execution time
    (iv) Large-volume production

P11.3 Why is the input/output definition so crucial to the success of both the hardware and software development. Explain the possible solutions and their ramifications should the hardware I/O system not match the software requirements.

P11.4 A product comprises a 4-digit display, thumbwheel switches, push putton switches, indicator lamps, solenoid drives and photosensors. Suggest simple tests to check out the I/O wiring, and in particular the order in which the tests should be performed to minimize interaction of tests.

P11.5 How can the designer ensure that the I/O definition supplied to the programmers is met by the hardware in the tests of P11.4?

References

General (referred to in more than one chapter)

D. W. Barron, *Assemblers and Loaders,* American-Elsevier, (1969).

C. G. Bell and A. Newell, *Computer Structures: Readings and Examples,* McGraw-Hill, (1971).

P. J. Brown, *Macroprocessors and Techniques for Portable Software,* Wiley, (1975).

M. Campbell-Kelly, *An Introduction to Macros,* American-Elsevier, (1973).

O. J. Dahl, E. W. Dijkstra and C. A. R. Hoare, *Structured Programming,* Academic Press, (1972).

E. W. Dijkstra, *A Discipline of Programming,* Prentice-Hall, (1976).

Intel Corporation, *MCS-85 User Manual 1978* (9800366E).

Intel Corporation, *8080 User Manual.*

D. Lewin, *Theory and Design of Digital Computers,* Nelson, (1972).

Motorola (UK) Ltd, *6800 Systems Reference and Data Sheets.*

Chapter 8

G. R. Johnson and R. A. Mueller, The automated generation of cross-system software for supporting micro/mini computer systems, *ACM SIGPLAN Notices,* **11,** pp 45–57 (1976).

D. Morris, T. G. Kennedy and L. Last, FLOCODER, *Computer Journal,* **14,** 221–8 (1971).

M. Whitbread, Software development and system testing techniques, *Microprocessors,* **3,** pp 15–18 (1979).

Chapter 9

Intel Corporation, *PL/M User Manual.*

For further reading

C. G. Bell, J. Grason and A. Newell, *Designing Computers and Digital Systems,* Digital Press, (1972).

C. C. Clare, *Designing Logic Systems using State Machines,* McGraw-Hill, (1973).

E. W. Dijkstra, *A Discipline of Programming,* Prentice Hall (1976).

J. J. Donovan, *Systems Programming,* McGraw-Hill, (1972).

S. S. Husson, *Microprogramming: Principles and Practices,* Prentice-Hall, (1970).

M. A. Jackson, *Principles of Program Design,* Academic Press, (1975).

A. M. Lister, *Fundamentals of Operating Systems,* Macmillan, (1975).

Appendix 1 **Number conversion**

The tables below provide simple conversion rules for up to 16-bit binary numbers represented in hexadecimal, octal and split octal. The tables provide conversion in both directions.

Convert to decimal: Taking each digit position in turn, find the decimal number from the table at the intersection of digit position and digit value. Sum all the terms for each digit position to obtain the decimal number.

Convert from decimal: Find the highest number in the table that is less than, or equal to, the decimal number to be converted. The digit value and its position are the co-ordinates of the intersection point. (All the higher digit positions are zero.) Subtract the value on the table from the decimal number and, by using the result as the new decimal number, repeat the operations from the beginning until all digit values are found.

Hexadecimal digit	Digit position			
	4th	3rd	2nd	1st
0	0	0	0	0
1	4096	256	16	1
2	8192	512	32	2
3	12288	768	48	3
4	16384	1024	64	4
5	20480	1280	80	5
6	24576	1536	96	6
7	28672	1792	112	7
8	32768	2048	128	8
9	36864	2304	144	9
A	40960	2560	160	10
B	45056	2816	176	11
C	49152	3072	192	12
D	53248	3328	208	13
E	57344	3584	224	14
F	61440	3840	240	15

Fig. A1.1 Hexadecimal–decimal

Octal digit	6th	5th	Digit position 4th	3rd	2nd	1st
0	0	0	0	0	0	0
1	32768	4096	512	64	8	1
2	—	8192	1024	128	16	2
3	—	12288	1536	192	24	3
4	—	16384	2048	256	32	4
5	—	20488	2560	320	40	5
6	—	24576	3072	384	48	6
7	—	28672	3584	448	56	7

Fig. A1.2 Octal–decimal

Octal digit	6th	Digit position Page 5th	4th	3rd	Line 2nd	1st
0	0	0	0	0	0	0
1	16384	2048	256	64	8	1
2	32768	4096	512	128	16	2
3	49152	6144	768	192	24	3
4	—	8192	1024	—	32	4
5	—	10240	1280	—	40	5
6	—	12288	1536	—	48	6
7	—	14336	1792	—	56	7

Fig. A1.3 Split octal–decimal

Note: Split octal uses two 8-bit numbers each expressed in octal form

Appendix 2 **Peripherals**

Peripheral hardware components

To enable readers to complete design exercises, the wiring details and operational characteristics of a selection of peripheral devices are provided. Connectors are numbered J1 to J5 and the pin numbers given for each. The input-output configuration for a small 8085 system is given as a basis for an I/O system.

A memory and I/O map is presented to show a real system for use in the design exercises.

Address range	Chip type	Function	Size
0000–07FFH	8755	PROM	2K
4700H–47FFH	8155	RWM	256
4800H–48FFH	8155	RWM	256

Fig. A2.1 Memory map of a small 8085 computer

I/O Address	Chip type	Function	Comments
00	8251	USART	Data read/write
01			Control/write—Status/read
08	8755	Digital I/O	Port AA ⎱ programmed by
09			Port BB ⎰ direction register
0A		(Unit A)	Direction A
0B			Direction B
10	8155	Digital I/O	Control/write—Status/read
11		and timer	Port BA ⎱ Read/write
12		(Unit B)	Port BB ⎬ programmed by
13			Port BC ⎰ Control register
14			TL Timer low byte
15			TH Timer high byte

Fig. A2.2 Input/Output port address map for a small 8085 computer

The connector J1 contains the I/O signals from all of the I/O ports shown in Fig. A2.2. The port directions are not defined since all may be programmed to be input or output by writing suitable commands to the appropriate control or direction registers (complete details of programming is given in Appendix 5). J1 connections are shown below, the connector has two columns of pins, Side A and Side B. Only those showing I/O signals are given.

Connector J1

Port AA bits 0–7	Side B pins 15–22
Port AB bits 0–7	Side B pins 23–30
Port BA bits 0–7	Side A pins 11–18
Port BB bits 0–7	Side A pins 19–26
Port BC bits 0–5	Side A pins 27–32
Timer output	Side B pin 33
Timer input connected to 3.072 MHz clock	

Fig. A2.3 Connector assignment for I/O signals

Peripheral devices

A selection of suitable peripheral devices is shown below.

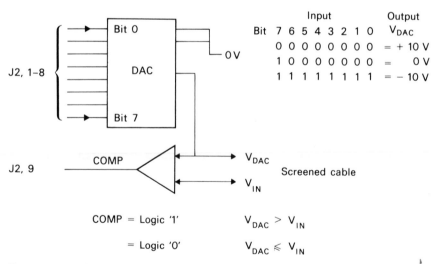

Fig. A2.4 DAC with comparator

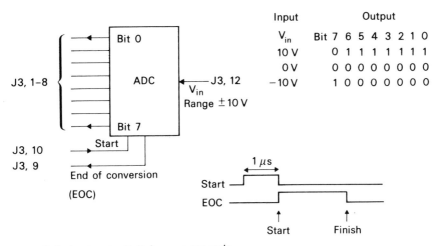

Fig. A2.5 Analog to digital converter unit

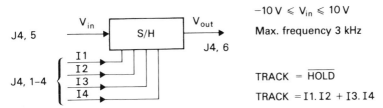

$-10\,V \leqslant V_{in} \leqslant 10\,V$

Max. frequency 3 kHz

$TRACK = \overline{HOLD}$

$TRACK = I1.I2 + I3.I4$

Fig. A2.6 Sample hold module

J5, 1	Red	North–South
2	Red	East–West
3	Amber	North–South
4	Amber	East–West
5	Green	North–South
6	Green	East–West
7	Pedestrian	Wait
8	Pedestrian	Go
9	Pedestrian	Request
10	North–South	Pad
11	East–West	Pad

Signals that control/monitor functions of a traffic-light model

Fig. A2.7 Traffic-light module

Appendix 3 8080/85 Instruction set summary

The information in Chapter 3 is presented so that the structure of the processor and the organization of the instruction set can be described in a clear, logical and structured manner. When working with programs, and especially when testing them, a more concise working document is desirable. The information in Fig. A3.1 presents the instructions in symbolic form for assembler programming and in hexadecimal machine code. Additionally assembler directives and operators are summarized as an aide-memoire. This diagram contains no explanatory material but does enable the user to identify machine code instructions quickly, for hand code assembly, and to check on the mnemonics while writing assembly programs.

Another useful aid is given, Fig. A3.2, which is a listing of all machine code instructions in numerical order, giving the symbolic instruction. This is useful when debugging a machine code program on the target machine.

The instruction execution time is given in Fig. A3.1 in italics after the machine code. The times are given for the 8085, the 8080 differs slightly in a few cases.

DATA TRANSFER GROUP

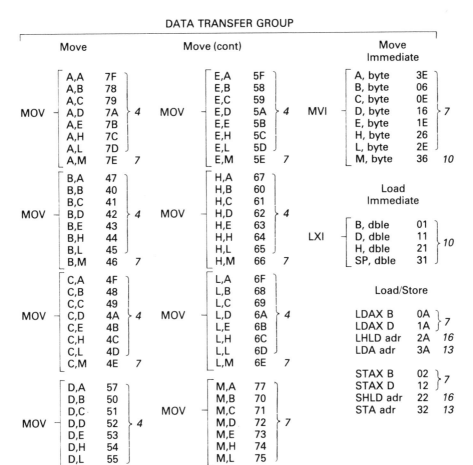

byte = constant or logical/arithmetic expression that evaluates to an 8-bit data quantity. (Second byte of 2-byte instructions).

dble = constant or logical/arithmetic expression that evaluates to a 16-bit data quantity. (Second and third bytes of 3-byte instructions).

adr = 16-bit address (Second and third bytes of 3-byte instructions).

* = all flags (C, Z, S, P, AC) affected.

** = all flags except CARRY affected: (exception: INX and DCX affect no flags).

† = only CARRY affected.

All mnemonics copyright © Intel Corporation 1978

Fig. A3.1 Summary of the 8085 instruction set, in functional groupings

ARITHMETIC AND LOGICAL GROUP

Add*

ADD
A	87
B	80
C	81
D	82	} 4
E	83
H	84
L	85
M	86	7

ADC
A	8F
B	88
C	89
D	8A	} 4
E	8B
H	8C
L	8D
M	8E	7

Subtract*

SUB
A	97
B	90
C	91
D	92	} 4
E	93
H	94
L	95
M	96	7

SBB
A	9F
B	98
C	99
D	9A	} 4
E	9B
H	9C
L	9D
M	9E	7

Double add†

DAD
| B | 09 |
| D | 19 | } 10
| H | 29 |
| SP | 39 |

Increment**

INR
A	3C
B	04
C	0C
D	14	} 4
E	1C
H	24
L	2C
M	34	10

INX
| B | 03 |
| D | 13 | } 6
| H | 23 |
| SP | 33 |

Decrement**

DCR
A	3D
B	05
C	0D
D	15	} 4
E	1D
H	25
L	2D
M	35	10

DCX
| B | 0B |
| D | 1B | } 6
| H | 2B |
| SP | 3B |

Specials

| DAA* | 27 |
| CMA | 2F |
| STC† | 37 | } 4
| CMC† | 3F |

Rotate†

| RLC | 07 |
| RRC | 0F |
| RAL | 17 | } 4
| RAR | 1F |

Logical*

ANA
A	A7
B	A0
C	A1
D	A2	} 4
E	A3
H	A4
L	A5
M	A6	7

XRA
A	AF
B	A8
C	A9
D	AA	} 4
E	AB
H	AC
L	AD
M	AE	7

ORA
A	B7
B	B0
C	B1
D	B2	} 4
E	B3
H	B4
L	B5
M	B6	7

CMP
A	BF
B	B8
C	B9
D	BA	} 4
E	BB
H	BC
L	BD
M	BE	7

Arith & logical immediate

ADI byte	C6
ACI byte	CE
SUI byte	D6
SBI byte	DE
ANI byte	E6	} 7
XRI byte	EE
ORI byte	F6
CPI byte	FE

Fig. A3.1 Contd.

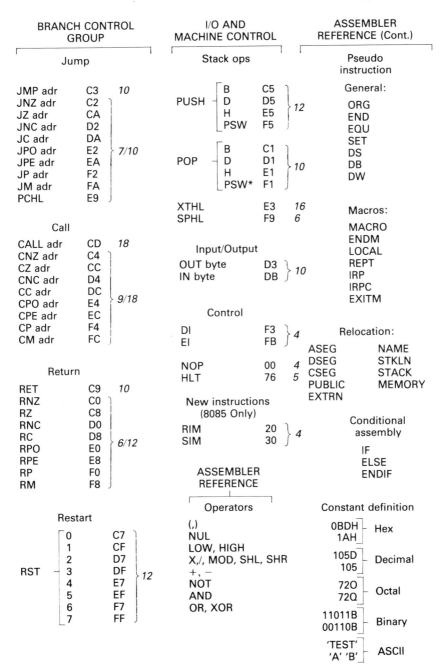

BRANCH CONTROL
GROUP

Jump

JMP adr	C3	10
JNZ adr	C2	
JZ adr	CA	
JNC adr	D2	
JC adr	DA	
JPO adr	E2	7/10
JPE adr	EA	
JP adr	F2	
JM adr	FA	
PCHL	E9	

Call

CALL adr	CD	18
CNZ adr	C4	
CZ adr	CC	
CNC adr	D4	
CC adr	DC	9/18
CPO adr	E4	
CPE adr	EC	
CP adr	F4	
CM adr	FC	

Return

RET	C9	10
RNZ	C0	
RZ	C8	
RNC	D0	
RC	D8	6/12
RPO	E0	
RPE	E8	
RP	F0	
RM	F8	

Restart

	0	C7	
	1	CF	
	2	D7	
RST	3	DF	12
	4	E7	
	5	EF	
	6	F7	
	7	FF	

I/O AND
MACHINE CONTROL

Stack ops

PUSH	B	C5	
	D	D5	12
	H	E5	
	PSW	F5	

POP	B	C1	
	D	D1	10
	H	E1	
	PSW*	F1	

| XTHL | E3 | 16 |
| SPHL | F9 | 6 |

Input/Output

| OUT byte | D3 | 10 |
| IN byte | DB | |

Control

| DI | F3 | 4 |
| EI | FB | |

| NOP | 00 | 4 |
| HLT | 76 | 5 |

New instructions
(8085 Only)

| RIM | 20 | 4 |
| SIM | 30 | |

ASSEMBLER
REFERENCE

Operators

(,)
NUL
LOW, HIGH
X,/, MOD, SHL, SHR
+, −
NOT
AND
OR, XOR

ASSEMBLER
REFERENCE (Cont.)

Pseudo
instruction

General:

ORG
END
EQU
SET
DS
DB
DW

Macros:

MACRO
ENDM
LOCAL
REPT
IRP
IRPC
EXITM

Relocation:

ASEG	NAME
DSEG	STKLN
CSEG	STACK
PUBLIC	MEMORY
EXTRN	

Conditional
assembly

IF
ELSE
ENDIF

Constant definition

0BDH	Hex
1AH	
105D	Decimal
105	
72O	Octal
72Q	
11011B	Binary
00110B	
'TEST'	ASCII
'A' 'B'	

Fig. A3.1 Contd.

Code	Instruction	Code	Instruction	Code	Instruction	Code	Instruction
00	NOP	2B	DCX H	81	ADD C	D7	RST 2
01	LXI B,bdle	2C	INR L	82	ADD D	D8	RC
02	STAX B	2D	DCR L	83	ADD E	D9	
03	INX B	2E	MVI L,byte	84	ADD H	DA	JC adr
04	INR B	2F	CMA	85	ADD L	DB	IN byte
05	DCR B	30	SIM*	86	ADD M	DC	CC adr
06	MVI B,byte	31	LXI Sp,dble	87	ADD A	DD	
07	RLC	32	STA adr	88	ADC B	DE	SBI byte
08		33	INX SP	89	ADC C	DF	RST 3
09	DAD B	34	INR M	8A	ADC D	E0	RPO
0A	LDAX B	35	DCR M	8B	ADC E	E1	POP H
0B	DCX B	36	MVI M,byte	8C	ADC H	E2	JPO adr
0C	INR C	37	STC	8D	ADC L	E3	XTHL
0D	DCR C	38		8E	ADC M	E4	CPO adr
0E	MVI C,byte	39	DAD SP	8F	ADC A	E5	PUSH H
0F	RRC	3A	LDA adr	90	SUB B	E6	ANI byte
10		3B	DCX SP	91	SUB C	E7	RST 4
11	LXI D,dble	3C	INR A	92	SUB D	E8	RPE
12	STAX D	3D	DCR A	93	SUB E	E9	PCHL
13	INX D	3E	MVI A,byte	94	SUB H	EA	JPE adr
14	INR D	3F	CMC	95	SUB L	EB	XCHG
15	DCR D	40	MOV B,B	96	SUB M	EC	CPE adr
16	MVI D,byte	41	MOV B,C	97	SUB A	ED	
17	RAL	42	MOV B,D	98	SBB B	EE	XRI byte
18		43	MOV B,E	99	SBB C	EF	RST 5
19	DAD D	44	MOV B,H	9A	SBB D	F0	RP
1A	LDAX D	45	MOV B,L	9B	SBB E	F1	POP PSW
1B	DCX D	46	MOV B,M	9C	SBB H	F2	JP adr
1C	INR E	47	MOV B,A	9D	SBB L	F3	DI
1D	DCR E	48	MOV C,B	9E	SBB M	F4	CP adr
1E	MVI E,byte	49	MOV C,C	9F	SBB A	F5	PUSH PSW
1F	RAR	4A	MOV C,D	A0	ANA B	F6	ORI byte
20	RIM*	4B	MOV C,E	A1	ANA C	F7	RST 6
21	LXI H,bdle	4C	MOV C,H	A2	ANA D	F8	RM
22	SHLD adr	4D	MOV C,L	A3	ANA E	F9	SPHL
23	INX H	4E	MOV C,M	A4	ANA H	FA	JM adr
24	INR H	4F	MOV C,A	A5	ANA L	FB	EI
25	DCR H	50	MOV D,B	A6	ANA M	FC	CM adr
26	MVI H,byte	51	MOV D,C	A7	ANA A	FD	
27	DAA	52	MOV D,D	A8	XRA B	FE	CPI byte
28		53	MOV D,E	A9	XRA C	FF	RST 7
29	DAD H	54	MOV D,H	AA	XRA D		
2A	LHLD adr	55	MOV D,L	AB	XRA E		
		56	MOV D,M	AC	XRA H		
		57	MOV D,A	AD	XRA L		
		58	MOV E,B	AE	XRA M		
		59	MOV E,C	AF	XRA A		
		5A	MOV E,D	B0	ORA B		
		5B	MOV E,E	B1	ORA C		
		5C	MOV E,L	B2	ORA D		
		5D	MOV E,M	B3	ORA E		
		5E	MOV E,A	B4	ORA H		
		5F	MOV H,B	B5	ORA L		
		60	MOV H,C	B6	ORA M		
		61	MOV H,D	B7	ORA A		
		62	MOV H,E	B8	CMP B		
		63	MOV H,H	B9	CMP C		
		64	MOV H,L	BA	CMP D		
		65	MOV H,M	BB	CMP E		
		66	MOV H,A	BC	CMP H		
		67	MOV L,B	BD	CMP L		
		68	MOV L,C	BE	CMP M		
		69	MOV L,D	BF	CMP A		
		6A	MOV L,E	C0	RNZ		
		6B	MOV L,H	C1	POP B		
		6C	MOV L,L	C2	JNZ adr		
		6D	MOV L,M	C3	JMP adr		
		6E	MOV L,A	C4	CNZ adr		
		6F	MOV M,B	C5	PUSH B		
		70	MOV M,C	C6	ADI byte		
		71	MOV M,D	C7	RST 0		
		72	MOV M,E	C8	RZ		
		73	MOV M,H	C9	RET		
		74	MOV M,L	CA	JZ adr		
		75	HLT	CB			
		76	MOV M,A	CC	CZ adr		
		77	MOV A,B	CD	CALL adr		
		78	MOV A,C	CE	ACI byte		
		79	MOV A,D	CF	RST 1		
		7A	MOV A,E	D0	RNC		
		7B	MOV A,H	D1	POP D		
		7C	MOV A,L	D2	JNC adr		
		7D	MOV A,M	D3	OUT byte		
		7E	MOV A,A	D4	CNC adr		
		7F		D5	PUSH D		
		80	ADD B	D6	SUI byte		

*8085 Only

All mnemonics copyright © Intel Corporation 1976

Fig. A3.2 Summary of 8085 instruction set in numerical order.

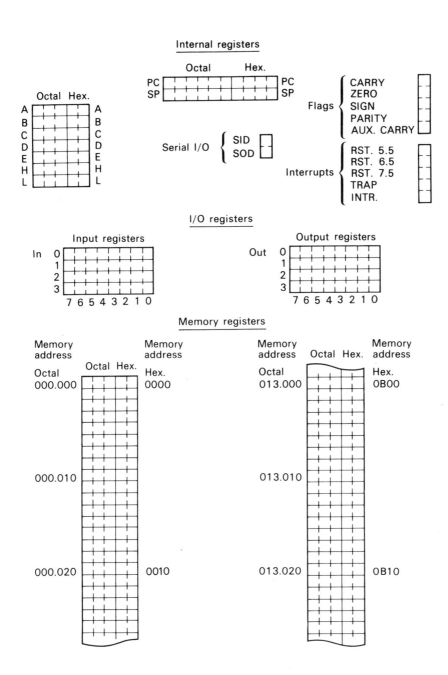

(Copies of the register structure and memory locations are included here for use while working on tutorial questions)

Appendix 4 **6800 Microprocessor**

In an earlier version of this book the 6800 was described in the main text to supply a comparative assessment of two processors. To avoid clutter and longer chapters the 6800 is presented, in a form identical to the 8080/85 in Chapters 2 and 3, in this appendix. The equivalent figures in those chapters are cited for easy reference. Additional text is given where this is felt to be necessary but the reader is directed to the many other texts for detailed information on the 6800 microprocessor.

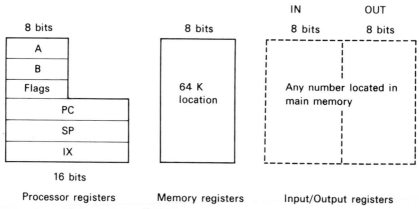

Fig. A4.1 6800 operand register structure

Operands of the 6800

The register structure is much simpler than the 8080/85 and is shown above in Fig. A4.1 (equivalent to Fig. 2.4).
Notable differences are:

(1) Two accumulators, or destination registers for operation orders
(2) An index register (IX) which provides indirect addressing and a version of indexed addressing.
(3) No dedicated input/output registers. Instead these must be located somewhere in the main memory (thereby reducing space for operands or instructions).

Operand addressing

Since there are so few registers there is no value in presenting the register identifiers in diagram form (see equivalents in Fig. 2.5(*a*) and Fig. 2.5(*b*).) The two 8-bit registers are designated by symbols, A and B while the 16-bit index register is represented by the symbol X. The index register is used to access memory operands in the indexed addressing mode but may also be loaded and stored.

Unlike the 8080/85, however, the 6800 has a more regular memory operand addressing structure. The addressing modes are summarized below in Fig. A4.2.

D 1	Register	D 2	Location	S	Location
0	A	0 0	Reg . A	0 0	Immediate
1	B	0 1	Reg . B	0 1	Direct normal
		1 0	Indexed	1 0	Indexed
		1 1	Direct extended	1 1	Direct extended

Fig. A4.2 Operand addressing codes (D1, D2 and S refer to fields in the instructions)

The normal direct addressing uses an 8-bit address concatenated with an upper byte of all zeros, allowing direct addressing to the first 356 locations in memory. Extended addressing provides the full 16-bit direct address.

b or u code	Binary Operator (b)	Unary Operator (u)
0 0 0 0	Subtract	Negate
0 0 0 1	Compare	*
0 0 1 0	Subtract with borrow	*
0 0 1 1	*	Complement
0 1 0 0	Logical AND	Logical shift right
0 1 0 1	Bit test	*
0 1 1 0	Load (1)	Rotate right
0 1 1 1	Store (1)	Arithmetic shift R
1 0 0 0	Logical EX–OR	Arithmetic shift L
1 0 0 1	Add with carry	Rotate left
1 0 1 0	Logical OR	Decrement
1 0 1 1	Add	*
1 1 0 0	Compare Index Reg.	Increment
1 1 0 1	*	Test
1 1 1 0	Load SP + INX (1)	*
1 1 1 1	Store SP + INX (1)	Clear

* Codes unused for normal operator orders

Fig. A4.3 Binary and unary operators of the 6800 (operators (1) are unary ones needing two operands)

Eight-bit operators

All the ALU operators are eight bits in length and are shown in Fig. A4.3 (equivalent to Figs 2.7 and 2.10). Useful additions are negate, which performs a 2's complement subtraction from zero, and the arithmetic shifts which maintain sign integrity on right shifts. Test is equivalent to an 'AND' operation with eight ones, i.e., FFH.

Sixteen-bit operators

The 16-bit operators include moves, increment, decrement and compare using the memory, stack pointer and index register.

One-bit operators

Clear and set operators are provided for unconditionally setting and flag register bits.

Instruction	Type and function	Mnemonic	Machine code (Hex)
Zero-address A4.1A	Clear carry C ← O	CLC	O C
A4.1B	Clear interrupt mask IM ← O	CLI	O E
A4.1C	Clear overflow OVF ← O	CLV	O A
A4.1D	Set carry C ← I	SEC	O D
A4.1E	Set interrupt mask IM ← I	SEI	O F
A4.1F	Set overflow	SEV	O B

Fig. A4.4(a) One-bit instructions for 6800 (equivalent to Fig. 3.1(a))

Instruction set

One-bit operation orders

These operate on the flags carry, overflow and the interrupt mask.

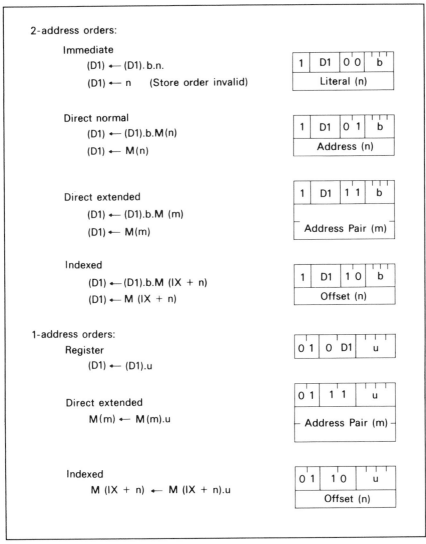

Fig. A4.4(b) Main operation instructions of 6800 (Note: D1, D2, b, u refer to Figs A4.2 and A4.3)

Eight and sixteen-bit operator orders

The orders for the 6800 are best described in one block as shown in Fig. A4.4(*b*).

These tables show the bulk of the 6800 orders. The rest are given in the summary at the end of this appendix.

Control orders

The 6800 uses relative, indexed and direct extended addressing to define the destination address for control instructions.

Both jump and jump to subroutine mechanisms are supported; in the latter case the return address stack is in main memory, addressed by the stack pointer.

A rich selection of conditional tests, summarized below in Fig. A4.5, can be performed.

Condition function	Set Mnemonic (C)	Code (K)	Cleared Mnemonic (c)	Code (K)
Carry	CS	5	CC	4
Zero	EQ	7	NE	6
Greater or equal	GE	C	LT	D
Less or equal	LE	F	GT	E
Sign	MI	B	PL	A
Overflow	VS	9	VC	8
Lower or same	LS	3	HI	2

Fig. A4.5 6800 condition codes

The main programmed control orders are shown below. In addition there are interrupt control orders which involve automatically storing the machine state. These are left for the more dedicated reader to explore personally.

A complete summary of all the 6800 instructions is given in Fig A4.7. This not only gives the machine code, but also flags affected and an explanation of the instruction.

Control type/	Unconditional		Conditional	
Destination address	Mnemonic and description	Machine code (Hex)	Mnemonic and description	Machine code (Hex)
Jump/relative (branch)	BRA X (PC) ← (PC) + X	2 O XL	Bc X **if** c = true **then** (PC) ← (PC) + 2 + X **else** (PC) ← (PC) + 2 (for value of c and K see fig A4.5)	2 K XL
direct (extended)	JMP X (PC) ← X	7 E XL XH		
indexed	JMP X, IX (PC) ← (IX) + X	6 E XL		
Jump to subroutine/ relative (branch)	BSR X Store ← (PC) (PC) ← (PC) + X	8 D XL		
direct (extended)	JSR X Store ← (PC) (PC) ← X	B D XL XH		
indexed	JSR X, IX Store ← (PC) (PC) ← (IX) + X	A D XL		
Return from sub-routine	RTS (PC) ← store	3 9		

Fig. A4.6 Control instructions of the 6800

ACCUMULATOR AND MEMORY INSTRUCTIONS

		IMMED			DIRECT			INDEX			EXTND			IMPLIED			BOOLEAN/ARITHMETIC OPERATION (All register labels refer to contents)	5 H	4 I	3 N	2 Z	1 V	0 C
OPERATIONS	MNEMONIC	OP	~	=	OP	~	=	OP	~	=	OP	~	=	OP	~	=							
Add	ADDA	3B	2	2	9B	3	2	AB	5	2	BB	4	3				A + M → A	:	●	:	:	:	:
	ADDB	CB	2	2	DB	3	2	EB	5	2	FB	4	3				B + M → B	:	●	:	:	:	:
Add Acmltrs	ABA													1B	2	1	A + B → A	:	●	:	:	:	:
Add with Carry	ADCA	89	2	2	99	3	2	A9	5	2	B9	4	3				A + M + C → A	:	●	:	:	:	:
	ADCB	C9	2	2	D9	3	2	E9	5	2	F9	4	3				B + M + C → B	:	●	:	:	:	:
And	ANDA	84	2	2	94	3	2	A4	5	2	B4	4	3				A · M → A	●	●	:	:	R	●
	ANDB	C4	2	2	D4	3	2	E4	5	2	F4	4	3				B · M → B	●	●	:	:	R	●
Bit Test	BITA	85	2	2	95	3	2	A5	5	2	B5	4	3				A · M	●	●	:	:	R	●
	BITB	C5	2	2	D5	3	2	E5	5	2	F5	4	3				B · M	●	●	:	:	R	●
Clear	CLR							6F	7	2	7F	6	3				00 → M	●	●	R	S	R	R
	CLRA													4F	2	1	00 → A	●	●	R	S	R	R
	CLRB													5F	2	1	00 → B	●	●	R	S	R	R
Compare	CMPA	81	2	2	91	3	2	A1	5	2	B1	4	3				A - M	●	●	:	:	:	:
	CMPB	C1	2	2	D1	3	2	E1	5	2	F1	4	3				B - M	●	●	:	:	:	:
Compare Acmltrs	CBA													11	2	1	A - B	●	●	:	:	:	:
Complement, 1's	COM							63	7	2	73	6	3				M̄ → M	●	●	:	:	R	S
	COMA													43	2	1	Ā → A	●	●	:	:	R	S
	COMB													53	2	1	B̄ → B	●	●	:	:	R	S
Complement, 2's	NEG							60	7	2	70	6	3				00 - M → M	●	●	:	:	①	②
(Negate)	NEGA													40	2	1	00 - A → A	●	●	:	:	①	②
	NEGB													50	2	1	00 - B → B	●	●	:	:	①	②
Decimal Adjust, A	DAA													19	2	1	Converts Binary Add. of BCD Characters into BCD Format	●	●	:	:	:	③
Decrement	DEC							6A	7	2	7A	6	3				M - 1 → M	●	●	:	:	4	●
	DECA													4A	2	1	A - 1 → A	●	●	:	:	4	●
	DECB													5A	2	1	B - 1 → B	●	●	:	:	4	●
Exclusive OR	EORA	88	2	2	98	3	2	A8	5	2	B8	4	3				A ⊕ M → A	●	●	:	:	R	●
	EORB	C8	2	2	D8	3	2	E8	5	2	F8	4	3				B ⊕ M → B	●	●	:	:	R	●
Increment	INC							6C	7	2	7C	6	3				M + 1 → M	●	●	:	:	⑤	●
	INCA													4C	2	1	A + 1 → A	●	●	:	:	⑤	●
	INCB													5C	2	1	B + 1 → B	●	●	:	:	⑤	●
Load Acmltr	LDAA	86	2	2	96	3	2	A6	5	2	B6	4	3				M → A	●	●	:	:	R	●
	LDAB	C6	2	2	D6	3	2	E6	5	2	F6	4	3				M → B	●	●	:	:	R	●
Or, Inclusive	ORAA	8A	2	2	9A	3	2	AA	5	2	BA	4	3				A + M → A	●	●	:	:	R	●
	ORAB	CA	2	2	DA	3	2	EA	5	2	FA	4	3				B + M → B	●	●	:	:	R	●
Push Data	PSHA													36	4	1	A → M$_{SP}$, SP - 1 → SP	●	●	●	●	●	●
	PSHB													37	4	1	B → M$_{SP}$, SP - 1 → SP	●	●	●	●	●	●
Pull Data	PULA													32	4	1	SP + 1 → SP, M$_{SP}$ → A	●	●	●	●	●	●
	PULB													33	4	1	SP + 1 → SP, M$_{SP}$ → B	●	●	●	●	●	●
Rotate Left	ROL							69	7	2	79	6	3				M	●	●	:	:	⑥	:
	ROLA													49	2	1	A	●	●	:	:	⑥	:
	ROLB													59	2	1	B	●	●	:	:	⑥	:
Rotate Right	ROR							66	7	2	76	6	3				M	●	●	:	:	⑥	:
	RORA													46	2	1	A	●	●	:	:	⑥	:
	RORB													56	2	1	B	●	●	:	:	⑥	:
Shift Left, Arithmetic	ASL							68	7	2	78	6	3				M	●	●	:	:	⑥	:
	ASLA													48	2	1	A	●	●	:	:	⑥	:
	ASLB													58	2	1	B	●	●	:	:	⑥	:
Shift Right, Arithmetic	ASR							67	7	2	77	6	3				M	●	●	:	:	⑥	:
	ASRA													47	2	1	A	●	●	:	:	⑥	:
	ASRB													57	2	1	B	●	●	:	:	⑥	:
Shift Right, Logic	LSR							64	7	2	74	6	3				M	●	●	R	:	⑥	:
	LSRA													44	2	1	A	●	●	R	:	⑥	:
	LSRB													54	2	1	B	●	●	R	:	⑥	:
Store Acmltr	STAA				97	4	2	A7	6	2	B7	5	3				A → M	●	●	:	:	R	●
	STAB				D7	4	2	E7	6	2	F7	5	3				B → M	●	●	:	:	R	●
Subtract	SUBA	80	2	2	90	3	2	A0	5	2	B0	4	3				A - M → A	●	●	:	:	:	:
	SUBB	C0	2	2	D0	3	2	E0	5	2	F0	4	3				B - M → B	●	●	:	:	:	:
Subtract Acmltrs	SBA													10	2	1	A - B → A	●	●	:	:	:	:
Subtr with Carry	SBCA	82	2	2	92	3	2	A2	5	2	B2	4	3				A - M - C → A	●	●	:	:	:	:
	SBCB	C2	2	2	D2	3	2	E2	5	2	F2	4	3				B - M - C → B	●	●	:	:	:	:
Transfer Acmltrs	TAB													16	2	1	A → B	●	●	:	:	R	●
	TBA													17	2	1	B → A	●	●	:	:	R	●
Test, Zero or Minus	TST							6D	7	2	7D	6	3				M - 00	●	●	:	:	R	R
	TSTA													4D	2	1	A - 00	●	●	:	:	R	R
	TSTB													5D	2	1	B - 00	●	●	:	:	R	R
																		H	I	N	Z	V	C

LEGEND:

OP   Operation Code (Hexadecimal).
~   Number of MPU Cycles.
=   Number of Program Bytes.
+   Arithmetic Plus.
-    Arithmetic Minus.
·   Boolean AND.
M$_{SP}$ Contents of memory location pointed to be Stack Pointer.

+   Boolean Inclusive OR.
⊙   Boolean Exclusive OR.
M̄   Complement of M.
→   Transfer Into.
0   Bit = Zero.
00   Byte = Zero.

CONDITION CODE SYMBOLS:

H   Half carry from bit 3.
I   Interrupt mask
N   Negative (sign bit)
Z   Zero (byte)
V   Overflow, 2's complement
C   Carry from bit 7
R   Reset Always
S   Set Always
:   Test and set if true, cleared otherwise
●   Not Affected

Note - Accumulator addressing mode instructions are included in the column for IMPLIED addressing

Fig. A4.7(a) 6800 Accumulator and memory instructions (reproduced from Motorola Manual with kind permission of Motorola (UK) Ltd)

INDEX REGISTER AND STACK MANIPULATION INSTRUCTIONS

POINTER OPERATIONS	MNEMONIC	IMMED			DIRECT			INDEX			EXTND			IMPLIED			BOOLEAN/ARITHMETIC OPERATION	H	I	N	Z	V	C
		OP	~	#	OP	~	#	OP	~	#	OP	~	#	OP	~	#				5	4	3	2	1	0
																		H	I	N	Z	V	C
Compare Index Reg	CPX	8C	3	3	9C	4	2	AC	6	2	BC	5	3				$X_H - M, X_L - (M+1)$	•	•	⑦	:	⑦	•
Decrement Index Reg	DEX													09	4	1	$X - 1 \to X$	•	•	•	:	•	•
Decrement Stack Pntr	DES													34	4	1	$SP - 1 \to SP$	•	•	•	:	•	•
Increment Index Reg	INX													08	4	1	$X + 1 \to X$	•	•	•	:	•	•
Increment Stack Pntr	INS													31	4	1	$SP + 1 \to SP$	•	•	•	:	•	•
Load Index Reg	LDX	CE	3	3	DE	4	2	EE	6	2	FE	5	3				$M \to X_H, (M+1) \to X_L$	•	•	⑨	:	R	•
Load Stack Pntr	LDS	8E	3	3	9E	4	2	AE	6	2	BE	5	3				$M \to SP_H, (M+1) \to SP_L$	•	•	⑨	:	R	•
Store Index Reg	STX				DF	5	2	EF	7	2	FF	6	3				$X_H \to M, X_L \to (M+1)$	•	•	⑨	:	R	•
Store Stack Pntr	STS				9F	5	2	AF	7	2	BF	6	3				$SP_H \to M, SP_L \to (M+1)$	•	•	⑨	:	R	•
Indx Reg → Stack Pntr	TXS													35	4	1	$X - 1 \to SP$	•	•	•	:	•	•
Stack Pntr → Indx Reg	TSX													30	4	1	$SP + 1 \to X$	•	•	•	:	•	•

JUMP AND BRANCH INSTRUCTIONS

OPERATIONS	MNEMONIC	RELATIVE			INDEX			EXTND			IMPLIED			BRANCH TEST	H	I	N	Z	V	C
		OP	~	#	OP	~	#	OP	~	#	OP	~	#		5	4	3	2	1	0
															H	I	N	Z	V	C
Branch Always	BRA	20	4	2										None	•	•	•	•	•	•
Branch If Carry Clear	BCC	24	4	2										$C = 0$	•	•	•	•	•	•
Branch If Carry Set	BCS	25	4	2										$C = 1$	•	•	•	•	•	•
Branch If = Zero	BEQ	27	4	2										$Z = 1$	•	•	•	•	•	•
Branch If ≥ Zero	BGE	2C	4	2										$N \oplus V = 0$	•	•	•	•	•	•
Branch If > Zero	BGT	2E	4	2										$Z + (N \oplus V) = 0$	•	•	•	•	•	•
Branch If Higher	BHI	22	4	2										$C + Z = 0$	•	•	•	•	•	•
Branch If ≤ Zero	BLE	2F	4	2										$Z + (N \oplus V) = 1$	•	•	•	•	•	•
Branch If Lower Or Same	BLS	23	4	2										$C + Z = 1$	•	•	•	•	•	•
Branch If < Zero	BLT	2D	4	2										$N \oplus V = 1$	•	•	•	•	•	•
Branch If Minus	BMI	2B	4	2										$N = 1$	•	•	•	•	•	•
Branch If Not Equal Zero	BNE	26	4	2										$Z = 0$	•	•	•	•	•	•
Branch If Overflow Clear	BVC	28	4	2										$V = 0$	•	•	•	•	•	•
Branch If Overflow Set	BVS	29	4	2										$V = 1$	•	•	•	•	•	•
Branch If Plus	BPL	2A	4	2										$N = 0$	•	•	•	•	•	•
Branch To Subroutine	BSR	8D	8	2											•	•	•	•	•	•
Jump	JMP				6E	4	2	7E	3	3				See Special Operations	•	•	•	•	•	•
Jump To Subroutine	JSR				AD	8	2	BD	9	3					•	•	•	•	•	•
No Operation	NOP										01	2	1	Advances Prog. Cntr. Only	•	•	⑩			
Return From Interrupt	RTI										3B	10	1							
Return From Subroutine	RTS										39	5	1		•	•	•	•	•	•
Software Interrupt	SWI										3F	12	1	See Special Operations	•	•	•	•	•	•
Wait for Interrupt	WAI										3E	9	1		•	⑪	•	•	•	•

CONDITION CODE REGISTER MANIPULATION INSTRUCTIONS

OPERATIONS	MNEMONIC	IMPLIED			BOOLEAN OPERATION	H	I	N	Z	V	C
		OP	~	#		5	4	3	2	1	0
						H	I	N	Z	V	C
Clear Carry	CLC	0C	2	1	$0 \to C$	•	•	•	•	•	R
Clear Interrupt Mask	CLI	0E	2	1	$0 \to I$	•	R	•	•	•	•
Clear Overflow	CLV	0A	2	1	$0 \to V$	•	•	•	•	R	•
Set Carry	SEC	0D	2	1	$1 \to C$	•	•	•	•	•	S
Set Interrupt Mask	SEI	0F	2	1	$1 \to I$	•	S	•	•	•	•
Set Overflow	SEV	0B	2	1	$1 \to V$	•	•	•	•	S	•
Acmltr A → CCR	TAP	06	2	1	$A \to CCR$	⑫					
CCR → Acmltr A	TPA	07	2	1	$CCR \to A$	•	•	•	•	•	•

CONDITION CODE REGISTER NOTES:

(Bit set if test is true and cleared otherwise)

1 (Bit V) Test: Result = 10000000?
2 (Bit C) Test: Result = 00000000?
3 (Bit C) Test: Decimal value of most significant BCD Character greater than nine? (Not cleared if previously set.)
4 (Bit V) Test: Operand = 10000000 prior to execution?
5 (Bit V) Test: Operand = 01111111 prior to execution?
6 (Bit V) Test: Set equal to result of N⊕C after shift has occurred.
7 (Bit N) Test: Sign bit of most significant (MS) byte = 1?
8 (Bit V) Test: 2's complement overflow from subtraction of MS bytes?
9 (Bit N) Test: Result less than zero? (Bit 15 = 1)
10 (All) Load Condition Code Register from Stack. (See Special Operations)
11 (Bit I) Set when interrupt occurs. If previously set, a Non-Maskable Interrupt is required to exit the wait state.
12 (All) Set according to the contents of Accumulator A.

Fig. A4.7(b) 6800 Index, stack, control and condition flag instructions (reproduced from Motorola Manual with kind permission of Motorola (UK) Ltd)

Appendix 5 **Programmable input/output**

The following figures show how the 8155/6 and the 8755 combination memory and I/O devices can be programmed for setting up the input/output. Finally the programming of the 6820 programmable I/O chip is given.

8755 Input/output ports

Each bit of the two 8-bit ports may be programmed individually by setting or clearing the appropriate bit in the direction register. A logic '0' in the direction register will set the corresponding bit of the port as an input circuit.

The address details are shown in Fig. A2.2.

Example

The following program sets Port A as all output and the top 4 bits of Port B as input and the bottom 4 bits as output.

MVI	A, 0FFH	;	All bits output
OUT	0AH	;	Direction reg. A
MVI	A, 0FH	;	Bit 0–3 out, 4–7 in
OUT	0BH	;	Direction reg. B

Fig. A5.1 Setting up ports on the 8755

8155/6 Combination input/output and timer

Input/output ports

The 8155/6 has two 8-bit ports, A and B, and one 6-bit port, C. They are programmed so that each port is either all input or all output by writing a code into the control register (see Fig. A2.2 for Address details).

The programming details are elaborated below.

Bit 0	of control word— 0; A input, 1; A output
Bit 1	of control word— 0; B input, 1; B output
Bits 2 and 3	of control word—00; C input, 11; C output

Fig. A5.2 I/O port programming on the 8155/6 The two other combinations of bits 2 and 3 provide a control mode of operation on port C. Details may be found in the data books

Timer

The timer is 14 bits long and, in the example cited in Appendix 2, is connected to an input clock of 3.072 MHz. The timer registers may be loaded with a count and this will be decremented to zero, which is called the terminal count. The action of the timer at terminal count is dictated by mode bits. The operation of the timer is controlled by command bits written into the control register. The program can examine the status of the timer by reading the status register.

Bits	7 6	Of the control register
	0 0	Do nothing
	0 1	Stop immediately
	1 0	Stop after terminal count
	1 1	Start timer after loading mode bits and counter value

Fig. A5.3 Command programming

Note that the timer command bits are in the same register as the I/O control bits. The latter must not be changed when issuing commands to the timer. The example below gives a further illustration.

Bits	13–0	14 bit binary count value
Bits	15 14	Mode control
	0 0	Single period square wave
	0 1	Continuous square wave
	1 0	Single pulse at terminal count
	1 1	Continuous pulse stream

Fig. A5.4 Mode and count programming

The mode bits control the waveform at the timer output pin. The waveform starts at a logic '1' level, the pulses going to logic '0' then returning one clock period later, while the square wave is low for the second half of the time period.

In continuous modes the timer automatically reloads the original count value at the terminal count. If a new count value has been written then this value will be used. Changing the value near the terminal count in continuous mode is dangerous since two bytes must be written and the counter may be loaded after the first and so operate with an erroneous value.

Status information

The timer status bit is located in bit 6 of the status word. It is set by the occurrence of terminal count. The bit is cleared by reading the status register.

The status register is also used when port C is used in control mode. Care must be taken when reading the control signals since the status bit will be cleared if set.

Examples of programming the 8155/6

Because of the problems of using this device some examples of programs are provided as illustrations.

```
MVI    A, 02H;            A in, B out, C in, timer NOP
STA    PORTSTATUS
OUT    10H;               8155/6 control register
```

Fig. A5.5 Programming the 8155/6 input/output ports

The location PORTSTATUS contains the current programming state. This must be used when operating the timer device. An example is given below.

```
SINGSW        EQU   00H       ;   define counter
CONTSW        EQU   40H       ;   mode labels
SINGPL        EQU   80H       ;   for later use
CONTPL        EQU   0C0 H     ;   remember bits 6 + 7 used
STARTTIM      EQU   0C0 H     ;   label for start command
              .
              .
              .

              MVI   A, 5
              OUT   14 H          ;   load timer count
              MVI   A, 2 + SINGPL ;   With 517 in single
              OUT   15 H          ;   pulse mode
              LDA   PORTSTATUS    ;   read current command,
              ANI   3FH           ;   clear timer bits,
              ORI   STARTTIM      ;   add start command
              STA   PORTSTATUS    ;   and return to memory
              OUT   10 H          ;   start timer.
              .
              .
              .
```

Fig. A5.6 Programming the 8155/6 timer

The 6820 programmable I/O device

As the first of its type the 6820 programmable input/output port device deserves a brief mention. Like the ports on the 8755 each bit of the two 8-bit ports may be programmed. An example program and the corresponding address map are given in Figs A5.7 and A5.8. These are referred to in the worked examples in Appendix 6.

Assembly code			Comments	Address	machine code	
LDA	A	#28	SET CONTROL WORDS	0100	86	28
STA	A	8009	FOR WRITING	0102	B7	8009
STA	A	800B	DIRECTION TO	0105	B7	800B
STA	A	800D	PORTS 1 to 4.	0108	B7	800D
STA	A	800F		010B	B7	800F
LDA	A	#00	SET PORTS 3 AND 4	010E	86	00
STA	A	800B	TO INPUT	0110	B7	8008
STA	A	800C	MODE	0113	B7	800C
LDA	A	#FF		0116	86	FF
STA	A	800A	SET PORTS 1 AND 2	0118	B7	800A
STA	A	800E	TO OUTPUT MODE	011B	B7	800E
LDA	A	#2C	SET CONTROL	011E	86	20
STA	A	8009	WORDS FOR	0120	B7	8009
STA	A	800B	NORMAL ACCESS	0123	B7	800B
STA	A	800D	TO PORTS 1 AND 4	0126	B7	800D
STA	A	800F		0129	B7	800F
RTS				012C	39	

(Hexadecimal used throughout)

Fig. A5.7 Subroutine for programming the 6820

Address Hexadecimal		
8008	Port A	
8009	Control A	PIA 1
800A	Port B	
800B	Control B	
800C	Port A	
800D	Control A	PIA 2
800E	Port B	
800F	Control B	

Fig. A5.8 Address map of 6820 used above

Appendix 6 **Worked examples**

Introduction

As with most design activities, program design is very subjective, and a computer program to perform a specified task will reflect greatly the thoughts and ideas of the designer. Thus, no two solutions independently derived for a given example are likely to be identical; the solutions to the four examples presented below are typical—not the best—and hopefully, not the worst. That is not to say, however, that good design procedure is arbitrary—far from it—and Chapter 9 describes principles which can prove invaluable, especially for large programming projects.

One interpretation of design procedure is to view each stage as producing a different *form* of definition or description; often, a textual description is the starting point, followed perhaps by flow diagrams or their equivalent, right down to the machine code. Each form defines the system but at a new and usually more detailed level, encompassing new design decisions. For the examples below, textual descriptions are followed by flow diagrams, memory maps, and assembly codes. These last three are tools of the designer, used to transform from the functional definition through to the program and hardware system, and record the important decisions. Production of the assembly code is the last stage of the design. Here one brings together the software in the form of a program and the hardware in terms of the processor instruction set, the input/output allocation and memory requirements. The combination is then tested. The memory maps indicate areas reserved for the main programs and sub-routines, the data, general work space, specific job allocations to registers and memory locations, and input/output requirements.

The development systems used for the solutions are described in Chapter 11, and more details of the individual modules are given in Appendix 2. The solutions for the 6800 and 8080 all assume the first 256 memory locations (0000 up to 00FF hexadecimal and 000.000 to 000.377 octal respectively) are reserved for the stack. For 6800, the input/output subroutine SETPIA occupies the area 0100 hexadecimal up to 013F hexadecimal. This subroutine, which initializes the input/output (see Appendix 5) is called at the beginning of each program, immediately after loading the stack pointer. This allocation is not shown explicitly in the memory maps. The numbering system for the 6800 is hexadecimal, and for the 8080 split octal.

The I/O registers for the 8080/5 examples are hardwired and no programming is required. It is suggested that readers try to modify the solutions to run on the system described in Appendix 2.

Four examples are given, a waveform generator, data logger, traffic light controller and analog to digital converter using a DAC.

Example 1: Waveform generator

Specification
Display repetitively on an oscilloscope the ramp functions illustrated in Fig. A6.1.

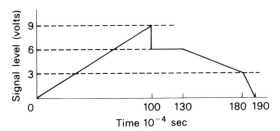

Fig. A6.1 Specification of waveform generator

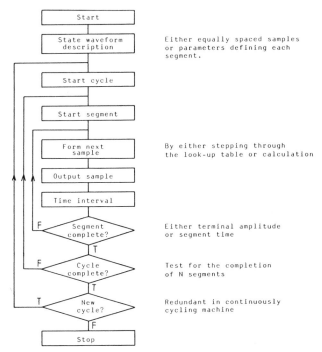

Fig. A6.2 Flow diagram for waveform generator

Solution

How is the waveform to be generated? Alternatives include either a look-up table approach, similar to that used for the sinewave in Chapter 4, or a simple calculation for each sample along the time course. The first flow diagram (Fig. A6.2) reflects the first level of design; note that the two alternatives are still open. However, the second flow diagram (Fig. A6.3)

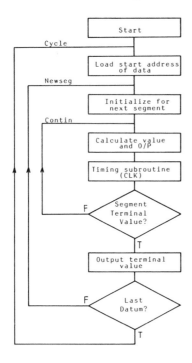

Fig. A6.3 Second flow diagram for waveform generator

indicates the decision that an appropriate increment is to be added to the accumulator and then output to form the ramps. The waveform is split up into four segments, and parameters defining each are stored in a data block. The program switches from one set of data to the next as each segment is complete. The second flow diagram details the principal actions of the program, and it is from this that the assembly codes are derived. The memory map for the three solutions is shown in Fig. A6.4 and the data structure in Fig. A6.5.

The assembly program in Fig. A6.6 is for the 8080/5: note that at the beginning of each new segment the four relevant parameters are transferred from memory to the internal registers to give easy access. The time loop is 22 clock cycles, or 11 μs at 0.5 μs clock period for the processor. The

8080 and 8085	Memory Map	6800
Page.line (Octal)		(Hexadecimal)
001.000 ⎫	Main program and subroutine	⎧ 0140
001.100 ⎬	Table of segment definitions	⎧ 0180
001.140 ⎭		⎩ 01A0

Registers		Special locations
A	O/P sample	
B	Time interval	
C	Increment for accumulator	
D	Segment final value	
H	Data block	Index
L	Address	Register
I/O		Memory mapped
Port 12	8 bits to DAC	800A

Fig. A6.4 Memory map for waveform generator

Location (split octal)	Value (octal)	Function	Segment Output
001.100	177	start value	
1	008	Time step	
2	377	step value $(+, 0, -)$	
3	015	End value	
4	063		
5	377		
6	000		
7	063		
10	063		
11	014		
12	001		
13	132		
14	132		
15	002		
16	001		
17	177		

Fig. A6.5 Table for function generator

time values in the table shown in Fig. A6.5 assume this clock calculation. (Deduce the error in time in each segment from the values given in Fig. A6.5.) The DAC used is that shown in Fig. A2.4, i.e., 8-bit input with output in the range +10V to −10V. Remember −1 step value is 377 in octal (i.e., all 1's in 2's complement).

Another version of the program is shown for the 8080/85 in Fig. A6.7. The algorithm is based on indexed addressing but uses a form of pseudo-index addressing. For while the version which utilizes the four internal registers is compact and efficient, the approach would prove very difficult in the event of the segment definitions requiring more than the four parameters. However, with the indexing method, the number of stored parameters could be extended readily.

	Assembly Code		Comments
	LXI	SP, 000.377	Set stack pointer
	MVI	M, 001	Address of first
CYCLE:	MVI	L, 100	data
NEWSEG:	MOV	A,M	Acc A ← initial value
	INR	L	
	MOV	B,M	Register B ← time interval
	INR	L	
	MOV	C,M	Register C ← increment (+ or −)
	INR	L	
	MOV	D,M	Register D ← final value
	INR	L	
	OUT	14	O/P initial value
CONTIN	ADD	C	Add increment (+ or −)
	OUT	14	O/P to port (12)
	MOV	E,B	Form time
	CALL	CLK	interval
	CMP	D	Test for segment termination
	JNZ	CONTIN	False: continue
	MVI	A, 120	Acc A ← final data address +1
	CMP	L	Data exhausted ?
	JNZ	NEWSEG	False: New segment
	JMP	CYCLE	Start new cycle
* Subroutine			
CLK:	NOP		No operations to
	NOP		give time interval
	DCR	E	unit
	JNZ	CLK	
	RET		

(Octal used in assembly code)

Fig. A6.6 Waveform generator 8080

Example 2: Data logger

Specification

A data logging system is required to store one thousand samples from a continuous waveform, at a sampling rate ranging from 500 Hz up to 5 kHz.

A flow diagram of the solution, a memory map and the program listings are shown in Figs. A6.8–11 respectively.

	Assembly Code		Comments
	LXI	SP, 000.377	Set stack pointer
CYCLE:	LXI	H, 100.001	H,L ← start address of data
NEWSEG:	MOV	A,	Acc A ←initial value
	XCHG		H,L ⟷ D,E
CONTIN:	OUT	14	O/P to port 14
	LXI	H, 001.000	Load immediate H,L
	DAD	D	H,L ← H,L + D,E
	MOV	B,M	B ← time interval
	CALL	CLK	Form time interval
	INX	H	Increment data address
	ADD	M	Acc A←Acc A + increment
	INX	H	Increment data address
	CMP	M	Segment terminal amplitude?
	JNZ	CONTIN	False: → CONTIN
	OUT	14	O/P terminal amplitude
	INX	H	Increment data address
	MOV	A,L	Is data
	CPI	120	exhausted?
	JNZ	NEWSEG	False: → NEWSEG
	JMP	CYCLE	Start new cycle
* Subroutine			
CLK:	NOP		No operations to form
	NOP		time interval
	DCR	B	
	JNZ	CLK	
	RET		

(Octal used throughout)

The solution uses a form of pseudo-index addressing, where register pair D and E is used as a global or base address and the pair H and L as a local modified address.

Fig. A6.7 Waveform generator 8080 with pseudo-index addressing

Equalizing inter-sample time

Clearly, it is important that the samples are regularly spaced in time. For the 8080, since the test for the upper address limit has to be performed in two stages (m.s.b. and l.s.b. separately), it is necessary to include the dummy operations following the label EQTI. This situation does not arise with the 6800 version (Fig. A6.11).

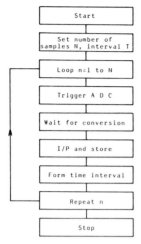

Fig. A6.8 Flow diagram for data logger

8080	Memory map	6800
Page.Line (Octal)		(Hexadecimal)
001.000 ⎱ 002.000 ⎰	Main program and subroutine	⎧ 0140 ⎨ ⎩ 0200
002.000 ⎱ 006.000 ⎰	I/P Data	⎰ ⎱ 0600
Registers		Special locations
D	Subroutine CLK	Acc B
E	Time interval	01FF
H ⎱ L ⎰	Current Data address	⎰ Index ⎱ Register
I/O		Memory mapped
Port 2	8 bits to ADC	8008
Port 8	1 bit to trigger	800A

Fig. A6.9 Memory map for data logger

Flexibility

While both programs meet the specification, they could be enhanced to give greater flexibility and simpler operation. As they stand, to change either the sampling rate or the total number of samples, instructions in the program have to be changed. But before modifications are made, one should ask whether flexibility is really necessary. Is the instrument to be used invariably at one speed and for 1000 samples? If so, the solutions given are the simplest and sufficient. Modifications aimed at improving the operation can prove very costly in program development and testing.

	Assembly code		Comments
	LXI	SP, 000.377	Set stack pointer
	MVI	E, 001	Register E ← time interval
	LXI	H, 002.000	H,L ← start address of data
NEXT:	MVI	A, 001	Trigger
	OUT	10	ADC
	NOP		Wait for conversion
	IN	2	I/P from ADC
	MOV	M,A	Store sample
	INX	H	Increment data address
	MOV	D,E	Form time
	CALL	CLK	interval
	MOV	A,H	Compare m.s.b. with
	CPI	006	upper limit
	JNZ	EQTI	False: return via EQTI
	MOV	A,L	Compare l.s.b. with
	CPI	350	upper limit
	JNZ	NEXT	False: return for next sample
	HLT		Stop
EQTI:	MOV	A,L	Equalize time for
	CPI	0	l.s.b. comparison
	JMP	NEXT	
* Subroutine			
CLK:	DCR	D	Control time
	JNZ	CLK	interval between
	RET		samples
	(Octal used throughout)		

Fig. A6.10 Data logger 8080

	Assembly code		Comments
	LDS	#00FF	Set stack pointer
	JSR	SETPIA	I/O
	LDAB	#01	Acc B ← time interval
	LDX	#01FF	Index register ← data address
	STAB	0,X	Store time interval
NEXT:	LDAA	#01	Trigger
	STAA	800A	ADC
	LDAB	01FF	Acc B ← time interval ⎫ ADC time to
	INX		Increment data address ⎬ convert
	LDAA	8080	⌃ :c A ← I/P sample
	STAA	0,X	ore sample
	JSR	CLK	:rement data address
	CPX	#05E8	1000 limit? i.e. 0200 + $(1000)_{10}$
	BNE	NEXT	False: → next sample
	SWI		Halt
* Subroutine			
CLK:	DECB		Control time interval
	BNE	CLK	between samples
	RTS		
	(Hexadecimal used in assembly code)		

Fig. A6.11 Data logger 6800

Here, of course, it is very simple to make the parameters variable at run time by using either special locations or input statements. Considering the 8080, the instructions to change are, for the sampling interval:

MVI	E,01	to	LDA	007.000	or	IN	W1
			MOV	E,A		MOV	E,A

and for the number of samples:

MOV	A,H	to	LDA	007.002	or	IN	W2 (MSB)
CPI	006		CMP	H		CMP	H

and

MOV	A,L	to	LDA	007.001	or	IN	W3 (LSB)
CPI	350		CMP	L		CMP	L

In the first alternative, the special locations (007.000, 007.001 and 007.002) are used to store the parameters; these are set by the user at run time, and the program accesses them directly. The second approach implies the use of input devices—a digital switch or teletype—and permits the number of samples to be changed during the logging process. These are simple, and may be useful modifications, but one step further—for example, permitting the input parameters to be given in decimal rather than octal—proves that enhancement generally is not quite so simple. This case is left for the reader to examine.

Sampling rate
8080: Number of clock cycles $= 104 + 15\ e$.
where $e = $ contents of register $(E)_{10}$ for $0 < (E) < 256$
and when Register $E = 0$, $e = 256$
6800: It is a simple exercise to check the sampling rates in terms of machine clock cycles, as has been done for the 8080. A more accurate calibration could be achieved by running the program and plotting a calibration curve.

Example 3: Traffic-light controller

Specification
Design a traffic light controller for a single intersection of two roads to provide the following features:

Abbreviations
Lights North/South denoted by $(RAG)_N$ Pads North/South denoted by P_N
Lights East/West denoted by $(RAG)_E$ Pads East/West denoted by P_E
R is red light, A is amber light and G is green light.

	State	*Time in state* (seconds)

Arbitrary starting state; stays in
this state until P_N $\qquad$ $(R\bar{A}\bar{G})_N$ $\quad (\bar{R}\bar{A}G)_E$

It then changes, following the
sequence: $\qquad$ $(R\bar{A}\bar{G})_N$ $\quad (\bar{R}\bar{A}G)_E$

If P_E occurs in this sequence,
it is ignored.

Stays in this state until P_E

It then changes, following the
sequence:

If P_N occurs during this
sequence, it is ignored.

State (N)	State (E)	Time
$(R\bar{A}\bar{G})_N$	$(\bar{R}A\bar{G})_E$	6
$(R\bar{A}\bar{G})_N$	$(\bar{R}\bar{A}G)_E$	2
$(RA\bar{G})_N$	$(\bar{R}\bar{A}G)_E$	6
$(\bar{R}\bar{A}G)_N$	$(\bar{R}\bar{A}G)_E$	18 (minimum)
$(\bar{R}\bar{A}G)_N$	$(R\bar{A}\bar{G})_E$	
$(\bar{R}A\bar{G})_N$	$(R\bar{A}\bar{G})_E$	6
$(\bar{R}\bar{A}G)_N$	$(R\bar{A}\bar{G})_E$	2
$(\bar{R}\bar{A}G)_N$	$(RA\bar{G})_E$	6
$(R\bar{A}\bar{G})_N$	$(\bar{R}\bar{A}G)_E$	18 (minimum)

While there is obvious symmetry in the two transition sequences
(interchange of lights), this does not appear to be useful immediately; the
solution below assigns to each of the six lights one bit of an output port
(port 12), and then identifies the bit pattern for each state. The flow
diagram, memory map and program listing are shown in Figs A6.12–
A6.14. (Note: Pad N/S is connected to bit 0 while pad E/W is connected to
bit 2)

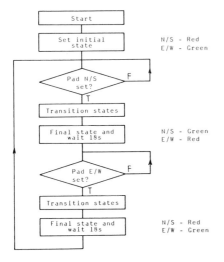

Fig. A6.12 Flow diagram for traffic-light controller

Memory Map 8080		Registers
	Main Program	B
Page 1	and Subroutine	C Subroutine CLK
		D
		E Argument for CLK

I/O

Input: Port 2—1 bit to N/S pad; Port 4—1 bit to E/W pad.
Out: Port 10—6 bits to the lights as follows:

Green E/W to bit 0	Green N/S to bit 3
Amber E/W to bit 1	Amber N/S to bit 4
Red E/W to bit 2	Red N/S to bit 5

Fig. A6.13 Memory map for traffic-light controller

Example 4: Analog to Digital Conversion

Specification

Given a digital to analog converter, a comparator, and a sample/hold circuit (see Appendix 2 for details), implement an analog to digital converter and calculate the time for one conversion. The result is required as a 2's complement signed integer of 8 bits.

A basic flow diagram is shown in Fig. A6.15. Notice that the conversion algorithm is unspecified at this stage. The operation 'convert data' changes the offset binary code of the DAC into 2's complement.

Before elaborating any further, the algorithm must be specified. Alternatives are successive approximation or counter-ramp. The former consists of making successive binary approximations, starting at the most significant bit, until all 8 bits have been tested.

A flow chart of the elaboration only is shown in Fig. A6.16. A solution for the counter ramp is shown in Fig. A6.17.

A memory map of the two solutions is shown in Fig. A6.18, and the program listing is shown in Fig. A6.19.

Timing

The analog circuitry will take a finite time to respond to new inputs; say the DAC takes 4 μs to settle to 1 l.s.b. accuracy, and the comparator will take 1 μs to respond. The time between the output order to the DAC and the input from the comparator must be sufficient for both to settle. These two instructions take 4 μs for a 1 μs processor clock cycle time, and this assumes that the output and input occur at the same point in the instruction cycle. For the DAC and comparator specified, this is too short, and dummy instructions are needed: 2 NOP orders between STA and LDA should be sufficient.

Assembly code			Comments
	LXI	SP, 000.377	Set stack pointer
START:	MVI	A, 041	Acc A ← $(100001)_2$
	OUT	12	O/P R$\bar{A}\bar{G}$ R$\bar{A}\bar{G}$
SEQ1:	IN	2	
	ANI	001	
	JNZ	S$\bar{E}$Q1	
	MVI	A, 042	Acc A ← $(100010)_2$
	OUT	12	O/P R$\bar{A}$$\bar{G}$ R$\bar{A}$G
	MVI	E, 006	Register E ← 6
	CALL	CLOCK	Form time interval 6s
	MVI	A, 044	Acc A ← $(100100)_2$
	OUT	12	O/P R$\bar{A}\bar{G}$ R$\bar{A}\bar{G}$
	MVI	E, 002	Form time
	CALL	CLOCK	interval 2s
	MVI	A, 064	Acc A ← $(110100)_2$
	OUT	12	O/P RA$\bar{G}$ R$\bar{A}\bar{G}$
	MVI	E, 006	Form time
	CALL	CLOCK	interval 6 s
	MVI	A, 014	Acc A ← $(001100)_2$
	OUT	12	O/P R$\bar{A}\bar{G}$R$\bar{A}\bar{G}$
	MVI	E, 022	Form time
	CALL	CLOCK	interval 18 s
SEQ2:	IN	4	
	ANI	004	
	JNZ	SEQ2	
	MVI	A, 024	
	OUT	12	
	MVI	E, 006	
	CALL	CLOCK	
	MVI	A, 044	
	OUT	12	
	MVI	E, 002	
	CALL	CLOCK	
	MVI	A, 046	
	OUT	12	
	MVI	E, 006	
	CALL	CLOCK	
	MVI	A, 041	
	OUT	12	
	MVI	E, 022	
	CALL	CLOCK	
	JMP	SEQ1	
* Subroutine			
CLOCK:	MVI	B, 002	
CLK1:	MVI	C, 000	
CLK2:	MVI	D, 000	
CLK3:	DCR	D	
	JNZ	CLK3	Subroutine to give units of 1 second
	DCR	C	
	JNZ	CLK2	i.e. delay = e seconds
	DCR	B	
	JNZ	CLK1	e = (Register E)$_{10}$
	DCR	E	$0 < e \leq 256$
	JNZ	CLOCK	
	RET		

(Octal used in assembly code)

Fig. A6.14 Traffic-light controller 8080

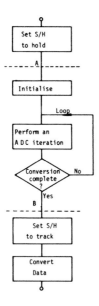

Fig. A6.15 Flow diagram for ADC

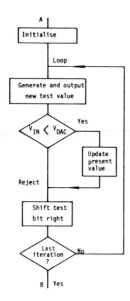

Fig. A6.16 Successive approximation—ADC subroutine

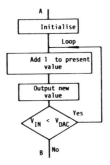

Fig. A6.17 Counter ramp—ADC subroutine

6800 Memory map Successive approx.	Address Hexadecimal	Counter-ramp
Program and subroutines	$\begin{Bmatrix} 0200 \\ 02FF \end{Bmatrix}$	Program and subroutines
Test bit	0300	
	Registers	
Test datum	A	Current datum
Current datum	B	Work register
	I/O	
(OUT) S/H control (bit 0)	800A	(OUT) S/H control (bit 0)
(OUT) DAC (bits 0–7)	800E	(OUT) DAC (bits 0–7)
(IN) Comparator (bit 0)	8008	(IN) Comparator (bit 0)

Fig. A6.18 Memory map for ADC

Another timing problem occurs with the sample-hold device which will have a minimum track time. Having converted one sample, sufficient time must elapse before converting the next. This depends on the program using the ADC routine.

Conversion time
The time to perform an 8-bit conversion is dependent on the locus of control through the loop. The longest path occurs if the result is 11111111, the shortest for 00000000, i.e. 302 μs and 270 μs respectively for the successive approximation subroutine. A similar calculation can be carried out for the counter-ramp.

Assembly code		Comments
LDS	#00FF	Initialize stack pointer
JSR	SETPIA	Initialize I/O
LDAA	#00	Set sample hold
STAA	800A	to hold
JSR	ADC	Call ADC algorithm
LDAA	#01	Set sample hold
STAA	800A	to track
CMPB	#80	Convert offset
BEQ	TEND	binary results
SUBB	#01	to
EORB	#7F	2's complement
BRA	FIN	and return
TEND: LDAB	#00	
FIN: RTS		

Successive approximation solution

ADC:	LDAA	#80	Initialize most
	STAA	TSTBIT	significant test bit
	CLRB		Initialize current value (Reg. B)
LOOP:	TBA		Generate new
	ORA	TSTBIT	test datum
	STAA	800E	Output to DAC ⎫ See note on timing.
	LDAA	8008	Input comparator value ⎭
	BITA	#01	Test for one
	BEQ	REJECT	Jump if zero
	ORAB	TSTBIT	Up-date value
REJECT:	ROR	TSTBIT	Shift test bit
	BCC	LOOP	Jump if not last iteration
	RTS		Return

Counter ramp solution

ADC:	CLRA		Initialize current value
LOOP:	INCA		Add 1 to current value
	STAA	800E	Out to DAC ⎫ See note on timing.
	LDAA	8008	Input comparator value ⎭
	BITB	#01	Test for one
	BEQ	LOOP	Repeat if zero
	RTS		Return

(Hexadecimal used throughout)

Fig. A6.19 ADC—6800

Glossary

Accumulator: A register in which the result of an arithmetic operation is deposited. Frequently part of the arithmetic unit of the computer.

ADC: Analog to Digital Converter is a component which produces a digital representation of an analogue voltage.

Addressing modes: Different methods for specifying the address of an operand to be used in an instruction. Much of the power of a processor depends on the addressing modes available. Common ones are:

> *Immediate*: The operand is in the instruction, usually the 2nd byte for 8-bit and the 2nd and 3rd byte for 16-bit operands.
> *Direct*: The instruction contains the address of the operand.
> *Indirect*: The instruction contains the address of a register or memory location that contains the address of the operand.
> *Indexed*: The operand address is formed by adding two operand addresses together.
> *Relative*: Indexed addressing where one of the addresses is the value of the program counter.

Assembler: The program which translates from mnemonic code to machine code.

BCD: Binary Coded Decimal is a method of representation where four bits are used to represent each decimal digit in the number.

Bit: Binary digit. The basic unit of information in a computer, having two possible values, represented by 0 and 1.

Bus: A common set of signals that interconnect many devices so that any device may communicate to any other.

Byte: A unit of information normally comprising of 8 bits.

CAM: Content Addressable Memory is a memory whose locations are identified by their content, rather than their address.

Code: A representation of information.

Compiler: A program which translates a high-level language into a low-level language.

Condition flags: Single bits which 'remember' the result of the previous operation. Flags are normally used to indicate zero, carry, sign, over-flow, etc.

CPU: Central Processing Unit, the unit which co-ordinates and controls the activities of all the other units and performs all the logical and arithmetic processes to be applied to data. It comprises internal memory, arithmetic unit, and a control section.

Cross-: Software which runs on one computer producing output which will run on another, e.g. cross-assembler.

DAC: Digital to Analog Converter is a component which produces a voltage proportional to a binary number which is presented at its input.

Development system: The computer system on which is carried out both program and hardware development usually for microcomputer based product.

Direct addressing: See Addressing modes.

Disk: A flat magnetic medium for storing programs and data. Disk drives for both fixed and removable disks are available. An essential part of a development system.

DMA: Direct Memory Access, a technique by which data may be transferred to and from main memory without involving the central processing unit.

ECL: Emitter Coupled Logic, a high-speed logic family.

Floppy disk: A low-cost flexible disk medium now extremely popular in microcomputer development systems.

Flowchart: A graphical representation of the interaction between parts of a problem.

Full decoding: The decoding of address lines to generate enable signals for memories so that a single unique code selects a single block of memory (see partial decoding).

Functional memory: Equivalent to a Programmable Logic Array (PLA).

Hardware: That part of a computer system implemented by electronic circuitry.

Hexadecimal: A number system based on the radix 16, i.e. 0, 1, 2, 3, 4, 5, 6, 7, 8, 9, A, B, C, D, E, F.

High-level language: A language in which each statement corresponds to several machine code instructions. Statements bear some resemblance to spoken language.

Host computer: The machine on which program development is carried out for a different, target, computer.

Image memory: The memory of a processor that is connected to peripheral devices, so presenting a digital image of the peripheral system to the processor.

Immediate addressing: See Addressing modes.

Index register: A register which holds a modifier to be used indirectly to access data normally in a table.

Indexed addressing: See Addressing modes.

Indirect addressing: See Addressing modes.

Instruction: The bit pattern which drives the 'central processing unit'

(CPU) comprising an operation code and (possibly) some operands.

Instruction set: The repertoire of operations available from a particular computer.

Interpreter: A program which directly executes instructions in a given language on some specified hardware.

Interrupt: A break in the execution of a program which requires that control should pass temporarily to another program, e.g. a peripheral device demanding attention.

I/O ports: Input/output registers which allow the central processing unit to communicate with peripherals.

K: Multiples of 1024, e.g. 2K = 2 × 1024.

Literal: Any symbolic value which represents a constant, rather than the address of a location in memory.

Low-level language: A language in which each statement translates into a few machine code instructions, typically one or two.

LSI: Large Scale Integration, integrated circuit technology which has more than 100 gates on a single silicon chip.

Macroprocessor: A program which effects textual substitution by replacing one source instruction by many object instructions.

Machine code: A representation of the bit pattern of an instruction, normally in octal or hexadecimal.

Memory: An array of registers used to store the program and operands for use by the central processing unit.

Memory mapped I/O: If the peripheral image memory is accessed as part of the processors memory it is said to be memory mapped.

Microcomputer: A computer system fabricated on a single integrated circuit or from a selection of LSI circuits including a microprocessor.

Microprocessor: A processing unit constructed as one or more chips, using LSI.

Microprogramming: The technique of programming a computer at a level under that of the normal machine instructions, i.e. each machine instruction is several microcode instructions.

Mnemonic: An aid to memory; a mnemonic here refers to a symbolic character string used to represent the machine code of a computer.

MOS: Metal Oxide Semiconductor, refers to the structure of the transistor used in an integrated circuit. Used to distinguish it from conventional (bipolar) transistor.

MSI: Medium Scale Integration, integrated circuit technology which has between 20 and 100 gates on a single silicon chip.

Object code: The output from a translator, frequently machine code.

Octal: A number system based on the radix 8, i.e. 0, 1, 2, 3, 4, 5, 6, 7.

Operand: The data, identified by part of the instruction, used by the operator.

Operator: That part of the instruction which defines the operation to be performed.

Partial decoding: A decoding scheme where only a few of the address lines select a block of memory. Thus a single block may be selected by a number of different address patterns (see full decoding).

Peripheral: Any device that is connected to a computer whose activity is under the control of the computer.

PLA: Programmable Logic Array, a regular array of memory cells used to implement combinatorial logic functions. The address decoder of the PLA is non-exhaustive.

Polling: A scheme for scanning peripheral devices to determine if they require servicing. Each device is interrogated in sequence and served if necessary otherwise the next in line is interrogated. The poll must be repeated frequently enough to ensure each device is serviced adequately.

Port: The term used to define the gateway between the computer and the peripherals; i.e. input port and output port. Often used to describe any access point in a digital system, e.g. memory port on a large memory system.

Processor: Any device capable of carrying out operations on data.

Program: An ordered set of instructions which perform some specified task. A computer program defines a task to be executed by a central processor.

Program counter: A register containing the address of the next instruction to be obeyed.

Programmable I/O: This refers to input/output circuits which can perform both the input and the output function. They must first be programmed to define the mode of operation before being used to transfer information. Common on LSI microcomputer systems.

PROM: Programmable read only memory.

PROM programmer: A hardware system used to program the contents of PROM's. Usually a part of the development system.

RAM: Random Access Memory is memory in which all locations may be accessed in any random order. Now synonymous with RWM.

Real-time programs: Programs which must interact with the external world, responding to events whose activation is time dependent, are real time programs. Most microcomputer applications need real time programs.

Register: A storage unit of one or more bits; frequently refers to special locations in the processor.

Relative addressing: See Addressing modes.

ROM: Read Only Memory is memory which may be read, but not written, and hence normally contains instructions or permanent data (e.g. look-up tables, character converters).

RWM: Read Write Memory is a memory which may be written and read, and is used to store information that is modified by a program. Has become synonymous with RAM.

Simulator: A device, either in hardware or software, which imitates the action of some process.

Software: That part of a computer system realized by programs.

Source code: The input to a translator.

Stack: A storage mechanism which works on the basis of Last In, First Out (LIFO). Used as a subroutine return address storage area and also for operand storage.

Structured programming: A methodology of designing computer programs.

Subroutine: Part of a program which performs some logical part of the overall task. It normally has some well-defined structure in any particular programming language.

Target computer: The computer system on which the developed software will ultimately run. For microcomputer products the target machine is very seldom the machine on which the programs are developed.

Timer: A counter driven by an external clock and incorporated in the image memory which can be initialized and controlled by program is called a timer. It can provide a variety of timing events so saving the programmer from generating them by program.

ULA: Uncommitted Logic Array is an integrated circuit fabricated with an assembly of logic gates whose interconnection may be defined by the user.

USART: Universal Synchronous Asychronous Receiver Transmitter is a peripheral device which converts parallel digital words into a serial format suitable for transmission and reception from devices such as VDUs, Teletypes and modems. This was one of the first widely used LSI components.

Word: A unit of information normally comprising of one or more bytes (See Bit; Byte).

2's Complement: A number representation scheme used in the arithmetic unit of a computer.

6800: An 8-bit N–MOS microprocessor, first produced by Motorola. Also being produced by other manufacturers and an accepted standard.

6820: A programmable input/output device giving two 8-bit parallel digital ports. Called a peripheral interface adapter (PIA) by Motorola, it was the first of its type and designed to work with the 6800 microprocessor.

8080: An 8-bit N–MOS microprocessor, designed to supersede the 8008 and upwards and compatible with it. A processor that is an industry standard, and produced first by Intel.

8085: An N–MOS successor to the 8080, identical in most respects. This device achieves a higher level of integration and has a narrower communication path to its memory and I/O system than its predecessor.

8155/6: A combination memory, input/output, timer circuit which operates with the 8085.

8755: A combination PROM and input/output device which works with the 8085. In conjunction with the last two devices it can be used to make a small powerful complete computer.

Index

Internal registers

Octal Hex.

A B C D E H L

PC SP

Serial I/O { SID SOD }

Flags { CARRY ZERO SIGN PARITY AUX. CARRY }

Interrupts { RST. 5.5 RST. 6.5 RST. 7.5 TRAP INTR. }

I/O registers

Input registers

In 0 1 2 3

7 6 5 4 3 2 1 0

Output registers

Out 0 1 2 3

7 6 5 4 3 2 1 0

Memory registers

Memory address Octal 000.000

Octal Hex.

Memory address Hex. 0000

000.010

000.020 0010

Memory address Octal 013.000

Octal Hex.

Memory address Hex. 0B00

013.010

013.020 0B10

Copies of the register structure and memory locations are included here for use while working on the tutorial questions.

Internal registers

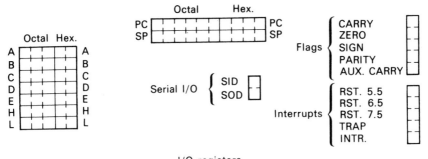

Octal Hex.

A A
B B
C C
D D
E E
H H
L L

PC Octal   Hex. PC
SP   SP

Serial I/O { SID
             SOD

Flags { CARRY
        ZERO
        SIGN
        PARITY
        AUX. CARRY

Interrupts { RST. 5.5
             RST. 6.5
             RST. 7.5
             TRAP
             INTR.

I/O registers

Input registers

In 0
    1
    2
    3
    7 6 5 4 3 2 1 0

Output registers

Out 0
    1
    2
    3
    7 6 5 4 3 2 1 0

Memory registers

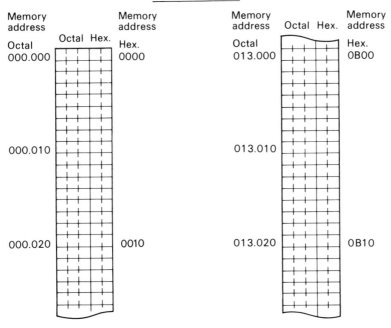

Memory address   Memory address   Memory address   Memory address

Octal   Octal Hex.   Hex.   Octal   Octal Hex.   Hex.
000.000   0000   013.000   0B00

000.010   013.010

000.020   0010   013.020   0B10

Internal registers

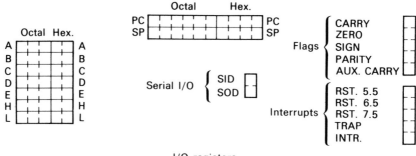

Octal Hex.

A A
B B
C C
D D
E E
H H
L L

PC PC
SP SP

Octal   Hex.

Serial I/O { SID / SOD }

Flags { CARRY / ZERO / SIGN / PARITY / AUX. CARRY }

Interrupts { RST. 5.5 / RST. 6.5 / RST. 7.5 / TRAP / INTR. }

I/O registers

Input registers

In   0
    1
    2
    3

7 6 5 4 3 2 1 0

Output registers

Out   0
     1
     2
     3

7 6 5 4 3 2 1 0

Memory registers

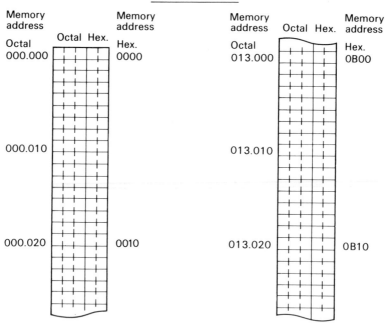

Memory address Octal	Octal Hex.	Memory address Hex.	Memory address Octal	Octal Hex.	Memory address Hex.
000.000		0000	013.000		0B00
000.010			013.010		
000.020		0010	013.020		0B10

Internal registers

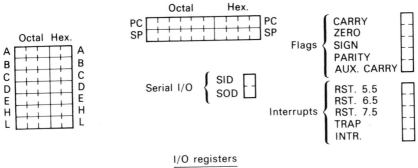

Octal   Hex.

PC   PC
SP   SP

Serial I/O   SID   SOD

Flags
CARRY
ZERO
SIGN
PARITY
AUX. CARRY

Interrupts
RST. 5.5
RST. 6.5
RST. 7.5
TRAP
INTR.

Octal   Hex.

A   A
B   B
C   C
D   D
E   E
H   H
L   L

I/O registers

Input registers

In   0
1
2
3

7 6 5 4 3 2 1 0

Output registers

Out   0
1
2
3

7 6 5 4 3 2 1 0

Memory registers

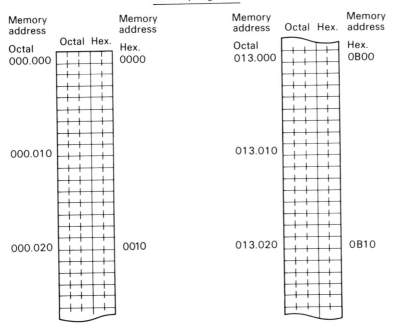

Memory address
Octal
000.000

Octal   Hex.

Memory address
Hex.
0000

000.010

000.020   0010

Memory address
Octal
013.000

Octal   Hex.

Memory address
Hex.
0B00

013.010

013.020   0B10

Internal registers

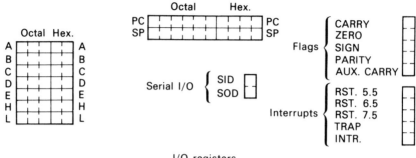

Octal   Hex.

A — A
B — B
C — C
D — D
E — E
H — H
L — L

PC — PC
SP — SP

Serial I/O { SID SOD }

Flags { CARRY ZERO SIGN PARITY AUX. CARRY }

Interrupts { RST. 5.5 RST. 6.5 RST. 7.5 TRAP INTR. }

I/O registers

Input registers

In 0
    1
    2
    3
    7 6 5 4 3 2 1 0

Output registers

Out 0
     1
     2
     3
     7 6 5 4 3 2 1 0

Memory registers

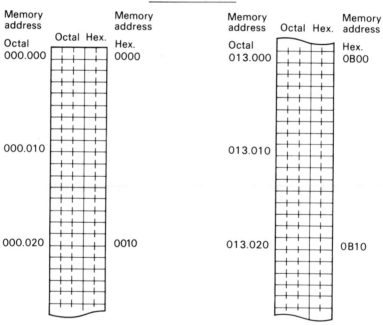

Memory address Octal	Octal Hex.	Memory address Hex.
000.000		0000
000.010		
000.020		0010

Memory address Octal	Octal Hex.	Memory address Hex.
013.000		0B00
013.010		
013.020		0B10

Internal registers

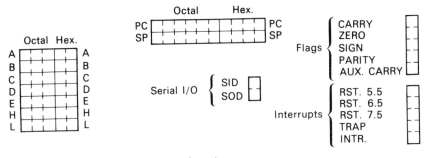

I/O registers

Memory registers

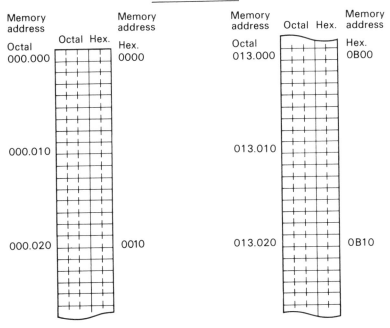

Internal registers

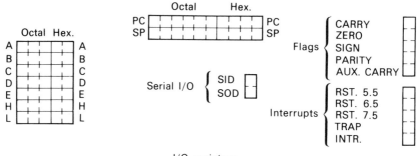

I/O registers

Memory registers

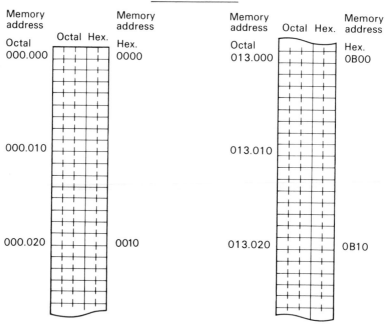

Internal registers

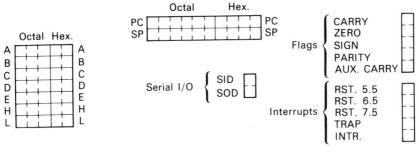

I/O registers

Memory registers

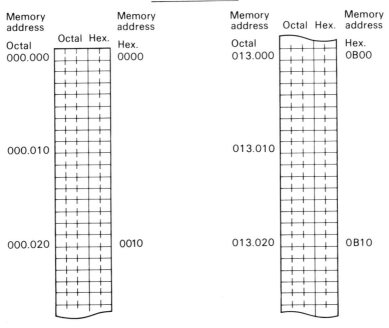

Internal registers

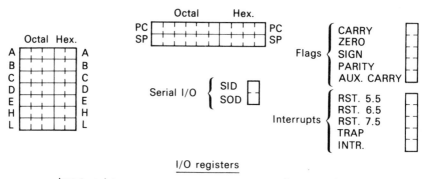

Octal Hex.

A B C D E H L (Octal / Hex.)

PC SP (Octal / Hex.)

Serial I/O { SID SOD }

Flags { CARRY ZERO SIGN PARITY AUX. CARRY }

Interrupts { RST. 5.5 RST. 6.5 RST. 7.5 TRAP INTR. }

I/O registers

Input registers

In 0 1 2 3
7 6 5 4 3 2 1 0

Output registers

Out 0 1 2 3
7 6 5 4 3 2 1 0

Memory registers

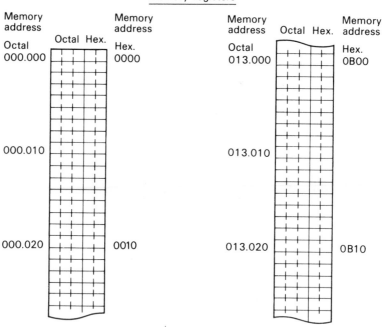

Memory address Octal 000.000
Octal Hex.
Memory address Hex. 0000

000.010

000.020   0010

Memory address Octal 013.000
Octal Hex.
Memory address Hex. 0B00

013.010

013.020   0B10

Internal registers

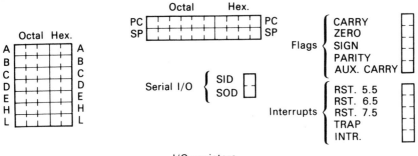

I/O registers

Memory registers

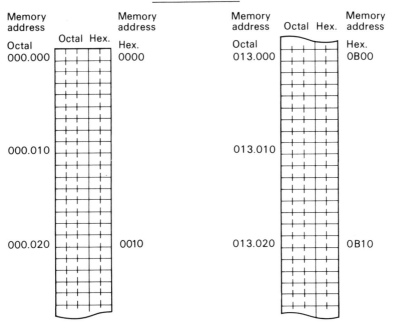